Three Cartularies from Thirteenth-Century Auxerre

Medieval Academy Books, No. 113

Three Cartularies from Thirteenth-Century Auxerre

Edited by Constance Brittain Bouchard

Published for the Medieval Academy of America by
University of Toronto Press 2012

University of Toronto Press
Toronto Buffalo London
www.utppublishing.com

ISBN 978-1-4426-4528-8

Library and Archives Canada Cataloguing in Publication

Three cartularies from thirteenth-century Auxerre /
edited by Constance Brittain Bouchard.
(Medieval Academy books ; no. 113)

Includes the Latin text of the cartularies with English annotations and summaries.
Includes bibliographical references and indexes.
ISBN 978-1-4426-4528-8

1. Catholic Church. Bishopric of Auxerre (France) – History – Sources.
2. Monasticism and religious orders for women – France – Auxerre – History –
Middle Ages, 600–1500 – Sources. 3. Auxerre (France) – Church history – Sources.
4. Cartularies. I. Bouchard, Constance Brittain II. Medieval Academy of America
III. Series: Medieval Academy books ; no. 113

BX2615.A98T57 2012 271.044'412 C2012-904805-4

University of Toronto Press acknowledges the financial assistance to its publishing program of the Canada Council for the Arts and the Ontario Arts Council.

University of Toronto Press acknowledges the financial support of the Government of Canada through the Canada Book Fund for its publishing activities.

CONTENTS

PREFACE

The episcopal cartulary of Auxerre, long assumed lost, was composed in the 1280s, reproducing the most important documents in the bishopric's archives. Confirmations by popes, quarrel settlements with counts, and agreements with the bishop's tenants all feature in its folia. I here give the first edition of this cartulary, many of whose documents were previously unknown. Joined to it are two other thirteenth-century cartularies, both much smaller, that of the nuns of St-Julien of Auxerre and that of the cathedral chapter – the latter existing only in fragmentary form.

One of the most pleasant aspects of this project was returning to Auxerre, both physically and intellectually. The Saint Patrick's Day, over thirty-five years ago, on which I left Chicago for Auxerre to do archival research for my dissertation is still vivid. In some ways I have never come back. In the mid-seventies Auxerre was a rather sleepy provincial capital, without a centre for medieval studies or even a *zone piétonne*, but with wonderful medieval monuments and medieval manuscripts. After my dissertation and first book focused on Auxerre in the twelfth century, the city has had a cameo appearance in several subsequent projects, but here I return fully to the city on the Yonne.

The preparation of this edition was generously supported by grants from the University of Akron Faculty Research Committee and from the University's Research Foundation, as well as by a Summer Stipend from the National Endowment for the Humanities. I am very grateful for their assistance. Librarians and archivists in Auxerre, Paris, and Berkeley were uniformly helpful. Wade Wilcox created a handsome map from my rough sketch. I would also like to express my gratitude to Karl Morrison and Ted Evergates for their encouragement and faith in this project.

ABBREVIATIONS

Arch. Yonne	Auxerre, Archives départementales de l'Yonne
Bibl. Auxerre	Auxerre, Bibliothèque municipale
BnF	Paris, Bibliothèque nationale de France
GC	*Gallia christiana in provincias ecclesiasticas distributa*
Gesta	*Gesta pontificum Autissiodorensium*, 3 vols., ed. Guy Lobrichon et al.
Lebeuf 2	Abbé Lebeuf, *Mémoires concernant l'histoire civile et ecclésiastique d'Auxerre*, vol. 2 [1743]
Lebeuf 4	Abbé Lebeuf, *Mémoires concernant l'histoire civile et ecclésiastique d'Auxerre et de son ancien diocèse*, new ed. by A[mbrose] Challe and M[aximilien] Quantin, vol. 4, *Recueil de monuments, chartes, titres et autres pièces inédites* [1855]
Philip's Register A	King Philip II's first register, consulted in the facsimile edition, *Le premier registre de Philippe-Auguste*
PL	J.-P. Migne, ed., *Patrologia cursus completus, series Latina*
Q 1, 2, 3	Maximilien Quantin, ed., *Cartulaire général de l'Yonne*, 2 vols.; *Recueil de pièces pour faire suite au Cartulaire général de l'Yonne*
RHGF	*Recueil des historiens de Gaule et de la France*

Three Cartularies from Thirteenth-Century Auxerre

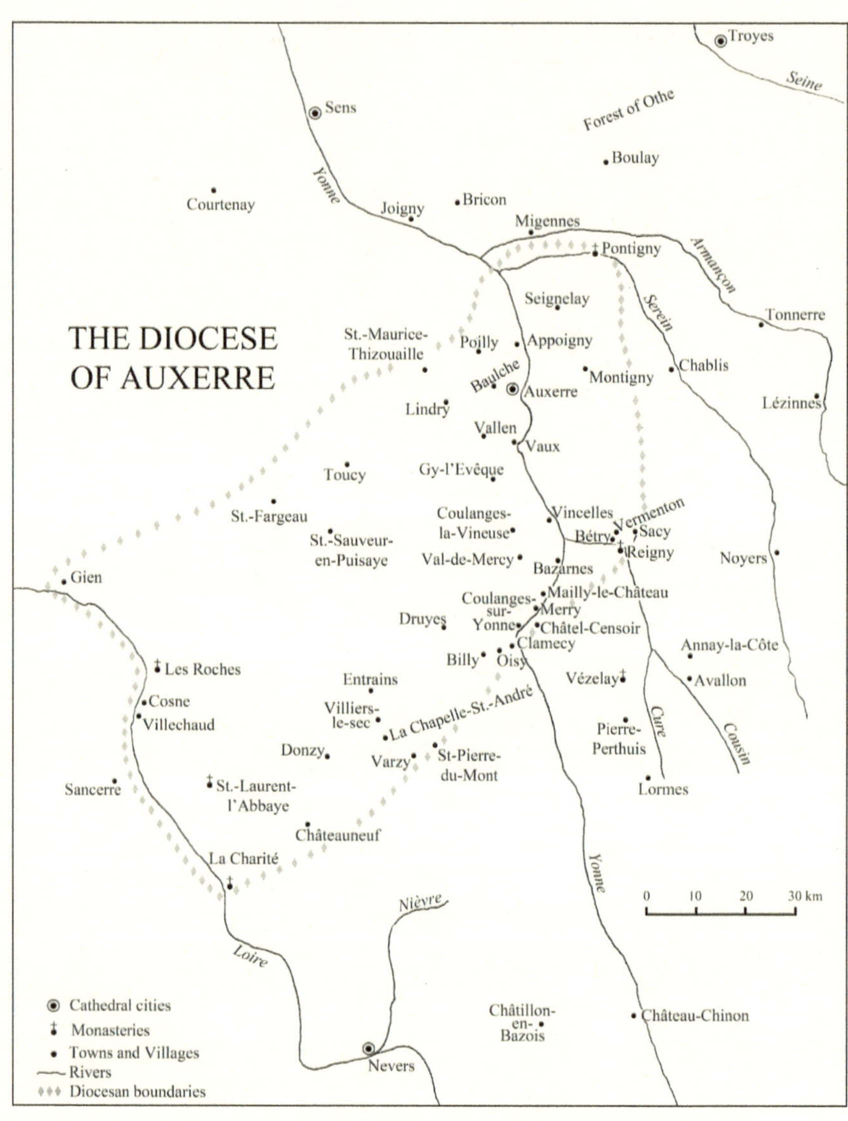

The diocese of Auxerre in the twelfth and thirteenth centuries

INTRODUCTION

Thirteenth-century Auxerre is curiously little known. An important Burgundian diocese since the Merovingian era, with *Gesta* of its bishops first composed in the Carolingian era and continued throughout the Middle Ages, and its region a centre for both Cistercian and Cluniac monasticism, it disappears into something of scholarly obscurity by the 1220s. Maximilien Quantin, the pioneering archivist of Auxerre in the nineteenth century, published in full all the documents he could find from the region from the Early Middle Ages and was fairly thorough for the twelfth century, but in his volume on the thirteenth century, the period when the total number of surviving documents from the Auxerrois greatly increases, he mostly contented himself with brief summaries. Two monographs on Auxerre published virtually simultaneously over thirty years ago, one focusing on the bishops and one on the counts, both stopped at the beginning of the thirteenth century.[1]

This volume makes many more sources available for thirteenth-century Auxerre by publishing three previously unedited cartularies, most notably the cartulary of the bishops, but also a fragmentary cartulary from the cathedral chapter and a small cartulary produced by the nuns of St-Julien of Auxerre, the three dating respectively from the 1280s, the 1230s, and the 1290s. The latter two, one short and the other (being a fragment) even shorter, have long been known, but only about half their contents have ever been published. The bishops' cartulary, long assumed lost, contains even more previously unedited documents. With these three cartularies, and the recent publication of new editions both of the episcopal *Gesta* and of the *Gesta* of the abbots of St-Germain,[2] it should be possible to continue the history of this important diocese past the twelfth century.

THE BISHOPS' CARTULARY

The thirteenth-century cartulary of the bishopric of Auxerre was lost and assumed destroyed for nearly two hundred years, from the French Revolution to the late twentieth century.[3] With the disappearance of the cartulary, much information on the bishops' property, rights, and prerogatives also disappeared, for the cartulary was among the few episcopal records to survive the sixteenth-century Wars of Religion, when the bishops' palace at Régennes, where the records were stored, was burned. None of the documents copied into the cartulary still survive as originals, and most of the other charters issued by the bishops were preserved (if at all) in the archives of the diocese's monasteries. Only the *Gesta* of the bishops, mostly written within a few years of their deaths, gave the cathedral's perspective on the bishops of the thirteenth century.

Fortunately for the history of the diocese, the bishops' cartulary was known in the seventeenth and eighteenth centuries, and copies were made of some of its contents. It was used by the editors of *Gallia christiana*, who published over half of the documents in it, often in abbreviated form; there are many more from the earlier than the later folios of the cartulary, suggesting a decreasing enthusiasm on the part of the copyist whose work was the basis of these editions. For example, for the final, very long document in the cartulary, *Gallia christiana* gives an edition of just a small portion. In addition, several of the charters were copied into larger manuscript collections of ecclesiastical documents. Local historians Dom Georges Viole in the seventeenth century and Abbé Jean Lebeuf in the eighteenth century made copies of a few more. Maximilien Quantin, however, had access to none of the cartulary's documents other than those copied by Viole or Lebeuf or printed in *Galllia christiana*; he reprinted Lebeuf's transcriptions in the new and revised edition of that scholar's works.

The long-lost cartulary of the bishops surfaced in private hands in the mid-twentieth century, being owned by M. Grignard of Dijon; it was used by the editors of the documents of Philip Augustus.[4] In 1974 it was bought for FF 5,000 by the law school (Boalt Hall) of the University of California, Berkeley, where it is presently catalogued as Robbins MS 48. Its existence there has barely been remarked, and it is here edited for the first time.

The cartulary contains transcriptions of 103 documents and summaries of many more. Some one-third of the documents have never before been edited, and many of those were printed only in abbreviated form or were misdated. Of those previously unedited, some have been known from the copies made in the early modern period, but others have remained completely unknown, including three papal bulls (documents 41, 85, and 86). All but fifteen date from after the year 1200. All appear authentic; there is no indication that any are forgeries.

Description

The cartulary volume consists of sixty-six parchment folios, plus a blank folio at front and back, added during binding. The folios are numbered in lead in a modern hand. The binding is brown leather. It is embossed in gold with a coat of arms. The spine reads, 'Cartulaire de l'evesche.' The leaves were slightly trimmed during binding, because the letters at the top of the folios, indicating the section of the cartulary, are often missing their tops. Also partially trimmed away are the words 'De Ste. Marthe,' in an early modern hand, at the top of fol. 1r. This is a reference to Denys de Ste-Marthe, governer general of the congregation of St-Maur (d. 1725), whose transcriptions the editors of *Gallia christiana* used for those documents they printed from the cartulary.[5] Presumably it was he who had the cartulary bound.

The volume now includes two gatherings at the front, one of seven and the second of eight folios, both added during the fourteenth century. The cartulary itself, now on fols. 16r to 66v, was written around 1282, for there are several charters from 1281 included but none from later. The cartulary consists of six gatherings of eight folios each, plus a gathering of three folios at the end. The back of the second gathering (fol. 31v) was originally blank, but an additional charter was copied there in the fourteenth century. The folios now measure 28 cm high and 21 cm wide. They are ruled in lead for between 28 and 31 lines per page. The written area measures 22.5 cm high and 16 cm wide. The writing is a late thirteenth-century bookhand, done in brown ink, with rubrics in red in the same hand.

Except for one charter (that on fol. 31v, added later), the entire cartulary was written in one hand, with occasional corrections in a contemporary cursive. For the most part the writing is clear, but a challenge is sometimes posed by the scribe's tendency to write m's, n's, and u's all as a series of minims, indistinguishable from a series of i's. (A word like 'munimine' poses an especial challenge.) The scribe himself seems occasionally to have miscounted his minims.

The first fifteen folios now in the codex were added to the front of the cartulary a generation or two after its composition. The first gathering (seven folios) consists of a list of revenues owed to the bishopric from various sources; it is headed in red, 'Hic sunt redditus episcopatus Autissiodorensis.' The second gathering (eight folios) begins with a summary listing of the documents in the episcopal archives; it is headed in red, 'Hic incipit inuentarium cartarum et priuilegiorum que faciunt ad ius et iurisdictionem episcopi Autissiodorensis et inuenientur in scriniis suis signatis per ordinem alphabeti et ita scripta sunt et signata in hoc libro.' This listing runs from fol. 8r to fol. 11r. Although at first glance it might appear to be a table of contents to the cartulary, it was based directly on the archival record rather than the cartulary itself, for it does not list all the documents the cartulary scribe copied – not even enumerating what was in box B, for example – it lists some in a different order, and includes box R, not even mentioned in the cartulary. The rest of the gathering, fols. 11v to 15v, is a further listing of revenues and customary requirements, without a heading.

These two preliminary gatherings are revelatory of how the cartulary was perceived in the early fourteenth century, as a clear, organized statement of episcopal rights. It was thus appropriate that a tidy list of revenues and customary obligations should be attached to it. However, because my interest here is the original thirteenth-century cartulary itself, rather than the later additions, I have not included in this edition most of the material in these first two gatherings. The lists of revenues from fols. 1r–7v and 11v–15v were printed by Lebeuf in the eighteenth century.[6] I do, however, give the fourteenth-century listing of the episcopal documents (found on fols. 8r–11r) in an appensix, as indicative of the boxes in the archives in which documents were stored and from which the cartulary scribe worked.

The Archives and the Cartulary

The episcopal cartulary from Auxerre provides one of the clearest indications of the scribe's methods of any French cartulary. According to the scribe and to the later listing of documents attached to the front of the cartulary, as already noted, the episcopal archives were arranged in boxes, *in scriniis*, each of which was labelled with a letter of the alphabet, A through T. Charters were here organized topically, not chronologically. The scribe began with box A, gave a very brief overview of the type of documents in the box, and then copied the individual charters in it, most likely following the order of the charters in the box. He then proceeded to box B and continued. It is possible that other people were also using the archives, and he did not have access to the full collection of documents, which was why he skipped over box R. Although at the end of the cartulary the scribe summarizes what was in boxes S and T, he made no attempt to copy any of the charters in the final two boxes, having apparently lost all enthusiasm for the enterprise.

Even earlier, when still not far into the cartulary, the scribe realized that there was little if any value to be found in identically worded charters, where the only differences lay in who had issued them. By the late twelfth and especially in the thirteenth century, it became common for an archbishop, or perhaps the son of the count, to issue his own charter, repeating an agreement essentially word for word. The scribe decided, after copying some twenty documents and getting well into box B, that it was no use copying simple confirmations or highly similar charters, so he merely noted their existence and moved on to the next.[7]

Thirteenth-century charters were also, on average, longer than documents from the twelfth century. The longest charter in the cartulary (document 39), an agreement, called a 'franchise,' between the bishop and the villagers of Appoigny and adjoining areas, is indicative of the reasons for this greater length: it is highly repetitive and what would now be called legalistic, covering every possible contingency and repeating its requirements and penalties at each turn. The scribe appears to have become very bored during the copying, as indicated by increasing sloppiness and heavier and heavier word abbreviations, as well as by his brisk summaries of most of the rest of the documents in the same box, with no effort to transcribe them. But he does not appear to have considered actually leaving anything out – if so, the document, already enormously long at over thirty-five hundred words, must have truly been massive. Indeed, it is possible that the scribe left enough room in his codex to go back and finish copying the charter later and then moved ahead, for fol. 41v was left blank. (The charter ends where one would expect, with its dating formula, so it may not have been quite as long as the scribe feared.) But because this was a unique charter, unlike the confirmations that he summarized, he still felt it necessary to copy the entire text.

Because no originals exist for the documents copied into the cartulary, it is difficult to say whether the scribe may have made some quiet deletions of passages he considered unnecessary, but overall he appears to have copied conscientiously. For only three documents, 24, 26, and 99, does a copy of the original exist independent of the cartulary. Documents 24 and 26 were copied in abbreviated form into the royal register at the time they were issued. Document 24 was also copied into the *Gesta* of the bishops two generations before the cartulary was compiled; the *Gesta* version is essentially identical, except for a few very minor variants. For document 99, a vidimus was made in the Late Middle Ages. It includes a few words and even a few sentences not found in the cartulary version, but then the cartulary also contains a few sentences not in the vidimus. Both the cartulary scribe and the vidimus scribe may have simply skipped a few words or phrases by accident, or they may each have consciously decided that the entire repetitive text was not necessary, but it is interesting to note that where they overlap (that is, almost everywhere) their texts are essentially identical except for some minor spelling variations in proper names. The evidence thus suggests that the cartulary scribe sought to transcribe everything in front of him – at least when he did not reduce a document to a simple summary.

The earliest two documents in the cartulary date from 1142 and 1145. The first is a confirmation by Pope Innocent II of the bishopric's rights and privileges. The second is an agreement, mediated by Bernard of Clairvaux, over the respective rights in the city of Auxerre of the bishop and the count. The issuing of this detailed, very influential charter, along with the papal privilege, may well have been the impetus for the bishopric to start keeping better track of its archival documents, for there is no indication that the episcopal archives went back any earlier than the 1140s.

Perhaps because the bishopric in essence started over with new personnel every time a new bishop was elected, there seems to have been little institutional memory. The cathedral chapter, on the other hand, as an undying institution had charters going back to its organizational establishment in the ninth century, and the local monasteries of St-Germain and St-Julien had charters in their cartularies from the Merovingian era. The bishops had certainly issued and, presumably, received many documents before 1142, for a number of episcopal charters exist from before then, but they were preserved in the archives of other churches, not the cathedral.

Starting in the middle of the twelfth century, however, successive bishops paid much more attention to the records of their predecessors – for one thing, earlier grants and confirmations could be brought out and shown to opponents to prove points in a dispute. The orderly system of boxes presumably came into effect fairly quickly, for twelfth-century documents were found in a number of boxes. New boxes were added as needed over the following decades. Box T, according to the cartulary, contained the decisions of Bishop William III, who had become bishop just a few years before the cartulary scribe worked; the scribe made no effort to copy its contents, even though he noted its presence.

THE NUNS AND THEIR ARCHIVES

The cartulary of the nunnery of St-Julien of Auxerre is now catalogued as H 1667 in the Archives départementales de l'Yonne. The purpose and method of the nuns who created the cartulary were very different from those of the almost exactly contemporary cartulary scribe who worked for the bishopric. The nuns' archives included much older documents than those of the cathedral: the house's seventh-century foundation charter, and privileges from Louis the Pious and Charles the Bald. But their cartulary was not meant to be a comprehensive overview of the nuns' documents, unlike the episcopal cartulary.

After copying the three oldest documents, the scribe at St-Julien gave the rest of her attention to quarrels with the counts of Joigny in the eleventh through thirteenth centuries, especially charters in which the count promised that he and his successors would never raise quarrels again. The documents starting with no. 9 are indeed virtually identical, although given over three generations. These repeated promises were arranged chronologically. The cartulary was thus intended as a tool in a specific quarrel. From their foundation, the nuns of St-Julien had had two centres of their property, located 30 km or more apart: in the forest of Othe, well north of Auxerre in the territory of the counts of Joigny, and south of Auxerre along the Yonne. Their northern holdings were the source of tension with the counts of Joigny for some two centuries.[8]

None of the original charters from which the cartulary scribe worked survive. However, there still exist a number of original twelfth- and thirteenth-century documents from St-Julien that were never copied into the cartulary, including some concessions issued by the counts of Joigny.[9] Only half of the fourteen documents included in the cartulary have been previously edited, primarily by Maximilien Quantin in the nineteenth century.

A nearly complete copy of the cartulary (omitting only the first charter) was made in the sixteenth century, now catalogued as Arch. Yonne H 1668. The modern catalogue mistakenly says that the sixteenth-century scribe collated the cartulary with the original documents, now lost. In fact, this scribe worked directly from the cartulary. The cataloguer was confused by the intermittent comment in this manuscript, 'facta est collatio cum originali.' In reality, the sixteenth-century scribe just copied the original nun's marginal comments to this effect along with the documents themselves.

Description

The nuns' cartulary is physically small, only 10 folios (the first is blank and not numbered, so 'fol. 1' is actually the second), consisting of five bifolia in a single gathering. It is on parchment, written in dark brown ink. Larger initials at the beginning of each individual charter are done in the same brown ink. The folios are 30 cm tall and 20 cm wide; the written area measures 26.5 by 16 cm. The outer edges of several of the folios are worn and have been mended with parchment. They are lightly ruled in lead for forty-six or forty-seven lines per page. The cartulary's cardboard binding is modern.

The cartulary is written in a neat but small book hand, doubtless by a nun of St-Julien. Every few documents the scribe seems to have stopped and rechecked her work so far, indicated by the marginal comment, 'facta est collatio cum originali.' The latest document in the cartulary is dated 1291, so the cartulary was doubtless compiled around 1292, a decade after the episcopal cartulary.

THE CHAPTER'S CARTULARY

The cartulary of the cathedral chapter of Auxerre, catalogued as Arch. Yonne G 1797, exists now only as a fragment. The documents in it date from between 1166 and 1230, and the cartulary doubtless dates from the middle decades of the thirteenth century. A bifolio is all that survives, both beginning and ending in the middle of documents.[10] Jean Lebeuf in the eighteenth century made periodic reference to charters in the chapter's cartulary that are either not in the surviving fragment or else not in complete form, so presumably it was damaged at the time of the French Revolution. None of its documents were printed in *Gallia christiana.* Of the eleven documents transcribed on the two surviving folios, four have not before been printed. None exist as originals.

Description

The cartulary is written on parchment in dark brown ink, thirty-two lines per page, in a very small hand. A space was left at the beginning of each charter for an initial, presumably in red, but the initials were never added. There is no binding, although holes in the back crease of the bifolio indicate that it was once sewn into the centre of a larger gathering. Each folio measures 22 cm tall and 15 cm wide; the written area is 16 by 13 cm.

OTHER MANUSCRIPTS

BnF MS lat 17048. A large collection of documents from various medieval collections, copied from cartularies and the like in 1680 by M. Gaignières, including documents from Auxerre on pp. 93–150. Most are given as brief summaries rather than full transcriptions. The heading on p. 93 reads 'ex cartulario ecclesie Autissiodorensis,' but in fact it mixes charters from the bishops' cartulary and charters from the chapter's cartulary, as well as some other documents. Some of these appear to come from the capitular cartulary but are not in the fragmentary existing cartulary, indicating that it was still intact in 1680.

BnF Collection de Bourgogne, vol. 3. An eighteenth-century copy of documents from various Burgundian sources. It includes, on fols. 2r–17v, copies of some of the charters in the bishopric's cartulary. The majority of the documents were summarized rather than given integral copies, and many were skipped entirely.

BnF MS fr. 18692. An inventory of the rights and titles of the bishopric of Auxerre, done in 1642 by Julian Chalopin, secretary to Bishop Pierre de Broc. A description of the cartulary begins the inventory (p. 5). A few of the documents from the cartulary were copied into the inventory, usually in abbreviated form. Formerly catalogued as St-Germain MS fr. 1595.

Arch Yonne G 1592. A copy of the preceding, done in 1861.

Arch. Yonne G 1708. A piece of paper on which documents 43–46 were copied in 1645, from the cartulary.

Arch. Yonne G 1832. Copies on paper of documents concerning episcopal regalia, done in the nineteenth century.

Auxerre, Bibliothèque municipale, MS 142. The 'Gesta' of the bishops of Auxerre, written on parchment in the twelfth and thirteenth centuries. It includes a near-contemporary copy of the original of document 24.[11]

Auxerre, Bibliothèque municipale, MS 152. Dom Georges Viole's manuscript history of the bishopric of Auxerre, part 1, including copies of many documents, done in the seventeenth century at St-Germain; formerly catalogued as MS 138, vol. 1. Paper, bound in calfskin.[12]

Auxerre, Bibliothèque municipale, MS 153. Dom Georges Viole's manuscript history of the bishopric of Auxerre, part 2, including copies of many documents, done in the seventeenth century at St-Germain; formerly catalogued as MS 138, vol. 2. Paper, bound in calfskin.

Auxerre, Bibliothèque municipale, MS 155. Dom Georges Viole's manuscript history of the churches of the Auxerrois, including copies of many documents, done in the seventeenth century at St-Germain; formerly catalogued as MS 138, vol. 4. Paper, bound in calfskin.

AUXERRE IN THE THIRTEENTH CENTURY

Besides the cartulary, the other major source of information on the thirteenth-century bishopric of Auxerre is the *Gesta* of the bishops. Originally composed in the 870s, the *Gesta* were continued throughout the Middle Ages, often describing a bishop's deeds shortly after his death, although in some cases only long after the fact.[13] The *Gesta* authors in the thirteenth century had access to the charters that were later copied into the cartulary, and they summarized a number of them.

Churches of the Auxerrois

The region of the Auxerrois had a large number of churches and monasteries. In the city itself, all were served by monks or canons by the thirteenth century. The bishops sought to maintain control over all of them, fairly successfully, although the relations between most of the monasteries and the bishops are better documented by charters in the monasteries' archives than in the episcopal cartulary.

The oldest monastery in the diocese, dating in at least some form to the fifth century, was St-Marien, located across the river from the cathedral, but it never had more than a small body of religious men attached to it; in the thirteenth century it was a house of Premonstratensian canons. The most important monastery of the region was St-Germain, a Benedictine house probably established in the sixth century, which was twice reformed to Cluny's *regula*, once at the end of the tenth century and again at the end of the eleventh. Located just north of the cathedral, on its own hill and behind its own walls, the abbey was the most influential spiritual presence in Auxerre besides the bishopric. Although St-Germain retained its own abbot, rather than becoming a Cluniac priory, it always had an especial relationship with Cluny. The bishop still insisted, from the late eleventh century on, that the abbot owed obedience to him first and foremost, a topic which merited its own section both in the archives and in the episcopal cartulary, but which is notably missing from St-Germain's own thirteenth-century cartulary. The oldest nunnery in the region, nearly as old as St-Germain, was St-Julien, located just south of Auxerre.

Like St-Marien, many of the other Merovingian-era churches in Auxerre were houses of Augustinian canons in the thirteenth century. St-Martin, like St-Marien, followed the Premonstratensian version of the Augustinian rule. St-Eusèbe, St-Pierre, Notre-Dame-la-Dehors, and St-Amâtre also had bodies of Augustinian canons; the latter house was subjected to St-Satur of Bourges in the 1160s (document 28). Although the cathedral dominated the bishop's *cité*, this section of Auxerre also housed the small churches of Notre-Dame-la-Cité and St-Regnobert.

There were few monasteries in the diocese outside of Auxerre itself that dated from before the eleventh century, and those had long been ruined or abandoned. During the eleventh century, a Cluniac priory became established at La Charité, and a house of Augustinian canons at St-Laurent-l'Abbaye. In the twelfth century, a number of Cistercian houses were founded in the region, beginning with Pontigny, one of Cîteaux's 'first four daughters.' The Cistercian houses of Reigny, Les Roches, and Bourras were also soon founded. The nunneries of Celles and Crisenon, the latter affiliated with Molesme, also became established in the diocese.

The Counts of Nevers

The most important laymen in the diocese of Auxerre were the counts of Nevers.[14] The three counties of Auxerre, Nevers, and Tonnerre had been held by the same family since the middle of the eleventh century, and Nevers was the most important of the three. In the twelfth century, Tonnerre generally went to a younger brother (or occasionally a dowager countess), while Nevers and Auxerre were reserved for the heir.

Starting in the late twelfth century, the three counties were inherited by a series of women for close to a hundred years. Their husbands took the titles of count of Nevers and Auxerre, but the wives wielded the true power in the counties. The counts and countesses were frequently in conflict with the bishops, in the twelfth century primarily over jurisdiction within the city of Auxerre, and in the thirteenth century primarily over the obligation to carry a new bishop from St-Germain to the cathedral on the day of his consecration, or 'enthronement' as the charters called it. The bishops also sometimes repeated this ceremony on special occasions. The first recorded instance of the ceremony was in the eleventh century, when the biographer of Bishop Heribert of Auxerre

(1039–52) said that this 'ecclesiastical custom' was observed at the time of his ordination. Although the bishops of Paris, Bordeaux, and Soissons observed similar customs in the twelfth century, it only became a contentious issue in Auxerre in the thirteenth century.[15]

The bishops insisted on tbeing carried, which clearly symbolized the subjection of the counts to the bishops, but the counts routinely avoided this duty. In the cartulary there are enough comital excuses, promises, legalistic quibblings, and grudging admissions of the necessity of the ceremony to suggest that the counts rarely performed it, if ever.

The Mello Family

Besides the counts of Nevers, the most important secular family in the region was those who called themselves 'of Mello,' originally from the Ile-de-France, who came to the Auxerrois with Peter of Courtenay, a membeer of the royal family who became count of Auxerre by marriage at the end of the twelfth century. Droco of Mello was royal constable in the late twelfth century. In the thirteenth century, his descendants became lords of castles of the Auxerrois, and they produced one bishop of Auxerre (Gui of Mello, 1247–70).

THIS EDITION

All three cartularies are written in a thirteenth-century book hand, quite small (one imagines nearsighted scribes bending close over the parchment) and fairly neat. The vocabulary is standard medieval Latin, varying from classical Latin in such common ways as substituting 'imperpetuum' for 'in perpetuum' or 'michi' for 'mihi.' The scribe of the bishops' cartulary especially routinely substituted c's for t's and vice versa. I have followed the cartularies' spelling, only correcting where there is clearly a mistake (such as 'peripiendo' for 'percipiendo') and noting my correction.

Capitalization and punctuation have been normalized. I have tried to respect the scribes' ideas of where sentences stopped and started, but the scribe of the bishops' cartulary especially was very lax in his use of punctuation. I have been sparing with commas, trying to use just enough to make the meaning clear. Longer charters I have broken up into paragraphs, generally following the cartulary scribe's indication (such as a large capital letter) that a new section has begun. Following the scribes' usage, I have used lower-case 'u' for both 'u' and 'v,' and capital 'V' for both. The only exception, again following the scribes, is 'v' for numbers, both upper and lower case.

I have retained the order of the documents in the cartularies, rather than reorganize the material chronologically, as modern cartulary editors once did routinely. Especially in the case of the bishops' cartulary, the organization itself is indicative of the way that the churchmen of Auxerre thought about their archives, and thus I have judged it important to retain the order.

I have sought to identify the people and places mentioned in all the documents. For the places, I have been aided by the work of Maximilien Quantin, who traced the names of a great many places in the Auxerrois through the centuries;[16] here as in his editions of medieval documents, he built the foundaiton on which all other scholars of the region have worked. Although I have not localized well-known places outside of the Auxerrois (e.g., Paris, Bourges, Lyon), I have located the *villae* of the region by distance and direction from Auxerre, or occasionally another well-known city. Here I have deliberately deviated from the French practice of locating places by department, arrondisement, and commune, which is anachronistic for the thirteenth century and can also make it hard to locate a place in a lightly populated region.

Because in most cases the cartulary is the earliest witness to the text of a charter, I have followed it in editing. Later copies and printed editions (such as *Gallia christiana*), being based on the cartulary, do not normally provide useful variants; they vary primarily in attempting to classicize the Latin or in abbreviating witness lists. I begin each document with a summary of its contents. Most documents in the edition are followed by a brief discussion, explaining, for example, why I have dated a document as I have.

Three indexes complete the edition, one of people, one of places, and one of topics (examples, 'tolls' or 'vineyards'). These are indexes to all three cartularies. A chronological list of the documents in the three cartularies completes this introduction.

NOTES

1 Constance Brittain Bouchard, *Spirituality and Administration*. Yves Sassier, *Recherches sur le pouvoir comtal en Auxerrois du Xe au début du XIIIe siècle*.

2 *Gesta pontificum Autissiodorensium*, 3 vols., ed. Guy Lobrichon et al. For the episcopal *Gesta*, see also Bouchard, *Spirituality and Administration*; and *Gesta abbatum Sancti Germani Autissiodorensis*, ed. Noëlle Deflou-Leca and Yves Sassier.

3 Henri Stein, *Bibliographie générale des cartulaires français*, p. 42, no. 295.

4 *Recueil des actes de Philippe Auguste, roi de France*, vol. 3, ed. Charles Samaran, J. Monicat, and J. Boussard, p. 11.

5 A portrait and biography of Denys de Ste-Marthe begin the fourth volume of *Gallia christiana*.

6 Lebeuf 2:73–81.

7 The scribe who created the cartulary of Byland Abbey, about a century later, similarly reduced a number of charters to brief summaries; *The Cartulary of Byland Abbey*, ed. Janet Burton.

8 For the economic importance of forests and forest products in this region in the thirteenth century, see Richard Keyser, 'The Transformation of Traditional Woodland Management.'

9 For example, Arch. Yonne H 1710, H 1738, H 1743.

10 Stein mentions this fragmentary cartulary but mistakenly says that it has thirty-one folios, when in fact it has only two; *Bibliographie des cartulaires*, p. 42, no. 294.

11 This manuscript is described in *Catalogue général des manuscrits des bibliothèques publiques de France*, 6:58–9.

12 For a description of this and the following manuscripts, ibid., p. 61.

13 Constance B. Bouchard, 'Episcopal *Gesta* and the Creation of a Useful Past in Ninth-Century Auxerre.'

14 For the counts, the very detailed history by René de Lespinasse, *Le Nivernais et les comtes de Nevers*, is old but still useful. See also Constance Brittain Bouchard, *Sword, Miter, and Cloister*, pp. 340–51.

15 *Gesta*, 1:263. Bouchard, *Spirituality and Administration*, pp. 129–30.

16 Maximilien Quantin, *Dictionnaire topographique du département de l'Yonne*.

CHRONOLOGICAL LIST OF DOCUMENTS

BISHOPS' CARTULARY

1142	96	1210	83
1145	1	1210	84
1148	93	1211	62
1154	95	1211	63
1157	99	1211	64
1157	101	1211	66
1163	28	1211	103
1164	2	1211	104
1168–75	4	1212	102
1173	42	1213	31
1175	25	1214	67
1175	5	1215	65
ca 1185	100	1215	90
1188	27	1215	9
1189	60	1216	7
1204	26	1216	59
1207	8	1216	94
1207	24	1219	85
1207	37	1221	22
1208	29	1224	21
1208	30	1226	56
1208	33	1226	71
1208	36	1228	72
1209	9	1229	97
1209	61	1232	45

1234	10	1258	57
1235	48	1258	70
1236	46	1258	78
1236	49	1260	98
1237	74	1263	50
1237	89	1263	92
1239	43	1266	3
1239	54	1266	41
1239	55	1267	51
1239	73	1267	58
1243	47	1269	80
1245	44	1269	81
1246	11	1269	82
1246	12	1271	14
1247	13	1271	87
1247	34	1271	88
1248	52	1272	15
1248	53	1272	16
1248	76	1274–6	86
1248	77	1275	23
1249	79	1275	69
1249	32	1276	39
1249	35	1276–81	6
1249	40	1280	19
1249	75	1281	17
1251	38	1281	18
1253	68	1281	20

CHAPTER'S CARTULARY

1166	1	1211	7
1191	10	1215	3
1193	6	1218	9
1208–20	11	1219	2
1209	8	1230	4
1210	5		

ST-JULIEN'S CARTULARY

631	1	1214	8
814–40	2	1236	9
840–77	3	1236	10
1043	4	1238	11
1164	5	1244	12
1182	6	1283	13
1209	7	1291	14

THE BISHOPS' CARTULARY

Fol. 16r.

Hic incipit liber cartarum episcopi Autissiodorensis que inuenientur in scriniis signatis per ordinem alphabeti, et primo continentur littere que faciunt ad ius et iuridictionem episcopi in ciuitate Autissiodorensis et pertinentiis in scriniis signatis per A.

1

Auxerre, 1145

Bernard, abbot of Clairvaux, settles a quarrel between Bishop Hugh of Auxerre and Count William II of Nevers. They will share in the upkeep of the woods of Bruyères, where they agree on the amends to be paid if animals do damage. Compromises are reached on their relative rights to capture and punish malefactors. The bishop retains his authority over all clerics and churches. The count agrees that he will yield to the bishop the four castles he holds from him, whenever the bishop wants. Most importantly, the count promises not to make any changes or innovations at Auxerre without episcopal permission and recognizes that almost everything he has at Auxerre is held in fief from the bishop, excepting only that which he holds from the king and the duke.

MANUSCRIPTS: Bishops' cartulary, fols. 16r–17r. Bibl. Auxerre, MS 153, fols. 103r–105v; seventeenth-century copy by Dom Viole. Coll. Bourgogne 3, fols. 2r–3v. BnF MS lat 17048, p. 111; highly abbreviated.

EDITIONS: Urbain Plancher, ed., *Histoire générale et particulière de Bourgogne*, 1:xlv–xlvi, no. 68; from the cartulary. GC 12, instr. cols. 115–16, no. 23. Q 1:393–7, no. 247.

In nomine sancte et individue trinitatis, ego Bernardus Clarevallensis vocatus abbas.[1] Cognita que inter Hugonem episcopum Autissiodorensis et Willelmum comitem Niuernensem[2] emerserat discordia pro quibusdam querelis que inter eos agebantur, Autissiodorum ueni, et pari amborum assensu et uoluntate querelas illas ad concordiam redactas fineui terminari hoc modo.

In bosco qui dicitur Brueria episcopi[3] facient communiter episcopus et comes haiam, factamque communiter custodietur, ita quod singuli singulos ministros eius custodie deputabunt, et uterque ab ambobus [*sic*] fidelitatem accipiet, eritque in sacramento eorum quod nullus homo siue animal in haia per occasionem capiatur. Forifacta haie communiter percipentur,[4] que etiam forifacta hac ratione determinantur. Porcus, ouis, uacce cum lasciuientes fugiunt tauros, si in ea deprehense fuerint nichil emendabunt. Boues, uacce, equi, asini, capre et similia animalia si sine custode in ea inuenta fuerint, pro singulis singuli denarii persoluentur. Si custos affuerit, iii solidos pro se emendabit. Pro pecudibus nichil exigetur. Si homo ligna cedens in ea inuentus fuerit, xv solidos emendabit, incendium faciens, lx. Itaque predicta forifacta haie numquam excedent prenominatas summas. Haia non extendetur in latum ultra xl perticas arpennales. Si autem eandem haiam contigerit aliquando seu uetustate seu aliqua occasione, ad id deuenire ut non sit. Si eam simul ibidem recipere uoluerint, licebit. Quod si noluerint, terra remanens siue culta sit siue inculta ad dominium episcopi reuertetur. Omnia alia forifacta que extra haiam fuerit siue parte comitis. episcopi sunt.

Statutum est de clericis, ut omnino a potestate comitis liberi et immunes existant, ita quod nec aliquid iuris uel dominacionis in eos ex aliqua occasione comes excercebit, nec rebus eorum ubicumque sint, manum aliquo modo mittere sibi uel alicui ministrorum suorum licebit. Quod si in aperto latrocinii forifacto clericus fuerit deprehensus, absque omni clericalis ordinis iniuria seu indignitate episcopo uel eius ministris reddetur. Ac deinceps si quidem contra ipsum a comite uel eius ministris aut hominibus expostulabitur, episcopus eis quantum ius et ratio dictauerit de eodem faciet.

Theloneum ciuitatis et suburbiorum eius, quia episcopo et comiti commune esse constat, si aliquod forifactum inde commissum fuerit, episcopus capitale suum per se recipiet cum ea lege qua quisque uiuit, et comes pro forifacto lx solidos. Si thelonarus comitis seu aliquid clientum primus ceperit eum qui capitale episcopi abstulit, capitale suum cum lege episcopo reddere faciet, et si

1 Bernard, abbot of Clairvaux (1115–53).

2 Hugh of Mâcon, bishop of Auxerre (1136–51), and William II, count of Nevers (1098–1149).

3 The forest of Bruyères is centred 9 km west of Auxerre.

4 The cartulary reads 'percientur.'

per eius incuriam cum eodem capitale euaserit, ipse pro illo episcopo de capitali et lege respondebit. Seruientes episcopi et quotquod erunt de familia eius, numquam iustitiabunt se per comitem.

Omnia forifacta claustrorum, uidelicet claustri Sancti Stephani et claustri Sancte Marie et claustri Sancti Eusebii et Sancti Petri et Sancti Amatoris[5] et ea que claustris continentur, iuris episcopalis sunt, nec aliquam in eis excercere poterit comes potestatem, nec pro aliquo forifacto cuiuslibet hominis res que in claustris sunt in suam transferiet potestatem. Si aliquis laicus deprehensus fuerit in claustris in latrocinio, cum unaquacumque ueste sua pro iusticia facienda comiti reddetur. Extra claustra autem quicumque laici latrones deprehensi fuerint et ipsi et res eorum comitis sunt, exceptis illis rebus que in claustris nominatis continentur que proprie ad episcopum pertinent.

De terris censualibus manifestum est quod nusquam licet comiti uel homini suo eas que de fundo sunt episcopi acquirere nisi per episcopum, nec etiam aliquam decimam.

Bannum comitis obseruabunt tribus diebus omnes tam clerici quam laici qui in claustris morantur, quibus transactis libere uendent. Si episcopus uinum aut annonam comparauerit, nichil gellagii uel alterius consuetudinis ab eo exigetur.

Episcopus seruientes et homines comitis tam per se quam ecclesiasticos ministros per Christianitatem submonebit et iusticiabunt se per eum.

Domus comitis et munitiones castrorum que ipse dinoscitur tenere ab episcopo, scilicet Castri Noui, Sancti Saluatoris, Conade, Mailliaci,[6] tradentur episcopo ad eius beneplacitum, ita tamen quod eo discedente comiti uel ministerialibus eius cum integritate restituentur.

In boscis comitis episcopus accipiet necessaria sibi et ecclesie Sancti Stephani. Dictum est et concessum de canonicis Sancti Stephani quod in bosco de Thul[7] usuarium suum plenarie habebunt.

Cognitum est et a comite concessum quod non licet ei Autissiodori aliquam mutacionem uel innouacionem facere absque licencia episcopi, de cuius feodo recognoscit se tenere quicquid habet Autissiodori et in circuitu eius, preter hoc quod continetur infra muros urbis extra claustrum quod tenet de domino rege et preter feodum ducis ultra pontem.

---

5 The cathedral and the houses of canons of Auxerre, Notre-Dame, St-Eusèbe, St-Pierre, and St-Amâtre.

6 These four castles were held by the counts from the bishops throughout the twelfth and thirteenth centuries: Châteauneuf (64 km south-southwest of Auxerre), St-Sauveur (35 km southwest of Auxerre), Cosne (65 km southwest of Auxerre), and Mailly-le-Château (23 km south of Auxerre). Within the next decade or so Bétry (20 km southeast of Auxerre) was added to this group of castles; see document 99.

7 Place not identified. It may be the woods of Thou, 55 km west-southwest of Auxerre.

Comes res episcopi custodire debet ut suas proprias. Si aliquis de potestate eius, aliquid de rebus episcopi aut hominum suorum ceperit, comes reddi faciet aut de suo recompensabit. Ad molendinos episcopi de Regioanne[8] tale debet esse bochellum, quod nauibus ascendentibus et descendentibus peruium sit.

De illis qui pisces uendunt, comes habet iiii creditarios, in quibus episcopus nichil accipit. Si ad alios thelonearius episcopi primus aduenerit et primus barguinauerit, tantum accipiet quantum curia episcopi necesse habebit et idem thelonearius comitis similiter faciet. Si pariter uenerint pariter accipient quod inuenerint. Similter in aliis uictualibus faciant. Creditariam habet episcopus in omnibus uictualibus xl diebus exinde donec reddiderit, ab eis quibus debetur nichil ei credetur.

Statutum est de mercatoribus qui in domibus suis uendunt, quod a quindecim in quindecim dies uel a mense in mensem, theolenario episcopi uentas reddent si quesite eis fuerint. In nundinis kalendarum Maiarum, thelonei et uentarum due partes sunt episcopi, tercia comitis. Illique hos redditus recipiunt, fidelitatem episcopo et comiti facient.

Episcopus in uineis suis propriis et in censualibus, si illi uoluerint quorum sunt uinee custodiam ponet, si noluerint non cogentur. Comes faciet similiter. In Brueria tota cuiuscumque fondus sit aut possessio episcopi et comitis uenacio communis est et forifacta ad uenationem pertinencia.

Actum Autissiodoro anno ab incarnacione Domini MCXLV, episcopatus Eugenii pape II primo.[9] Huic rei interfuerunt abbates Stephanus Renniacensis, Guido de Caroloco, Balduinus de Castellione, Gaufridus de Ruppibus,[10] Rainnaudus archidiaconus, Gauffridus cantor, Hugo decanus Meldensis,[11] Andreas de Baldement, Landricus, Bernardus, Hugo de Castro Censurii,[12] Hugo de Tociaco[13] presbiteri, Gaufridus cellarius, magister Anselmus, Guido de Bichiaco, Stephanus de Sancto Germano canonici, milites Guillelmus filius suprascripti comitis,[14] Hugo de Tilio, Humbertus de Sancto Germano, Siguinus

8 Régennes, 9 km north of Auxerre.

9 Not in fact Eugenius II but Eugenius III (1145–53).

10 Abbots Stephen of Reigny (1134–62), Gui of Charlieu, Baldwin of Châtillon (ca 1140–ca 1150), and Geoffrey of Les Roches (1137–52).

11 Meaux.

12 Châtel-Censoir, 30 km south-southeast of Auxerre.

13 Toucy, 22 km southwest of Auxerre. He may be a relative of the brothers Hugh and William of Toucy, respectively archbishop of Sens (1143–68) and bishop of Auxerre (1167–81). They had a nephew named Hugh who was a cathedral canon. See Constance Brittain Bouchard, *Spirituality and Administration*, pp. 83–4.

14 The future Count William III of Nevers (1149–61).

de Tornella,[15] Odo de Tociaco, Humbaudus Tortus seruientes, Robertus prepositus comitis, Humbaudus pistor, Erueus prepositus episcopi, Olannus cellarius, et alii quamplures hinc et inde.

This is the second oldest charter in the cartulary. Its placement at the beginning is indicative of its importance for the bishops; its provisions were referred to repeatedly over the next century and a half. The biographer of Bishop Gui of Mello (1247–70) referred to its provisions but said that for a century bishops had not been properly enforcing them.[16]

Although it was clearly a compromise, the biographer of the bishop described this agreement as a great episcopal victory over a count who had wrongly seized church revenues due to the weakness of the bishop's predecessor.[17] The bishop was a long-time friend of Bernard of Clairvaux, from even before they first became monks together at Cîteaux. Even though the counts of Nevers at this time were also counts of Auxerre, they rarely used that title, possibly because they held in fief from the bishops of Auxerre, who were thus their superiors.[18]

2

1164

Geoffrey, formerly bishop of Langres, settles a quarrel between Bishop Alain of Auxerre and Count William IV of Nevers, with the assistance of Abbots Guichard of Pontigny and Geoffrey of Clairvaux. The agreement reached before Bernard of Clairvaux almost twenty years earlier is reconfirmed.

MANUSCRIPTS: Bishops' cartulary, fols. 17r–18r. Bibl. Auxerre, MS 153, fol. 140r–v; seventeenth-century copy by Dom Viole. Coll. Bourgogne 3, fol. 3v. BnF MS lat 17048, p. 112; abbreviated.

EDITIONS: Urbain Plancher, ed., *Histoire générale et particulière de Bourgogne*, 1:xlvi–xlvii, no. 69, from the cartulary; abbreviated. GC 12, instr. cols. 127–8, no. 40. Q 2:164–5, no. 149, from GC and Viole.

---

15 Siguin of 'Tornella' founded a priory in the diocese of Nevers at the beginning of the twelfth century. At that time he gave his late father's name as Hugh. Surviving were his mother, Margarita, stepfather (*vitricus*) William, uncle Siguin, and sisters Agnes, Aanordis, and Petronilla. Siguin went on to have a wife named Agnes and sons named Hugh, Siguin, and Raynald, the last a cleric. GC 12, instr. cols. 341–3, no. 51.

16 *Gesta*, 2:311.

17 *Gesta*, 2:101. On this agreement, see Bouchard, *Spirituality and Administration*, pp. 54–5; and Yves Sassier, *Recherches sur le pouvoir comtal en Auxerrois*, pp. 127–8, 180–1.

18 René de Lespinasse, *Le Nivernais et les comtes de Nevers*, 1:295–7.

Ego Godefridus episcopus quondam Lingonensis.[1] Notum fieri uolo presentibus et futuris quod de quibusdem querelis que inter dominum Alanum uenerabilem episcopum Autissiodorensem et Vuillelmum illustrem comitem Niuernensem agitabantur[2] auxiliante Deo per manum nostram et Wichardi Pontiniaci et Gaufridi Clarevallensis abbatum,[3] de iure et consuetudinibus predictorum episcopi uidelicet et comitis inquisita diligencius, ueritate tali modo amicalibiliter facta est composicio.

Salua igitur in primis et approbata carta quam inter predecessorum huius dominum Hugonem episcopum et auum illius comitis, comitem scilicet et de Cartusia, sancte memorie Bernardus Clareuallensis abbas composuit.[4] Statutum est a nobis ut quicquid in ea diffinitum est et ipsorum sigillis firmatum ratum habeatur, et tam ab episcopo quam a comite cunctis diebus inuiolabiliter obseruetur. Igitur de terra mercati que tam episcopi quam comitis communis est, cognitum est quia neutri eorum eam dare alicui, uel aliquid ibi facere sine assensu alterius licet, excepto quod comes in ea stalla concedere solis cambiatoribus potest tantummodo ad cambiandum que tamen ab eis ad alios usus transferri non possunt, ita duntaxat ut si precium exinde comes habuerit episcopus medietatem habeat. De theloneo quod episcopus et uicecomes accipiunt, ministeriales comitis nichil se intromittere habeunt. Terra que Kalende Maii appellatur, liquet quia episcopi est, unde comes nichil ibi facere habet, et quod in ea construxerat edificium cadat. Similiter domus iuxta pontem quia cognitum est et manifestum constructam eam esse super aquam que a ponte inferius iuris episcopi est cadat.

Equitaturas hominum episcopi uel ecclesiarum ministerialibus comitis capere ad aliquod faciendum uel alicubi mittendum non licet. Sed pro municionibus faciendis uel reficiendis, nichil ab hominibus episcopi uel ecclesiarum est exigendum. Aliquociens homines episcopi apud ministeriales comitis conqueruntur et eis iustitiam facere nolunt nisi pro ipsis se iusticient, etiam hii quod non debent nisi de mercato uiuentes, unde manifestum est quia ideo non est eis iusticia subtrahenda seu neganda. Preterea contingere solebat quod homines comitis hominibus episcopi sua credebant, et cum non possent credita rehabere propter hoc res aliorum hominum episcopi capiebant, quod dictum est omnino fieri non debere. Credentie enim a nullo nisi ab eo cui sunt credite sunt requirende. Recognitum est pretera quod in feodatis seruientibus quos episcopus

1 Geoffrey, former bishop of Langres (1139–63). He retired to Clairvaux in 1163, where he lived another year.

2 Alain, bishop of Auxerre (1152–67), and Count William IV of Nevers (1161–8).

3 Abbots Guichard of Pontigny (1136–65) and Geoffrey of Clairvaux (1162–5).

4 This is a reference to document 1. Count William II was known to his posterity as William 'of Chartreuse' because he died at that monastery.

habet Autissiodori uel alibi etiam si de mercato uiuant, comes nullam omnino in foro aut alio in loco pro aliquo forifacto nisi per episcopum habet iusticiam seu potestatem.

Vt igitur prescripta compositio rata et inconcussa perpetuo maneat, episcopi comitis et nostro sigillo eam confirmauimus, bb,[5] notatis testibus qui nobiscum presentes interfuerunt, Henricus uenerabilis Trecensis episcopus[6] et Girardus eiusdem archidiaconus, Guido Autissiodorensis prepositus, Willelmus decanus, Stephanus cantor, Stephanus cellarius, Garnerius senescallus, Stephanus de Petra Pertussa miles,[7] Stephanus episcopi prepositus, Raaudus burgensis[8] Autissiodorensis. Actum anno ab incarnacione Domini Millesimo C sexagesimo quarto, regnante Ludouico Francorum rege Christianissimo.[9]

This document refers back to document 1, above. These two documents were the basis of all subsequent agreements between bishops and counts.

3

Viterbo, 15 May 1266

Pope Clement IV grants the bishop of Auxerre a privilege, confirming the bishopric's possessions and whatever property bishops may be given in the future. He refers to earlier popes' privileges and to the churches of the Auxerrois that are subject to the bishop, as well as to the castles held from the bishop. He gives especial attention to what the abbey of St-Germain owes both to the bishop and to the abbot of Cluny. He also details what will happen to the property of clerics who die intestate.

MANUSCRIPTS: Bishops' cartulary, fols. 18r–20r. Bibl. Auxerre, MS 153, fols. 412r–415r; seventeenth-century copy by Dom Viole.

EDITION: GC 12, instr. cols. 170–2, no. 105.

SUMMARIES: Q 3:393, no. 770. August Potthast, *Regesta pontificum Romanorum*, 2:1585, no. 19634.

---

5 In early medieval documents, a mark that looked like 'bb' with some added flourishes meant 'conscribi.'

6 Henry, bishop of Troyes (1145–69).

7 The cartulary erroneously reads 'milites.' The knight is Stephen of Pierre-Perthuis (d. ca 1175), brother of the lord of Seignelay. Pierre-Perthuis is 44 km southeast of Auxerre. See Constance Brittain Bouchard, *'Those of My Blood,'* p. 157.

8 The cartulary reads 'burgenses.'

9 King Louis VII of France (1137–80).

Clemens episcopus seruus seruorum Dei,[1] uenerabili fratri Autissiodorensis episcopo[2] eiusque successoribus canonice constituendis. In perpetuum.[3] In eminenti sedis apostolice specula disponente Domino constituti ex iniuncto nobis a Deo apostolatus officio fratres et coepiscopos nostros honorare debemus attentius, et sincera caritate diligere et loca eorum gubernacioni commissa Beati Petri patrocinio communire, ut de suscepti prosecucione officii tanto possint sollicitores existere quanto amplius a mundanorum fluctuum tempestatibus securi fuerint et quieti.

Eapropter uenerabilis in Christo frater episcope tuis iustis postulacionibus benigno concurrentes, assaisu[4] ad exemplar patrum et predecessorum nostrorum felicis memorie, Eugenii, Adriani, Alexandri et Clementis[5] in Romanorum pontificum Autissiodrensem ecclesiam cui auctore Deo presides presentis scripti privilegio communimus. Statuentes ut quascuque possessiones, quecunque bona eadem ecclesia iuste et canonice possidet aut in futurum largicione principum, oblacione fidelium, seu aliis iustis modis Deo propicio poterit adipisci, tibi tuisque successoribus firma et illibata permaneant. In quibus hec propriis duximus exprimenda uocabulis. Ecclesiam uidelicet S. Laurencii de abbacia,[6] ecclesiam S. Petri regularium, ecclesiam B. Marie extra muros, ecclesiam S. Amatoris, ecclesiam Sancti Mariani.[7] Sancimus eciam ut sine alicuius persone contradictione, liceat uobis in eisdem locis canonicum ordinem in melius reformare. Abbaciam sanctimonialium S. Iuliani in suburbio Autissiodorensi, abbaciam sanctimonialium de Crisannio.[8] Castellum Varziaci[9] cum omni immunitate sua et ecclesiis eiusdem loci, uidelicet Sancti Petri et Sancte Eugenie, Castellum de Conada[10] cum ecclesia Sancti Leurencii ibidem sita. Castellum de Toziaco[11] cum ecclesiis Beate Marie et Beati Petri, et hiis que a dominium castelli infra et extra, et ad ius ecclesiarum petinent. Ecclesiam de

---

1 Pope Clement IV (1265–8).

2 Gui of Mello, bishop of Auxerre (1247–70).

3 This phrase is represented by a series of capital letters, IN PPM.

4 GC suggests correcting to 'assensu.'

5 The reference to Pope Alexander is most likely a reference to document 57, issued by Alexander IV, but Alexander III had also issued bulls to the bishop of Auxerre; Q 2:138, no. 127; Alexander III, Letter 952, PL 200:834. The reference to Pope Eugenius is to document 93. The bulls of the other two popes, doubtless Hadrian IV and Clement III, do not survive.

6 St-Laurent-l'Abbaye, 66 km southwest of Auxerre.

7 The houses of canons regular in Auxerre, St-Pierre, Notre-Dame-la-Dehors, St-Amâtre, and St-Marien.

8 The nunneries in the diocese, St-Julien and Crisenon.

9 Varzy, 51 km south-southwest of Auxerre.

10 Cosne, 65 km southwest of Auxerre.

11 Toucy, 22 km southwest of Auxerre.

Fontanis cum decimis suis, ecclesiam Sancti Viuienni de Madriaco.[12] Redditus decimarum de Saciaco et Toriaco,[13] et de uillis eiusdem parrochie. Castellum de Apponiaco[14] cum terris et aquis, et eccelsia Beati Petri ibi sita cum decimis eiusdem parrochie. Ecclesiam de Baserna[15] cum decimarum redditibus, ecclesiam de Sancti Prisco[16] cum decimis eiusdem parrochie. Ecclesias de Liuinaco, de Teugeio,[17] de Venussia, de Montiniaco,[18] de Miscidis, et ecclesias de Valle.[19] Ecclesiam de Oratorio, preter illam partem oblacionum quam monachi de Boniaco ibidem accipiunt.[20] Illud quod quondam Stephanus cantor de castro Sancti Aniani in ecclesia de Boiaco a[21] uobis tenebat, ecclesiam Sancti Martini de Clamiciaco[22] cum omnibus ad eam pertinentibus, in loco qui dicitur de Caritate,[23] in ecclesiis in clero et populo, quicquid ad ius pontificale noscitur pertinere, preter interdictum in congregacione monachorum qui tamen excommunicatos uestros nulla racione recipiant.

Quod etiam quondam Petrus Cluniacensis abbas[24] in presencia predicti predecessoris nostri sancte recordacionis Eugenii pape et fratrum suorum, presentibus quoque suis fratribus, recognouit de singulis domibus eiusdem parrochie de Caritate habitatores earum in festiuitate Penteconstem, aut apud Varziacum singulos obolos, aut apud Caritatem singulos nummos ministerialibus uestris soluant, sicut antiquitus consuetum est, et de toto alio episcopatu uobis persoluuntur, preter castellum S. Saluatoris[25] et monasterium Merlenensis.[26] In abbacia S. Germani benedicionem abbatis et obedientiam et quicquid ad ius episcopale noscitur pertinere. In reditu consecracionis episcopi, suscepcionem eius in iamdicta abbacia cum processione conuentus, et in ipsa die procuracionem cum clericis et seruientibus suis, ceteris uero diebus cum priuata familia sua, usque ad diem quo in sedem episcopalem intronizandus fuerit, sicut predecessores tui et tu hactenus habuisti, de qua utique abbacia cum inter bone

12 Fontaines, 28 km southwest of Auxerre, and Merry, 28 km south of Auxerre.
13 Sacy, 24 km southeast of Auxerre; and Thory, 38 km southeast of Auxerre.
14 Appoigny, 10 km north-northwest of Auxerre.
15 Bazarnes, 16 km south-southeast of Auxerre.
16 St-Bris, 10 km southeast of Auxerre.
17 Leugny, 19 km southwest of Auxerre; and Thorigny, 56 km north-northwest of Auxerre.
18 Venouse, 14 km northeast of Auxerre, and Montigny, 12 km northeast of Auxerre
19 Misery, 32 km south of Auxerre; and Vaux, 5 km south-southeast of Auxerre.
20 Neither the church nor the monastery are identified.
21 Starting here, and continuing through the word 'qui' in the next line, this text is written in the margin in a contemporary hand, having been mistakenly skipped by the scribe.
22 Clamecy, 37 km south of Auxerre.
23 La Charité, 86 km southwest of Auxerre
24 Peter the Venerable, abbot of Cluny (1122–56). This is a reference to document 93.
25 St-Sauveur-en-Puisaye, 35 km southwest of Auxerre.
26 This monastery is not identified.

memorie Hugonem predecessorem tuum et predictum Petrum abbatem ac monachos Cluniacenses in presentia bone memorie predecessoris nostri pape Eugenii controuersia tractaretur, rationibus hinc inde cum fratribus diligenter auditis et plenarie cognitis, talis est sententia promulgata, ut uidelicet absque Cluniacensis abbatis consilio, qui ante ibi et receptionem et ordinis correctionem habuerat, abbas ibi nullatenus eligatur. Electum uero approbandi et reprobandi canonice, et si dignus fuerit benedicendi penes Autissiodorensem episcopum qui pro tempore fuerit, auctoritas maneat et facultas qui gratiam benedictionis adeptus obedienciam ei pertinebit. Depositio quoque ipsius, si depositione dignus extiterit, ordine iudiciario facienda, et canonica tam abbatis quam monachorum correctio ad episcopum nihilominus pertinebit. Ab eodem preterea episcopo abbas et monachi eiusdem loci crisma, oleum sanctum, consecraciones altarium seu basilicarum et ordinaciones monachorum uel clericorum, qui ad sacros ordines promouendi fuerint forcienter, donec idem episcopus gratiam apostolice sedis habuerit. Porro inuestituram ipsius abbacie de cetero per baculum predictus antecessor noster ab abbate Cluniacensi abbati S. Germani fieri interdixit. Huius nimirum uestigiis inherentes, eandem sententiam confirmamus et futuris temporibus ratam et inconcussam permanere sancimus.

Presenti quoque decreto statuimus ut clericorum uestrorum bona qui intestati decesserunt libere in uestra potestate permaneant et disposicione. Si quis uero de clericis ecclesie uestre in aliam ecclesiam ad episcopatum assumptus fuerit, quecumque beneficia de ipsa ecclesia habebat in libera uestra potestate consistant. Preterea que a predecessoribus uestris illicite sine assensu capituli eiusdem ecclesie de possessionibus seu consuetudinibus hominum atque terrarum laicis concessa sunt in irritum, auctoritate apostolica ducimus, et ad ius proprium Autissiodorensis ecclesie reuocari precipimus. Vnde etiam in Cartaginensi concilio noscitur institutum, 'Irrita erit episcopi donacio uel alienacio de rebus ecclesie nisi clericorum suorum coniuencia confirmetur. Episcopus enim rebus ecclesie non tanquam propriis, sed tanquam commendatis uti debet.' Nulli quoque persone uel ecclesie ea que de casamentis eiusdem ecclesie sunt liceat sine uestro et ecclesie ipsius assensu acquirere uel obtinere. Porro immunitates et consuetudines quas Autissiodorenses episcopi et homines habitantes Varziaci et in aliis castris ac uillis eidem ecclesie pertinentibus, necnon in claustro beatri prothomartyris et in claustris aliarum ecclesiarum suburbiarum hactenus habuistis, quiete uobis et in posterum obtinendas auctoritate nostra firmamus. Denique res decedentium episcoporum ab aliquo inquietari uel usurpari sub pena anathematis interdicimus, sed potius omnia substituendo episcopo integra et inconcussa seruari sancimus. Nulli ergo omnino hominum fas sit prefatam ecclesiam temere perturbare aut eius possessiones auferre, uel ablatas retinere, minuere seu quibuslibet molestiis fatigare, sed omnia integra conseruentur, eorum pro quorum gubernacione ac sustentatione concessa sunt usibus omnimodis profutura, salua sedis apostolice auctoritate, et in predictis decimis moderacione consilii generalis.

Si qua sane in posterum ecclesiastica secularisue persona hanc nostre constitutionis paginam sciens contra eam temere uenire temptauerit, secundo terioue commonita, si non satisfactione congrua emendauerit, potestatis honorisque sui dignitate careat, reamque se diuino iudicio existere de perpetrata iniquitate cognoscat, et a sacratissimo corpore ac sanguine Dei et Domini Redemptoris nostri Ihesu Christi aliena fiat, atque in extremo examine districte subiaceat ultioni. Cunctis autem eidem loco sua iura seruantibus sit pax Domini nostri Ihesu Christi, quatinus et hic fructum bone actionis percipiant, et apud districtum iudicem premia eterne pacis inueniant. Amen. Amen. Amen. Amen. Amen. Amen.[27]

Ego Clemens catholice ecclesie episcopus.
Ego Ancherus tituli Sancte Praxedis presbiter cardinalis.
Ego Guillermus tituli Sancti Marci presbiter cardinalis.
Ego frater Vnbaldus basilice xii apostolorum presbiter cardinalis.
Ego Odo Tusculanus episcopus.
Ego Stephanus Prenestinus episcopus.
Ego frater Iohannes Portuensis et Sancte Rustine episcopus.
Ego Heinricus Ostiensis et Weliternensis episcopus.
Ego Richardus Sancti Angeli diaconus cardinalis.
Ego Gaufridus Sancti Georgii[28] ad uelum aureum diaconus cardinalis.
Ego Vbertus Sancti Eustachii diaconus cardinalis.
Datum Viterbii per manum magistri Michaelis sancte Romane ecclesie uicecancellarii idibus Maii. Indictione viiii. Incarnacionis Dominice anno MCCLXVI, pontificatus uero Domini Clementis pape iiii, anno secundo.

Pope Clement issued another document for the bishop of Auxerre at about the same time; see document 41. The occasion was doubtless Bishop Gui's trip to Rome in 1266, in which he offered the pope his assistance in putting Charles of Anjou on the throne of Sicily.[29] Much of this privilege refers to what Eugenius III had granted the bishop a century earlier; see document 93.

27 On fol. 19v, below the text and above the signatures, the cartulary reproduces the *rota* of Pope Clement IV and the words 'Bene Valete,' done as a monograph.

28 The cartulary reads 'Georogii.'

29 *Gesta*, 2:325.

4

ca 1173

Count Gui of Nevers settles his quarrels with the bishop of Auxerre when the charters of his grandfather, father, and brother are read out in a council at Sens, called by the king. He promises to observe the previous agreements made by counts of Nevers.

MANUSCRIPT: Bishops' cartulary, fol. 20r–v.

Ego Guido comes Niuernensis,[1] notum esse uolo tam futuris quam presentibus quod cum esset discordia inter me et dominum meum W[illelmum] Autissiodorensis episcopum[2] et ecclesias super consuetudinibus nobis, assignato nobis die a domino Ludouico rege Francorum[3] apud Senonensem. Lecte sunt ibi in presencia domini regis et domini Willelmi Senonensis archiepiscopi[4] et apostolice sedis legati quedam carte continentes modum concordiarum olim factarum super eisdem consuetudiinibus inter meos predecessores et predecessores ipsius episcopi. Prima quidam carta continebat concordiam olim factam per manum Bernardi Clareuallensis abbatis inter dominus Hugonem episcopum Autissiodorensis et Willelmum auum meum, comitem scilicet de Cartusia.[5] Et hec confirmata erat eorumdam sigillis, Hugonis scilicet Autissiodorensis episcopi, Bernardi Clareuallensis abbatis, Willelmi aui mei. Secunda continebat concordiam factam inter dominum Alanum Autissiodorensis episcopum et Willelmum patrem meum super consuetudinibus Conade,[6] et super mellicus aliorum castrorum et uillarum tam episcopi quam comitis, et hec quoque munita erat utriusque sigillis. Tercia continebat modum concordie facte per manum Godefridi Lingonensis episcopi et Wicardi Pontiniacensis et Gaufridi Clareuallensis abbatum inter predictum Alanum Autissiodorensis episcopum et W[illelmum] fratrem meum,[7] et hec nichilominus roborata erat

---

1 Gui, count of Nevers (1168–75).

2 William of Toucy, bishop of Auxerre (1167–81).

3 King Louis VII of France (1137–80).

4 William, archbishop of Sens (1168–76), son of the count of Champagne.

5 This is a reference to document 1, in which Bernard, abbot of Clairvaux (1115–53), reached an agreement between Count Gui's grandfather, Count William II of Nevers (1098–1149), and Bishop Hugh of Auxerre (1136–51). William II was known as 'of Chartreuse' because he was buried there.

6 This is a reference to document 99. Cosne is 65 km southwest of Auxerre.

7 This is a reference to document 2, in which Geoffrey, formerly bishop of Langres (1139–63), settled a quarrel between Alain, bishop of Auxerre (1152–67), and Count William IV of Nevers (1161–8), Count Gui's older brother. Bishop Geoffrey was assisted by Abbots Guichard of Pontigny (1136–65) and Geoffrey of Clairvaux (1162–5).

erat sigillis predictorum, Alani scilicet Autissiodorenensis et Godefridi quondam Lingonensis episcoporum et Willelmi fratris mei.

Auditatas itaque cartas in presentia curie domini regis Ludouici laudaui et concessi et me eas de cetero obseruaturum promisi. Si quis etiam contra tenorem predictarum cartarum episcopo uel ecclesiis nocere attemptaret, bona fide promisi me eidem episcopo et ecclesiis pro posse meo fore auxiliatorem, et ne elapsu temporum uel mutacione personarum inter Autissiodorensis episcopos et me uel successores meos iterum super huiusmodi controuersia nasceretur, presentem paginam sigilli mei apposicione muniri. Huius rei testes sunt, Hugo Senonensis archidiaconus,[8] Siguinus decanus Eduensis, Magister Lambertus de Sedelogo,[9] Stephanus Autissiodorensis sacrista, Magister Thomas notarius comitis, Erardus comes Brene, Nargodus de Tociaco, Stephanus de Petra Petrussa,[10] Gautermus Berardi, Damianus de Mailliaco,[11] Guido Li Befors, Petrus de Cortenui,[12] Colinus prepositus de Tonorre,[13] Theobaldus de Conassa.

This document, not previously printed, can be dated between 1168 and 1175 by the regnal years of the count and the archbishop. The king referred to it in 1175 when he issued a ruling forbidding a commune at Auxerre (document 25). The most likely date is 1173, when Gui was known to have been at Sens (document 42); there is some overlap of the witnesses of the document he issued then and this one. The biographer of Bishop William links this close inspection of Gui's predecessors' 'privileges and charters' to the ending of a commune at Auxerre.[14]

5

1175

Countess Ida of Nevers makes gifts for the soul of her dying son, Gui, count of Nevers. She promises twenty pounds a year of revenue from her dotal property

8 Bishop William of Auxerre had a nephew named Hugh who was archdeacon of Sens; *Gesta*, 2:141.

9 These two witnesses were attached respectively to the churches of Autun and Saulieu.

10 Count Erard II of Brienne (1158–91), Lord Narjod II of Toucy (d. 1192), and Stephen of Pierre-Perthuis (d. ca 1175). For these lords, see Theodore Evergates, *Feudal Society in the Bailliage of Troyes*, pp. 164–5; Constance Brittain Bouchard, *Sword, Miter, and Cloister*, pp. 373–5; and Constance Brittain Bouchard, *'Those of My Blood,'* p. 157.

11 Mailly-le-Château, 23 km south of Auxerre.

12 Peter of Courtenay (d. ca 1183), younger brother of Louis VII. His son became count of Nevers and Auxerre a decade later. Courtenay is 48 km northwest of Auxerre.

13 Tonnerre, 30 km east-northeast of Auxerre.

14 *Gesta*, 2:117.

for the good of his soul and also gives the bishop of Auxerre all of her men at Varzy. Bishop William establishes a new altar at the cathedral, where masses shall be said for Gui.

MANUSCRIPTS: Bishops' cartulary, fols. 20v–21r. Coll. Bourgogne 3, fol. 4r (abbreviated).

EDITIONS: GC 12, instr. cols. 135–6, no. 51; abbreviated. Q 2:264–5, no. 246, from GC.

In nomine sancte et indiuidue trinitatis. Vsus litteratum repertus est propter memoriam rerum, inde est quod ea que in futurum manere uolumus litterarum custodie commandamus. Quantum ob rem ego Ida comitissa Niuernensis[1] per presentem paginam tam presentibus quam futuris notum facio, quod uidens Guidonem comitem Niuernensis[2] filium meum in extremis laborantem materna pietate commota, promisi ei me daturam xx libras in redditibus de terra dotalitii mei pro remedio anime sue et antecessorum eius. Quod ipse quidem gratissimum habuit et ut hoc ipsum opere complerem omnimoda prece postualuit. Ego igitur ad preces illius hanc eandem elemosinam uolens ordinare salubriter ad ecclesie tranquilitatem[3] et ad anime filii mei et antecessorum nostrorum salutem, hoc modo promissum compleui. Homines quos habebam tunc temporis Varziaci[4] cuiuscumque conditionis essent et eorum heredes qui ex illis nascerentur in perpetuum possidendos episcopis Autissiodorensibus donaui et concessi.

Willelmus uero tunc temporis episcopus in presentia Ludouici nobilissimi regis Francorum et Willelmi Senonensis archiepiscopi[5] pro hac elemosina sibi collata in ecclesia Beati Stephani Autissiodorensis altare nouum et duos presbiteros ab omni questu liberos constituit qui deinceps uicissim altare nouum singulis diebus missam pro remedio anime prefati G[uidonis] comitis filii mei et patris sui et antecessorum suorum omnium fidelium defunctorum celebrabunt.[6] Hanc siquidem predicte elemosine donacionem laudauerunt et

1 Ida, widowed countess of Nevers. Her husband, William III, had died in 1161. She was daughter of the duke of Carinthia and sister of the countess of Champagne; Constance Brittain Bouchard, *Sword, Miter, and Cloister*, p. 347 and n. 199.

2 Gui, count of Nevers (1168–75).

3 The cartulary reads 'transquilitatem.'

4 Varzy, 51 km south-southwest of Auxerre.

5 William of Toucy, bishop of Auxerre (1167–81); King Louis VII (1137–80); and Archbishop William of Sens (1168–76), son of the count of Champagne.

6 This establishment of perpetual masses for the count's soul is also mentioned by the bishop's biographer; *Gesta*, 2:129.

concesserunt Matildis comitissa[7] uxor scilicet G[uidonis] predicti comitis, et Reinaldus frater eiusdem comitis filius meus, et si quid iuris in hominibus de Varziaco habebant quittauerunt et Autissiodorensi episcopatui concesserunt.

Vt autem huius elemosine donacio et presbiterorum institucio rate et inconcusse permaneant, hanc cartam exinde fieri precepi et sigilli mei munimine roboraui, sub testimonio horum quorum nomina et signa subscripta sunt. S. Odonis abbatis Sancti Petri Autissiodorensis. S. Hugonis Senonensis archidiaconus.[8] S. Theobaudi[9] Niuernensis decani. S. Willelmi cantoris de Clamiciaco. S. Vichardi vicecomitis de Clamiciaco.[10] S. Willelmi Chacebor. S. Nicholai militis. S. Fornerii de Druia.[11] S. Odonis Beraudi. S. Sunonis camerarii. Actum est hoc anno ab incarnacione Domini Millesimo CLXXV.

Item consimilis littera G. archiepiscopi Senonesis apostolice sedis legati de eodem.
Item similis littera Matilidis comitisse super eodem.
Item similis littera regis Ludouici confirmatoria super eodem.
Item super eodem littera papalis confirmatoria.

Bishop William of Auxerre issued a charter the same year confirming Countess Ida's charter.[12] According to the biographer of Bishop William, the men at Varzy constituted 'thirty or more' families.[13] See also document 42.

Countess Ida in this charter seems like a tender mother, but the chronicler of Vézelay, writing a decade earlier, had described her as 'the instigator of all evils' in her enthusiastic support for the attacks on Vézelay by her older son, Count William IV of Nevers.[14]

7 For Countess Mathilda of Nevers (d. ca 1210), see Constance Brittain Bouchard, *Sword, Miter, and Cloister*, pp. 348–9.

8 Odo, abbot of St-Pierre of Auxerre; and Hugh, archdeacon of Sens and nephew of Bishop William; *Gesta*, 2:141.

9 The cartulary reads 'Ttheobaudi.'

10 Clamecy, 37 km south of Auxerre. For the viscounts of Clamecy, see Yves Sassier, *Recherches sur le pouvoir comtal en Auxerrois*, p. 69 and n. 32.

11 Druyes, 27 km south-southwest of Auxerre.

12 Lebeuf 4:58, no. 69 (Lebeuf 2:27, no. 55), said to be 'ex tabula' of the church of Auxerre.

13 *Gesta*, 2:119.

14 *Chronique* 4, in *Monumenta Vizeliacensia*, p. 568.

6

September 1276/September 1281

The officer of the Auxerre cathedral curia attests that Bishop Erard has reached an agreement with his cathedral chapter, granting them rights of justice in their property.

MANUSCRIPTS: Bishops' cartulary, fols. 21r–22v. Coll. Bourgogne 3, fol. 4r–v.
EDITION: GC 12, instr. cols. 178–9, no. 114; the embedded episcopal charter only.

Item littera de donatione iusticie domorum et familie claustri, quam fecit E[rardus] episcopus Autissiodorensis decano et capitulo Autissiodorensis ecclesie.

Omnibus presentes litteras inspecturis, officialis Autissiodorensis salutem in Domino, noueritis nos litteras que sequuntur uidisse in hec uerba.

Omnibus presentes litteras inspecturis, curie Autissiodorensis et curie decani Autissiodorensis officialis salutem in Domino. Noueritis nos litteras reuerendi patris E[rardi] Dei gratia episcopi Autissiodorensis uidisse et diligenter inspexisse in hoc uerba.

Omnibus presentibus litteras inspecturis, Erardus miseracione diuina Autissiodorensis episcopus,[1] salutem in Domino. Noueritis quod nos dilectis in Christo filiis decano et capitulo Autissiodorensis ecclesie eorumque successoribus canonicis eiusdem ecclesie illam totalem et omnimodam iuridicionem et iusticiam temporalem quam habemus seu habere possumus et debemus racione quacumque, et quam nos et predecessores nostri Autissiodorensis episcopi hactenus excercuimus aut excercere potuimus et debuimus quocunque modo et in quocunque casu in omnibus domibus et eorum porprisiis quas dicti decanus et capitulum haberent in presenciam et possiderent et acquisierunt hactenus et imposterum habebunt, possidebunt et acquirent, uacantes uel[2] inhabitatas, sitas infra claustrum nostrum Autissiodorense et quas suas uel gratis aut conductas inhabitant uel inhabitabunt ibidem, necnon in familia canonicorum ipsius ecclesie ac eciam in personis et in familiis aliorum domos ipsas, nunc et imposterum inhabitancium seu tenencium a decano et capitulo supradictis, exceptis murtro, homicidio, raptu et furto[3] et excepta confiscatione bonorum ubi propter delictum alicuius eius bona confiscari debebunt, excepta etiam tota magna iusticia quocumque genere censeatur ex mera gratia damus, concedimus ad perpetuitatem, remittimus pariter et quittamus, uolentes et concedentes quod quibus de

---

1 Erard, bishop of Auxerre (1270–8).

2 The text from 'uel' to 'inhabitant' is written interlinearly.

3 The cartulary reads 'fulto.'

canonicis ipsius ecclesie qui modo sunt et erunt ex nunc imperpetuum habeat, possideat, excerceat et exequatur libere per se uel per alium, prout sibi expedire uiderit in domibus suis et earum porprisiis predictis, et in tota familia sua necnon in quolibet extraneo in eisdem domibus et porprisiis delinquente, illam totalem et omnimodam iuridicionem et iustitiam quam prediximus, preter illa que superius sunt excepta, et omne commodum seu emolumentum quod ex hiis proueniet seu prouenire poterit in casibus in quibus eis concedimus, sicut predictum est, iuridicionem et iusticiam supradictas.

Nosque de toto iure predicte iuridictionis et iustitie deuestientes, uenerabilem uirum Hugonem decanum Autissiodorensis suo et predicti capituli nomine per nostri tradicionem inuestiuimus, de eodem animo transferendi in ipsos plenum dominium et ueram possessionem tocius iuris nostri predicti. ipsosque et eorum successores constituimus ex nunc tocius iuris predicti ueros dominos et legitimos possessores.

Concedimus insuper predictis decano et capitulo quod tota disposicio bonorum canonicorum ipsius capituli ab intestato decedentium ad ipsos decanum et capitulum iure pertineat, istud nobis specialiter retinentes quod si de bonis alicuius taliter decedentis eos minus sufficienter disposuisse credamus, ipsi decanus et capitulum de omnibus bonis predictis fidelem nobis uel nostris successoribus teneantur reddere racionem.

Ceterum ad perpetuam huius nostre concessionis et muneris firmitatem et sine interruptionis obstaculo ualituram uolumus et concedimus, quod si forte processu temporis per nostram aut nostrorum improbitatem seu per negligenciam dictorum decani et capituli uel canonicorum a nobis uel nostris aliquid in contrarium semel aut plures intercipi seu attemptari contingeret circa iusticiam et iuridictionem predictas, nullum proprietatis, saisine, usus uel possessionis commodus nobis aut succesoribus nostris per hoc de iuro acquiratur, quin pocius nobis et successoribus nostris ex tali usu seu possessione sequta prescripcio contra dictos decanum et capitulum et canonicos non prodesset, nec ipsos per hoc circa proprietatem et possessionem iuridictionis et iusticie predictarum preiudicium posset aliquod generari. Rogamus insuper et requirimus, reuerendum in Christo patrem dominum Dei gratia Senonem archiepiscopum qui pro tempore erit ut ad solam exhibicionem presencium litterarum et requisicionem dictorum decani et capituli huic nostre donacioni et concessioni benignum imperciatur assensum, et eas prout suprascripte sunt litterarum suarum patrocinio harum seriem continencium communiat et confirmet.

In cuius rei testimonium sigillum nostrum duximus apponendum. Actum et datum anno Domini Millesimo CC septuagesimo sexto, mense Septembri.

Quod autem in dictis litteris uidimus continentum de uerbo ad uerbum transcribi fecimus et sigillis curiarum uestrarum sigillari.

Datum anno Domini MCC septuagesimo sexto die sabbati post festum Beati Michaelis archangeli. Quod autem in predictis litteris de uerbo ad uerbum per litteris in presencia testium subscriptorum, uidelicet Iohannis de Ortis, Iacobi Pomtardi, Magistri Viuiani, Iohannis de Valle, et Galteri Blaud in predicta scribentis clericorum et magistorum curie Autissiodorensis uidimus continentis transcribi per dictum Galterium, fecimus et sigillo curie Autissiodorensis ad perpetuam memoriam sigillari. Datum anno Domini MCC ottagesimo primo, die Iouis ante natiuitatem Beate Marie uirginis.

This document was copied and then recopied five years after the agreement was originally issued, and it was this vidimus that the cartulary scribe included in his codex.

Fol. 22v.

Littera de portacionibus episcopi in scrinio signato per B inuenientur.

7

1216

Bishop William of Auxerre receives Countess Yolendis as his femina for Mailly-le-Château, Coulanges-sur-Yonne, and Bétry. Her husband, Count Peter, and son Philip both agree.

MANUSCRIPTS: Bishops' cartulary, fol. 22v. Coll. Bourgogne 3, fol. 4v. BnF MS fr. 18692, p. 99. Arch. Yonne G 1592, fol. 56r–v, from the preceding.
EDITION: GC 12, instr. col. 154, no. 78.
SUMMARY: Q 3:392, no. 752.

Ego Yolendis comitissa Autissiodorensis[1] notum facio universis quod dominus et pater meus Vuillelmus Dei gratia Autissiodorensis episcopus[2] [ad][3] petitionem Philippi filii mei comitis Niuernensis, domino et uiro meo Petro comite Autissiodorensi presente petente et consenciente, me recepit in feminam de

1 Yolendis, second wife of Peter of Courtenay (d. 1219). He had become count of Nevers, Auxerre, and Tonnerre by marriage, and even after his first wife died he retained title to the second two counties.

2 William of Seignelay, bishop of Auxerre (1207–20).

3 This word is missing in the cartulary.

Mailliaco castro, Colengiis super Yonnam, et Betriaco[4] cum eorum pertinenciis, in omnibus tam de dotalitio meo quam de omni iure quod ego in dicta terra habeo et quod Philippus filius meus in dicta terra habet quamdiu uixero, saluo tamen in omnibus iure episcopatus Autissiodorensis et quorumlibet aliorum qui in dicta terra ius habent, salua etiam uita P[etri] comitis uiri mei qui super hoc remanet homo dicti episcopi. Actum anno Domini MCC sexto decimo.

Count Peter, the countess's husband, was preparing to go east to take up the title of emperor of Constantinople, which was why his wife, who would rule in his absence, did homage to the bishop for their castles. This document is repeated as number 59 of the cartulary.

8

1207

Peter of Courtenay, count of Auxerre, recognizes that he, along with the other vassals of the bishop, is supposed to help carry new bishops on the day of their consecration. He excuses himself by saying he had to be at the royal court that day.

MANUSCRIPTS: Bishops' cartulary, fol. 22v. Coll. Bourgogne 3, fols. 4v–5r.
EDITION: GC 12, instr. col. 148, no. 66.
SUMMARY: Q 3:391, no. 744.

Item de eodem.

Ego Petrus comes Autissiodorensis[1] omnibus tam presentis quam futuriis, notum facio quod cum uenerabilis pater et dominus meus Vuillelmus Autissiodorensis episcopus[2] me ad diem intronisacionis sue uocauisset, ut ipsum cum aliis baronibus feodatis qui ad hoc tenentur portarem ut debebam, ego me excusaui quoniam eumdem diem habebam ante dominum meum regem, propter quod non poteram ad ipsum portandum uenire. Cum autem

---

4 Mailly-le-Château (23 km south of Auxerre), Coulanges-sur-Yonne (30 km south of Auxerre), and Bétry (20 km southeast of Auxerre). Count Peter had acquired Coulanges-sur-Yonne around 1190; Yves Sassier, *Recherches sur le pouvoir comtal en Auxerrois*, p. 67.

---

1 Peter of Courtenay (d. 1219) had become count of Nevers, Auxerre, and Tonnerre in 1184 by marrying the heiress. See *Recueil des actes de Philippe Auguste*, 1:134–5, no. 106. He retained the latter two counties even after his own daughter took Nevers to her husband when she married in 1199.

2 William of Seignelay, bishop of Auxerre (1207–20).

idem episcopus me postea propter hoc submonuisset sicut hominem suum et ego uenissem ante eum, facta diligenti inquisicione per uiros bonos qui ueritatem sciebant, certificatus sum, et publice recognoui et recognosco quod ego teneor episcopos Autissiodorenses in intronisacionibus suis cum aliis feodatis portare, et feci ipsi ego emendam de hoc quod ipsum non portaueram, non obstante excusatione mea. Et ne hoc ab aliquo imposterum dubitetur, litteras presentes sigillo meo muniri et ipsi ego tradi feci. Actum anno gratie MCC septimo.

The requirement that the counts of Auxerre and Nevers carry the newly consecrated bishop through the streets of Auxerre was a source of continued tension between the counts and the bishops. Each count and ruling countess eventually recognized that he or she was obligated to do so, but there seem to have been very few occasions when they actually did. Although Count Peter of Auxerre here made his excuses when Bishop William took office in 1207, his son-in-law, Count Hervé of Nevers, continued to deny for two more years that he was required to take part in the ceremony; see the following document.[3]

9

22 June 1209

Count Hervé of Nevers recognizes that he should carry the newly consecrated bishop of Auxerre, along with the other vassals of the bishops, and makes his excuses for not having done so when William became bishop by saying that he thought the obligation was attached to the fief of Gien, no longer his. Now, however, he agrees that he ought to carry the bishop, unless he can prove that the obligation really was attached to the fief of Gien.

MANUSCRIPTS: Bishops' cartulary, fol. 23r. Coll. Bourgogne 3, fol. 5r.
EDITION: GC 12, instr. col. 149, no. 68.
SUMMARY: Q 3:391, no. 746.

Item de eodem.

Herueus comes Niuerenensis[1] omnibus presentes litteras inspecturis, salutem in Domino. Nouerint uniuersi quod cum controuersia uerteretur inter uenerabilem patrem et dominum meum Vuillelmum Autissiodorensis episcopum[2] ex

3 See also Constance Brittain Bouchard, *Spirituality and Administration*, pp. 129–30.

1 Hervé of Donzy (d. 1222) became count of Nevers in 1199 by marrying the heiress.
2 William of Seignelay, bishop of Auxerre (1207–20).

una parte et me ex altera, eo quod die intronizacionis sue ipsum ad cathedralem ecclesiam cum aliis non portaui, licet nobilis uir pater meus Herueus bone memorie antecessorem eius portasset. Quod tamen ex contemptu uel superbia non omisi, sed quia michi dicebatur quod illa portacio mouebat siue dependebat de feodo Giemensis,[3] quod cum non tenerem tunc temporis, nec modo teneam uidebatur ad illam portacionem faciendam minime me teneri. Verumque dictus episcopus michi instanter opponebat quod bone recordacionis pater meus antecessorem eius portauerat, recognoui eumdem episcopum et successores suos esse in possessione memorate portacionis, tam a me quam a meis heredibus Autissiodorensi episcopo faciende, ratione feodi quod ab eodem tenuit pater meus. Saluo eo quod si ostendere potero uel probare quod dicta portacio moueat siue dependeat de feodo Giemensi, ego et heredes mei a dicta portacione facienda quitti remanebimus et liberi, nisi dictum feodum Giemensis ad me uel heredes meos reuertetur. Actum anno ab incarnacione Domini MCC nono, mense Iunnii, decimo kalendas Iunii.

Count Hervé had given Gien to the king in 1199 in return for royal permission to marry the heiress to Nevers (document 26). Throughout the thirteenth century, as indicated by the following documents, the counts continued to claim that the duty of carrying the bishop devolved from the fief of Gien, no longer theirs, but they were never able to support this assertion. The dating formula mistakenly gives June a second time where July is meant. The date was given correctly when countess Mathilda, Hervé's widow, confirmed this charter a generation later (document 11), suggesting the error was the cartulary scribe's.

10

April 1234

Wigo, count of Nevers and Forez, makes excuses for not carrying the bishop himself and sends a representative. He argues that this duty is attached to the fief of Gien, but sends a representative anyway, urging the bishop to free him and his successors from the ceremony if he can ascertain that it really does devolve from Gien.

MANUSCRIPT: Bishops' cartulary, fols. 23r–v.
EDITION: GC 12, instr. cols. 158–9, no. 85.
SUMMARY: Q 3:392, no. 757.

3 Gien, 76 km west-southwest of Auxerre.

Item de eodem.

Reuerendo patri et domino karissimo H[enrico] Dei gratia episcopo Autissiodorensis,[1] G[uigo] comes Niuernensis et Forensis,[2] salutem et paratam ad eius bene placita uoluntatem. Nouerit paternitas uestra quod nos uobis transmittimus dilectum et fidelem nostrum Humbaudum Cheurelli ad uos portandum, quia dominus de Donziaco[3] ut dicitis uos portare debet, et in saisina estis, et inde litteras habetis a comite Herueo,[4] prout uobis suggeritur a quibusdam. Sed nobis dictum est a pluribus quod uos portare debebat dominus Donziaci ratione feodi de Giemo. Sed quoque modo sit dictum Humbaudum ad uos transmittimus, ita tamen quod si inuenire possitis quod dominus predictus de Donziaco uos portare debebat pro Giemo, quod uos nos super hoc in pace dimittatis et quietis, et successores nostros. Datum anno Domini MCCXXX tercio, mense Aprilis.

This charter was given in 1234 in 'new style.' Although the counts of Nevers do not seem ever to have found proof that carrying the bishop was attached to the fief of Gien, they kept on so asserting over the generations; see the preceding document.

11

January 1246

Countess Mathilda of Nevers confirms the 1209 charter of her late husband, Count Hervé of Nevers, in which he recognized that he was obliged to carry a newly consecrated bishop of Auxerre. She says she now realizes she should have carried the new bishop herself but had not done so because she had not yet seen the charter.

MANUSCRIPTS: Bishops' cartulary, fols. 23v–24r. Coll. Bourgogne 3, fol. 5r (abbreviated).

Item de eodem.

Ego Matildis comitissa Niuernensis notum facio omnibus presentes litteras inspecturis me litteras bone memorie Heruei comitis Niuernensis quondam

---

1 Henry, bishop of Auxerre (1220–35). GC mistakenly reads the H as a B.

2 Wigo, count of Forez (d. 1241), became count of Nevers through his marriage to Countess Mathilda. See Constance Brittain Bouchard, *Sword, Miter, and Cloister*, p. 350.

3 Donzy, 58 km southwest of Auxerre.

4 This is a reference to document 9.

mariti mei[1] uidisse, sigillo ipsius sigillatas, non abolitas seu cancellatas aut in aliqua parte sui uiciatas, uerbo ad uerbum sub hac forma.[2]

Herueus comes Niuernensis omnibus presentibus litteras inspecturis, salutem in Domino. Nouerint uniuersi quod cum controuersia uerteretur inter uenerabilem patrem et dominum meum Vuillelum Autissiodorensis episcopum ex una parte et me ex altera eo quod die intronizacionis sue ipsum ad cathedralem ecclesiam cum aliis non portaui, licet nobilis uir pater meus Herueus bone memorie antecessorem eius portasset. Quod tamen ex contemptu uel superbia non omisi, sed quia michi dicebatur quod illa portacio mouebat siue dependabat de feodo Giemensis quod cum non tenerem tunc temporis nec modo teneam uidebatur ad illam portacionem faciendam minime me teneri. Verum quia dictus episcopus michi instanter opponebat, quod bone recordacionis pater meus antecessorem eius portauerat, recognoui eumdem episcopum et successores suos esse in possessione memorate portacionis, tam a me quam a meis heredibus Autissiodorensi episcopo faciende, racione feodi quod ab eodem tenuit pater meus. Saluo eo quod si ostendere potero uel probare quod dicta portacio moueat siue dependeat de feodo Giemensi, ego et heredes mei a dicta portacione facienda quitti remanebimus et liberi nisi dictum feodum Giemensis ad me uel heredes meos reuertetur. Actum anno ab incarnacione Domini MCC nono mense Iunii, decimo kalendas Iulii.

Quia uero per predictas litteras michi constitit euidenter episcopum Autissiodorensis esse in possessione memorate portacionis tam a predicto Herueo quam heredibus suis, recognoso me debuisse portare dominum meum regnandum Autissiodorensem episcopum racione feodi supradicti die intronizacionis, quod de contemptu uel superbia facere non obmisi sed quia non credebam me teneri ad predictam portacionem faciendam cum predictas litteras non uidissem. In cuius rei testimonium presentes litteras tradidi dicto episcopo sigilli mei munimine roboratas. Datum anno Domini MCC quadragesimo quinto, mense Ianuario.

Bishop Raynald had been consecrated a short time before Mathilda issued this document, not previously printed. It reprises the text of document 9 and was given at the same time as the following document. January 1245 is 1246 in 'new style.'

---

1 Hervé of Donzy (d. 1222) became count of Nevers in 1199 by marrying Mathilda, the heiress (d. ca 1257).

2 She here reiterates the text of document 9.

12

January 1246

Countess Mathilda of Nevers makes peace with Bishop Raynald of Auxerre, over her obligation to carry him on the day of his enthronement and over tolls she had been collecting. Their quarrel will be referred to two arbiters, or, if these cannot reach agreeement, to a third. She agrees to pay one hundred marks of silver if she does not keep the agreement.

MANUSCRIPT: Bishops' cartulary, fol. 24r–v.
EDITION: GC 12, instr. cols. 161–2, no. 90.
SUMMARY: Q 3:393, no. 760.

Item de eodem.

Omnibus presentes litteras inspecturis, Matildis comitissa Niuernensis[1] in Domino salutem. Notum facimus uniuersis quod cum contentio uerteretur coram uenerabili patre ac domino nostro Renaudo Dei gratia Autissiodorensis episcopo[2] inter ipsum ex una parte et nos ex altera, super hoc quod idem episcopus petebat a nobis quod nos emendaremus hoc, quod nos ipsum non deportauimus ad cathedralem ecclesiam Autissiodorensis die intronizacionis sue, cum aliis baronibus qui eum tenebantur deportare, cum ecclesia Autissiodorensis sit in possessione de portacione predicta a comite Autissiodorensi facienda, ut idem episcopus dicebat et super quod petebat a nobis quod iuraremus fidelitatem ecclesie Autissiodorensi, cum ipsa ecclesia sit in possessione fidelitatis predicte a comite Niuernensis faciende, sicut dicebat idem episcopus, et super hoc etiam quod petebat a nobis quod amoueri faceremus cicomolas,[3] quas leuari feceramus pro pedagio a transeuntibus leuando tempore predecessoris sui in preiudicium ecclesie Autissiodorensis. Cum comes Niuernensis absque assensu episcopi Autissiodorensis aliquam immutacionem uel innouacionem seu consuetudinem in uilla Autissiodorensi facere non posset,[4] ut dicebat dictus episcopus, de quibus omnibus dicebamus nos nullam iniuriam facere eidem domino episcopo, uel Autissiodorensi ecclesie.

Tandem mediantibus bonis uiris, de premissis querelis compromisimus in dilectos nostros dominum Iohannem Ruffini Autissiodorensem canonicum, et dominum Burellum de Riparia militem. Qui per iuramentum ab eisdem

1 Mathilda, countess of Nevers (d. ca 1257).

2 Raynald of Seignelay, bishop of Auxerre (1245–7). He would have very recently become bishop when this charter was issued.

3 This unusual word appears to be a form of toll.

4 This refers to document 1.

prestitum tenentur secundum rationes ab utraque parte coram eis propositas et proponendas, dictas contentiones terminare infra Penthecosten. Et si dicti arbitri in unam concordare sententiam nequiuerint, debent eligere tertium, qui tertius secundum rationes coram predictis duobus arbitris propositas, et eidem ab ipsis arbitris exhibendas, negotium mediante iustitia terminabit infra festum Beate Marie Magdalene. Nos autem arbitrium predictorum duorum, uel tertii si concordare nequiuerint, sub pena centum marcharum argenti promittimus nos firmiter et inuiolabiliter seruaturos. In cuius rei testimonium presentes litteras sigilli nostri munimine duximus roborandas. Actum anno Domini MCCXL quinto, mense Ianuario.

January 1245 is 1246 in 'new style.' This document was given at the same time as the preceding one.

13

Maundy Thursday, 1247

Countess Mathilda of Nevers confirms that she has seen Count Hervé's charter in which he agreed that all subsequent counts would have to carry the bishop of Auxerre on the day of their enthronement. She makes the excuse, however, that she will be otherwise occupied and thus will not be able to do so on Easter, but will instead send a representative.

MANUSCRIPT: Bishops' cartulary, fol. 24v.
EDITION: GC 12, instr. col. 162, no. 91.
SUMMARY: Q 3: 393, no. 761.

Reuerendo patri ac domino et amico suo in Christo karissimo G[uidoni] Dei gratia Autissiodorensis episcopo,[1] M[atildis] comitissa Niuerensis,[2] salutem et cum omni reuerencia et honore paratam ad eius bene placita uoluntatem. Cum per litteras bone memorie comitis Heruei Niuernensis quondam domini et mariti nostri[3] quas uidimus ipsius sigillo sigillatas, nobis constiterit euidenter episcopum Autissiodorensem esse in possessione portacionis die intronizacionis sue ab eodem comite Herueo faciende pro feodo hereditatis sue, quod

1 Gui of Mello, bishop of Auxerre (1247–70).

2 Mathilda, countess of Nevers (d. ca 1257). Her husband, Hervé IV of Donzy, became count of Nevers when she married him in 1199. See Constance Brittain Bouchard, *Sword, Miter, and Cloister*, p. 350.

3 This is a reference to document 9.

dictus comes Herueus et eius antecessores teneri dicebantur ab episcopo Autissiodorensis, uestre significamus paternitati quod nos ad hoc proximum festum Pasche ad uos apud Autissiodorum pro uestra portacione facienda non possumus personaliter interesse, pluribus negotiis impedite. Quare nos dilectum et fidelem nostrum dominum Hugonem de Varigniaco dominum Anlesiaci[4] pro uestra portacione dicta die Pasche facienda nostre possessionis supradicte loco nostri duximus transmittendum. Datum apud Montemonisum die Iouis benedicto, anno Domini millesimo CC quadragesimo sexto.

Although this document is dated 1246, it was issued in early 1247; the months before Easter were considered to belong to the previous year in thirteenth-century Auxerre. Gui of Mello became bishop of Auxerre early in 1247. In this charter Mathilda is no longer arguing, as she had a year earlier, that she had no idea she was expected to carry the bishop, but, given that she would have been in her sixties, it is not surprising that she did not want to help carry the bishop in person. Mathilda and Bishop Gui also quarrelled over the castles of Châteauneuf, St-Sauveur, Cosne, Mailly, and Bétry, which the counts had held in fief from the bishops for a century (see document 1).[5]

14

June 1271

Count Theobald of Bar recognizes that, because he holds the fief of Toucy, he is obligated to carry the bishop of Auxerre on the day of his enthronement. The fief comes to him via his wife Johanna.

MANUSCRIPTS: Bishops' cartulary, fol. 24v. Coll. Bourgogne 3, fol. 5r–v. BnF MS fr. 18692, p. 56, from the cartulary; slightly abbreviated. Arch. Yonne G 1592, fol. 32v, from the preceding.

Item de eodem.

Nous Thiebaus cuens de Bar le Duc sires de Saint Fergeaul[1] a touz ceus qui uerront ces presentes leittres, salut en nostre Seigneur. Saichent tuit que nous pour raison dou fie de Toci[2] et des autres choses que nous tenons en fie et en

4 Vergigny is 22 km northeast of Auxerre, and Anlezy is 26 km east of Nevers. See also René de Lespinasse, *Le Nivernais et les comtes de Nevers*, 2:201.

5 *Gesta*, 2:311.

1 Thibaud, count of Bar-le-Duc and lord of St-Fargeau, 42 km west-southwest of Auxerre.

2 Toucy, 22 km southwest of Auxerre.

homaige de l'euesque d'Auceurre, lesquelles choses meuuent[3] dou chief nostre chiere fame, Iohanne contesse de Bar et nostre hoiu qui la terre de Thouci et les autres choses qui meuuent de son fie teniuient sommes tenus a porter l'euesque d'Aucuerre quicunque soit le jour de l'intronizacion a Auceurre. En tesmoinguage de laquelle chose nous auons pendu nostre seaul en ces presentes leittres. Et nous Iohanne contesse de Bar de cuy chief ces choses meuuent en tesmoinaige de ceste chose auons mis nostre seaul auec le seaul nostre chier seigneur. Ce fut fait en l'an de l'incarnacion nostre seigneur Mil. II et sexante onze ou mois de Iuignet.

This document has not been previously printed. It is the first document in which the requirement that bishops be carried by their great feudatories is explicitly attached to Toucy. Most of the surviving documents involve those who held Nevers, Donzy, or Gien from the bishop, although all assume that a number of the bishop's vassals were expected to carry the bishop. It is one of the few documents in the cartulary in Old French; starting in the second half of the thirteenth century, aristocrats began in some cases to issue charters in the vernacular rather than Latin.

15

Auxerre, March 1272

Hugh IV, duke of Burgundy, attests to the end of a quarrel between Erard, bishop of Auxerre, and his granddaughter Yolendis, countess of Nevers and daughter of Odo, the duke's oldest son, now deceased. Yolendis, who holds the fief of Donzy, had asserted that the obligation to carry the bishop on the day of his enthronement devolved from Gien, not Donzy and Auxerre.

MANUSCRIPTS: Bishops' cartulary, fol. 25r. Coll. Bourgogne 3, fol. 5v.
EDITION: GC 12, instr. cols. 174–5, no. 110, erroneously dated 1261.
SUMMARIES: Q 3:394, no. 772. Ernest Petit, ed., *Histoire des ducs de Bourgogne de la race capétienne*, 5:328, no. 3783.

Nos Hugo dux Burgundie[1] omnibus presentes litteras inspecturis, salutem in Domino. Nouerint uniuersi quod cum controuersia uerteretur inter uenerabilem patrem E[rardum] Dei gratia Autissiodorensis episcopum[2] ex una parte et

3 The cartulary reads 'mueuent.'

1 Hugh IV, duke of Burgundy (d. 1272).
2 Erard, bishop of Auxerre (1270–8).

nobilem mulierem Yolandim comitissam Niuernensis[3] karissimam filiam defuncti[4] Odonis primogeniti nostri ex altera, eo quod ad diem intronizacionis sue citata ipsium ad cathedralem ecclesiam cum aliis non portauat, nec sufficienter miserat, predicto episcopo asserente quod ad ipsum portandum et successores suos die intronizacionis sue dicta comitissa tenebatur ratione feodi de Donziaco[5] et ratione feodi Autissiodorensis, ipsa comitissa concedente quod ratione feodi de Donziaco ad hoc tenebatur, nisi posset probare quod dicta portacio ratione feodi de Giemo[6] dicto episopo deberetur, non autem ratione feodi Autissiodorensis, quia tamen in presencia nostra dicte comitisse constitit per litteram bone memorie Petri quondam comitis Autissiodorensis, dictum episcopum et antecessores suos esse in possessione memorate portacionis racione feodi Autissiodorensis,[7] dicta comitissa recognouit publice coram nobis quod ipsa et successores sui teneretur portare predictum episcopum Autissiodorensis et successores suos cum idem episcopus et predecessores sui sint, et fuerint in possessione memorate portacionis tam ab ipsa quam ab heredibus suis Autissiodorensis episcopo faciende, non solum racione feodi Donziaci ut predictum est, sed etiam racione feodi Autissiodorensis quod ab ipso tenet.

In cuius rei testimonio nos Hugo dux Burgundie ad requisicionem dicte comitisse neptis nostre presentibus litteris sigillum nostrum apposuimus in testimonium ueritatis. Actum et datum apud Autissiodorum anno Domini M duecento septegesimo primo, die Martis post Brandones.

Because this document was given before Easter, the year is 1272. See also the following document.

16

Lézinnes, December 1272

Countess Yolendis of Nevers agrees that she is obliged to carry the bishop of Auxerre on the day of his enthronement, ending her quarrel with Bishop Erard. She accepts that this requirement devolves from the fiefs of Donzy and Auxerre, not Gien. Her husband, Robert, agrees.

---

3 Yolendis became countess of Nevers in 1257, after the death of her great-grandmother Mathilda.

4 The cartulary reads 'defundi.'

5 Donzy, 58 km southwest of Auxerre.

6 Gien, 76 km west-southwest of Auxerre.

7 This is a reference to document 8.

MANUSCRIPT: Bishops' cartulary, fol. 25r–v.
EDITIONS: Lebeuf 2, instr. pp. 290–1, no. 351. Lebeuf 4:124–5, no. 217.
SUMMARY: Q 3:423, no. 1044.

Vniuersis presentes litteras inspecturis, Yolendis comitissa Niuerensis,[1] salutem in Domino. Nouerint uniuersi quod cum controuersia uerteretur inter uenerabilem patrem E[rardum] Dei gratia Autissiodorensem episcopum[2] ex una parte et nos Yolendim comitissam Niuerensem ex altera, eo quod ad diem intronizacionis sue citata ipsum ad cathedralem ecclesiam cum aliis non portaueramus nec sufficienter miseramus, predicto episcopo asserente quod ad ipsum portandum et successores suos die intronizacionis sue nos tenebamur ratione feodi de Donziaco[3] et ratione feodi Autissiodorensis. Nos concedentes quod ratione feodi de Donziaco ad hoc tenebamur, nisi possemur probare quod dicta portatio ratione feodi de Giemo dicto episcopo deberetur, non autem ratione feodi Autissiodorensis. Quia tamen nobis constitit per litteram bone memorie Petri quondam comitis Autissiodorensis[4] dictum episcopum et[5] antecessores suos esse in possessione memorate portacionis ratione feodi Autissiodorensis. Nos recognoscimus quod nos et successores nostri tenemur portare predictum episcopum Autissiodorensem et successores suos, cum idem episcopus et successores sui sint et fuerint in possessione memorate portacionis, tam a nobis quam ab heredibus nostris Autissiodorensi episcopo faciende, non solum ratione feodi Donziaci ut predictum est, sed etiam ratione feodi Autissiodorensis, quod ab ipso tenemus.

In cuius rei testimonio nos Yolandis comitissa Niuernensis sigillum nostrum presentibus litteris duximus apponendum. Datum apud Lisinias[6] die Iouis post inuentionem Beati Stephani. Anno Domini M II septuagesimo secundo. Nos autem Robertus aduocatus Bitunie et comes Niuernensis[7] maritus dicte Yolendis omnia singula premissa rata habentes ac etiam confirmantes, sigillum nostrum presentibus litteris una cum sigillo dicte Yolendis, anno et die predictis, in testimonium premissorum duximus apponendum.

---

1 Yolendis, heiress to Nevers.
2 Erard, bishop of Auxerre (1270–8).
3 Donzy, 58 km southwest of Auxerre.
4 This is a reference to document 8.
5 The cartulary reads 'et et.'
6 Lézinnes, Bishop Erard's family home, 39 km east of Auxerre
7 Robert was son of the count of Flanders and advocate of Bethune. He became count of Nevers by marrying Countess Yolendis.

This document confirms the preceding one. At this point Yolendis was countess of Auxerre as well as Nevers, although the next year her younger sister, Adelaide, would successfully challenge her in court and obtain Auxerre.[8]

17

1281

Robert, son of the count of Flanders, recognizes that he is obliged to carry the bishop of Auxerre on the day of his enthronement, and that this obligation comes from the fief of Donzy. He makes his excuses for not having done so.

MANUSCRIPT: Bishops' cartulary, fol. 25v.

Vniversis presentes litteras inspecturis, Robertus primogenitus comitis Flandrie comes Niuernensis, salutem in Domino.[1] Notum facimus quod nos recognoscimus nos debuisse portare reuerendum patrem Guillelmum Autissiodorensis episcopum[2] dominum nostrum racione feodi de Donziaco[3] quod ab eodem et Autissiodorensis ecclesia tenemus die intronizacionis sue, quod pro libris et ardius negotiis prepediti facere non ponimus nec personaliter interesse, rogantes ipsum dominum[4] episcopum quatinus nos si placet super hoc habeat excusatos. Datum anno Domini MCC octagesimo primo, die Mercurii post festum Pentechosti.

This document has not been previously printed. Countess Yolendis, Robert's wife, had died in 1280; she had made her own excuses to the bishop nine years earlier (document 16). Because his wife was countess of Nevers alone after 1273, not both Nevers and Auxerre, the bishop had argued that Robert's carrying obligation was attached strictly to Donzy, not to Auxerre and Donzy both.

---

8 Q 3:340–1, no. 678.

---

1 Robert, son of the count of Flanders and count of Nevers through his marriage with Countess Yolendis.

2 William III of Grez, bishop of Auxerre (1279–93).

3 Donzy, 58 km southwest of Auxerre.

4 The cartulary reads 'dominum dominum.'

Fol. 26r

In scrinio signato per C inuenientur littere de homagio comitum et baronum.

18

November 1281

Abbot Felix of Montier-la-Celle and several canons of Auxerre attest that Count Edmund of Champagne has done homage to Bishop William of Auxerre for all that his predecessors held from the bishop.

MANUSCRIPTS: Bishops' cartulary, fol. 26r. Coll. Bourgogne 3, fol. 5v.

EDITION: GC 12, instr. cols. 180–1, no. 117.

SUMMARIES: Q 3:394, no. 778. H. d'Arbois de Jubainville, *Histoire des ducs et des comtes de Champagne*, vol. 6 (1866), p. 101, no. 3853.

Vniversis presentes litteras inspecturis, Felisius humilis abbas de Cella Trecensis,[1] Guillermus archidiaconus, Thomas officialis, magister Anselmus archipresbiter Autissiodorensis, magister Petrus de Appoigniaco archipresbiter de Varziaco,[2] magistri H. de Hermanto, Andreas de Sancto Germano canonici Autissiodorensis, salutem in Domino. Notum facimus quod nobilis uir Haymundus comes Campanie[3] nobis presentibus, die Lune post festum omnium sanctorum, fecit homagium apud pontem de Naiselles reuerendo patri ac domino Guillelmo Dei gratia Autissiodorensis episcopo[4] per hec uerba.

Domine ego facio uobis homagium de his omnibus de quibus predecessores mei alias fecerunt homagium predecessoribus uestris episcopis Autissiodorensis qui pro tempore prefuerunt ecclesie memorate, et eodem modo quo fecerunt. De quibus certificabo uos in breui.

In quorum memorariam et testimonium presentibus litteris sigilla nostra duximus apponenda. Datum die et loco predictis, anno Domini MCC octagesimo primo.

Item due littere de eodem homagio sigillo eiusdem comitis sigillate.
Item alia littera sub sigillo testium de eodem homagio.

---

1 Felix, abbot of Montier-la-Celle (1262–84).

2 Appoigny, 10 km north-northwest of Auxerre; and Varzy, 51 km south-southwest of Auxerre.

3 Edmund of England, brother of King Edward, had become count of Champagne 1275.

4 William III of Grez, bishop of Auxerre (1279–93). The count does homage here at the Natiaux bridge, near Pontigny; it crosses the Armançon, and was considered to be at the boundaries of the diocese of Auxerre, Sens, Langres, and Troyes.

19

Auxerre, September 1280

The abbots of St-Satur of Bourges, St-Pierre and St-Marien of Auxerre, and of Reigny, and the heads of the Dominicans and Franciscans at Auxerre attest that John of Chalon, count of Auxerre, has done homage to Bishop Willliam of Auxerre in the same form that he had done homage to Bishop William's predecessor Erard. The bishop invests John with the county of Auxerre and the castle of Coulanges-sur-Yonne.

MANUSCRIPTS: Bishops' cartulary, fol. 26r–v. Bibl. Auxerre, MS 153, fol. 464r–v; seventeenth-century copy by Dom Viole. Coll. Bourgogne 3, fol. 6r (abbreviated).

EDITION: GC 12, instr. cols. 179–80, no. 115.

SUMMARY: Q 3:394, no. 776.

Omnibus presentes litteras inspecturis. Nos Iohannes abbas Sancti Saturi Bituricensis dyocesis ordinis Sancti Augustini, Iohannes abbas Sancti Petri Autissiodorensis eiusdem ordinis,[1] Iohannes abbas Sancti Mariani Autissiodorensis ordinis Premonstratensis,[2] Stephanus abbas Regniaci ordinis Cisterciensis,[3] frater Guillelmus de Guerthi prior fratrum predicatorum, frater Iohannes de Sancto Geruasio gardianus fratrum minorum, salutem in Domino. Notum facimus uniuersis presentibus et futuris quod anno Domini MCC octuagesimo, die Iouis post festum Beatri Gregorii pape, nobis presentibus in aula superiori reuerendi patris Guillelmi Dei gratia Autissiodorensis episcopi[4] apud Autissiodorum, uidimus et audiuimus quod nobilis uir Iohannes dictus de Cabilone comes Autissiodorensis[5] fecit memorato episcopo homagium ligium de comitatu Autissiodorensis et de omnibus pertinentibus ad dictum comitatum, sub modis et forma quibus fecit dictum homagium bone memorie domino Erardo predecessori episcopi antedicti.[6] Quo facto dictus dominus episcopus de dicto feodo inuestiuit eumdem. Denique predictus comes secundo fecit homagium prefacto episcopo de castro de Colengiis super Yonam[7] et omnibus pertinentiis eius. Quo facto prefactus episcopus eum de dicto feodo inuestiuit.

1 John, abbot of St-Satur of Bourges, and John, abbot of St-Pierre of Auxerre (1271–ca 1295), both Augustinian houses.

2 John, abbot of St-Marien of Auxerre (ca 1275–90), a Premonstratensian house.

3 Stephen, abbot of the Cistercian house of Reigny (ca 1266–ca 1285).

4 William III of Grez, bishop of Auxerre (1279–93).

5 John of Chalon, count of Auxerre through his marriage with the countess.

6 Erard of Lézinnes, bishop of Auxerre (1270–8).

7 Coulanges-sur-Yonne, 30 km south of Auxerre.

Quibus sit peractis prefatus comes iuramentum prestitit ad sancta Dei euuangelia memorato episcopo quod corpus ipsius episcopi, ut pote domini sui custodiet et iura Autissiodorensis ecclesie pro uiribus tueretur.

Hec autem omnia facta fuerunt nobis uidentibus et audientibus, presentibus nobilibus uiris Hugone domino de Sancto Verano, Guillelmo de Sancto Fidolo, Guillelmo de Sancto Ferreolo, Stephano de Nououico, Ymbaudi de Corrigiaco, Milone de Autissiodoro militibus, presentibus etiam uenerabilis uiris Guillelmo archidiacono Autissiodorensis, Stephanus succentore eiusdem ecclesie, magistris Guillelmo de Noa, Iacobo de Sancto Germano, Hugone de Armento, Hugone de Sancto Iangulfo, Vincentio de Mena, Ansello de Mailliaco canonicis Autissiodorensis et pluribus aliis religiosis, secularibus, et clericis ad hoc specialiter uocatis. In cuius rei testimonium presentibus litteris sigilla nostra duximus apponenda. Actum et datum anno et die superius nominatis.

Although this document is phrased peaceably, according to the biographer of Bishop William's predecessor Bishop Erard, Count John had given the bishop a great deal of trouble and only yielded when faced with anathema.[8] Presumably the count had renewed his attacks on episcopal authority when a new bishop was elected in 1279. According to the biography of Bishop William, written close to a century later, William peacefully ended all quarrels with the counts.[9] There is no charter attesting to Count John's homage to Bishop Erard. Many of the witnesses, canons of Auxerre, are found again in the following document.

20

Auxerre, 1281

John, abbot of St-Marien, John, abbot of St-Pierre, and other ecclesiastical officials of Auxerre attest that Robert of Flanders, count of Nevers, has done liege homage to Bishop William of Auxerre for Donzy, Cosne, St-Sauveur, and Murat.

MANUSCRIPTS: Bishops' cartulary, fols. 26v–27r. Bibl. Auxerre, MS 153, fol. 467r; seventeenth-century copy by Dom Viole. Coll. Bourgogne 3, fol. 6r (abbreviated).

EDITIONS: GC 12, instr. col. 180, no. 116 (abbreviated). Lebeuf 2:68, no. 146. Lebeuf 4:131, no. 228.

SUMMARY: Q 3:394, no 777.

8 *Gesta*, 2:345.

9 *Gesta*, 3:13.

Omnibus presentes litteras inspecturis. Iohannes abbas Sancti Mariani ordinis Premonstratensis, Iohannes abbas Sancti Petri ordinis Sancti Augustini,[1] G. archidiaconus Autissiodorensis, M. archidiaconus in ecclesia Autissiodorensis prior S. Eusebii, Gaufridus prior de Testis, ciuitatis et dyocesis Autissiodorensis, salutem in Domino sempiternam. Notum facimus uniuersis presentibus et futuris quod anno Domini MCC octogesimo primo, die Mercurii post Penthecostes, nos omnes existentes in aula superiori reuerendi patris miseracione diuina Autitissiodorensis episcopi,[2] uidimus et audiuimus quod nobilis uir Robertus de Flandria comes Niuernensis[3] fecit homagium ligium dicto domino Autissiodorensis episcopo de feodo quod tenebat ab eodem episcopo, uidelicet de terra et omni baronia et castellania de Donziaco, de Conada, de Sancto Saluatore, et de Murato,[4] de dicto feodo et pertinenciis eorumdem, quo facto prefatus episcopus inuestiuit eundem comitem de dicto feodo. Hec autem omnia facta fuerunt nobis omnibus atque Stephano succentore ecclesie Autissiodorensis, magistro Hugone de Hermeto, Petro de Appoigniaco,[5] Guillelmo de Noa, Stephano sacrista, Henrico de Niuernis, Iacobo de Sancto Germano, Hugone de Sancto Iangulpho, Regnaudo de Mimochiis, Iohanne de Brayo, Petro Viarii, Guidone, Iacobo Romanis, et Girardo de Villa super Arciem canonicis Autissiodorensibus, Galtero de Arceyo uicecomite de Clameciaco,[6] Hugone de Perreria domino Sacleriarum, Iohanne de Montibus, Guillelmo de Arceyo uicecomite,[7] Iohanne de Viriaco, Petro de Penulo militibus, Adam dicto Bourdon, Regnaudo Pantin et magistro Guillelmo de Aurelianis laicis presentibus, uidentibus una cum nobis et audientibus. In cuius rei testimonium presentibus litteris sigilla nostra duximus apponenda. Datum anno et die predictis.

Item alia littera de homagio facto Erardo episcopo.[8]
Item littera nouiter facta de homagio de Ceposa.
Item littera de capellanis fundatis, a Magistro St[ephano] de Bona Valle.

---

1 Abbot John of St-Marien (ca 1275–90), a Premonstratensian house, and Abbot John of St-Pierre of Auxerre (1271–ca 95), an Augustinian house.

2 William III, bishop of Auxerre (1279–93).

3 Robert, son of the count of Flanders and count of Nevers through his marriage with Countess Yolendis.

4 Donzy, 58 km southwest of Auxerre; Cosne, 65 km southwest of Auxerre; St-Sauveur, 35 km southwest of Auxerre; and Murat, near Billy, 37 km south-southwest of Auxerre.

5 Appoigny, 10 km north-northwest of Auxerre.

6 Clamecy, 37 km south of Auxerre.

7 Arcy, 26 km southeast of Auxerre.

8 Erard, bishop of Auxerre (1270–8).

Item littera de comporacione inter dominum H[enricum] Autissiodorensis episcopum et M[ilonem] decanum.[9]

Item littera de burgensibus Conade[10] pro comite Niuernensis se aduo[c]antibus iusticiandis per episcopum secundum arrestum tempore bone memorie Guidonis episcopi Autissiodorensis et Odonis comitis Niuernensis[11] per dictum P. Autissiodorensis episcopum procurata et liberata.

Item littera de v solidis annui redditus debitis a uicarius altaris Sancte Eugenie de nouo fundati apud Varziaco[12] in honòre Beati Laurencii.

Item littera de parte terra empte a Iohanne de Pria pro ii libris Turonensis.

Item littera de emptore quaquid terrarum et pratorum apud Guacum et Valan[13] sitorum emptorum a Laurencio de Vallibus pro iiii-xx xv libris.

Item littera de iiii libris annui redditus emptis a Stephano de Hernianche pro xl libris.

Item littera de duabus peciis uinearum emptarum a Petro Mithael pro iiii-xx ii libris.

Item littera de x lb annui redditus emptis a Guillelmo de Mall[iaco][14] super domum suam ad fontem Sancti Amatoris pro c libris recusse fuerunt.

Although according to the scribe the documents in box B contained records of homage paid to the bishop and of the counts' duty to carry him on the day of his enthronement, there were clearly many other sorts of documents in it as well, especially sales records, which the scribe did not find worth copying. He did however copy the agreement between Bishop Henry and the dean of the chapter, referred to above.

21

Auxerre, September 1224

Walter, archbishop of Sens, attests to the end of a quarrel between Bishop Henry of Auxerre and the dean of the cathedral chapter. They settle their disagreements over relative jurisdictions in the city of Auxerre.

9 This agreement is document 21.

10 Cosne, 65 km southwest of Auxerre.

11 Gui of Mello, bishop of Auxerre (1247–70), and Odo of Burgundy, count of Nevers through his marriage with the countess.

12 Varzy, 51 km south-southwest of Auxerre.

13 Gy-l'Evêque and Vallan, both 7 km south-southwest of Auxerre.

14 Mailly, 23 km south of Auxerre.

MANUSCRIPTS: Bishops' cartulary, fols. 27v–29r. Bibl. Auxerre, MS 153, fols. 338r–339v; seventeenth-century copy by Dom Viole. Coll. Bourgogne 3, fols. 6r–7v.

EDITION: GC 12, instr. cols. 155–7, no. 82.

SUMMARY: Q 3:392, no. 755.

Galterus Dei gratia Senonensis archiepiscopus[1] uniuersis presentibus pariter et futuris ad quos presentes littere peruenerint, salutem in Domino sempiternam. Nouerint uniuersi quod cum esset contencio inter uenerabilem fratrem nostrum H[enricum] episcopum[2] ex una parte et dilectum filium M[ilonem] decanum Autissiodorensis ex alia, super remittendis causis hominum ciuitatis Autissiodorensis et parrochie Sancti Georgii[3] et abbacie de Cellis,[4] excepta parrochia Sancti Lupi que non est de iurisdictione decani, scilicet ab officio episcopi, ad decanum et super prouentibus siue explectis causarum predictorum locorum in utraque curia receptis et super ordinacione domus Dei de Monte Autrico,[5] et domus leprosorum Sancti Simeonis et super quibusdam aliis causis que inferius notabuntur. Tandem de consensu dictorum episcopi et decani, accedente eciam ad hoc consensu capituli Autissiodorensis ita sint pro bono pacis nobis mediantibus ordinatum quod de omnibus causis tam ciuilibus coram decano non inchoactis quam criminalibus predicti loci poterit cognoscere in propria persona dictus episcopus et etiam terminare et conuenti coram ipso non admittentur, si petierint ad curiam decani remitti, sed ibi tenebuntur litigare. Si autem fuerit querimonia coram ipso, poterit eam committere specialiter, pro uoluntate sua cuicunque uoluerit canonico uel non canonico, preter quam officiali suo, et conuenti tenebuntur coram huiusmodi delegato litigare, nec habebunt fori exceptionem, ut ad decanum remittantur.

De hominibus autem episcopi et ipsius familia ita est ordinatum, quod si conueniantur coram officiali episcopi, ibi habebunt litigare, si autem coram decano uel eius officiali conueniantur, si exceperint, quod sint de foro episcopi admittentur, et necesse habebit decanus et eius officialis eos remitere ad officialem episcopi, nisi conquerens sit, capitulum uel canonicus qui optionem habebit conueniendi hominem episcopi, et non familiam eius coram decano uel episcopo uel officiali eius de propriis causis suis. Si autem capitulum uel

1 Walter, archbishop of Sens (1223–41). For Walter, see Vincent Tabbagh, *Diocèse de Sens*, pp. 104–9.

2 Henry, bishop of Auxerre (1220–35).

3 St-Georges, 3 km west of Auxerre.

4 The Cistercian nunnery of Celles, just west of Auxerre, founded by Bishop William of Seignelay in 1219; GC 12, instr. cols. 154–5, nos. 79–80.

5 Montartre, just south of Auxerre.

canonicus conueniat aliquem de familia episcopi, episcopus uel eius officialis necesse habebit ius ei facere in ciuitate Autissiodorensi. De bailliuis et prepositis comitisse uel comitis, uel domini ciuitatis qui pro tempore fuerit, ita est ordinatum quod seu conueniantur coram officiali episcopi, uel in curia decani, ubi primo conuenti fuerint, ibi necesse habebunt litigare, et si obicierint exceptionem fori, nec admittentur, nec ad aliam curiam remittentur. Litigantes autem coram decano uel eius officiali quicumque fuerint, poterunt ad curiam episcopi appellare, clerici autem beneficiati ab episcopo, si coram officiali episcopi conueniantur de hiis que pertinent ad beneficia sua, ibi tenebuntur litigare, et allegantes fori excepcionem ad decanum non mittentur. Alii autem homines ciuitatis Autissiodorensis, ut puta homines ecclesiarum et homines comitisse, uel pro tempore domini ciuitatis uel quorumcunque aliorum, si conueniantur coram officiali curie episcopi et de foro decani exceperint petentes ad eum remitti, admittantur. De bedellis autem bailliuorum et prepositorum uerum si coram officiali episcopi conueniantur, ad excepcionem fori admittantur. Item et de hominibus episcopi et eius familia, si coram officiali episcopi aliquem conuenerint, uerum ad excepcionem fori admittantur, item et de clericis ciuitatis non beneficiatis uel beneficiatis, ab episcopo non a canonicis maioris ecclesie, si ratione contractuum uel delictorum conueniatur coram officiali episcopi, utrum ad excepcionem fori admittantur.

Item et de causis criminalibus ad quem spectant et quomodo, item et de prouentibus siue explectis causarum utriusque curie, uidelicet episcopi et decani quorum esse debeant, item et de ordinacione predictarum domorum ad quem spectet, in nos fuit ab utraque parte compromissum de uoluntate capituli Autissiodorensis, sicut per litteras eiusdem capituli nobis constitit euidenter. Ita quod supradicti episcopus et decanus firmiter promiserunt per litteras suas patentes, confirmantes id ipsum, quod quicquid supradictis articulis pro bono pacis uellemus statuere, siue ordinare, ratum haberent et gratum, et inuiolabiliter obseruarent.

Nos autem de bono et equo procedere cupientes, precognito utriusque partis assensu, de bonorum consilio ordinauimus in hunc modum. Si bedelli bailliuorum uel prepositorum deliquisse dicuntur in rebus memorati episcopi, uel hominibus eius uel familia uel rebus eorum, si super [hiis][6] conueniantur coram officiali episcopi, non habebunt excepcionem fori ut ad decanum remittantur. In aliis ante autem causis generaliter secundum communem legem aliorum hominum ciuitatis si excipiant iidem bedelli coram officiali episcopi, necesse habebit eos remittere ad curiam decani, de hominibus et familia episcopi ita pronunciamus, quod si conueniant homines qui sunt de iurisdictione

6 This word is missing in the cartulary.

decani, et illi excipiant de foro coram officiali episcopi, remittentur ad decanum. De clericis ciuitatis non beneficiatis uel beneficiatis ab episcopo non canonicis maioris ecclesie, si racione contractuum uel delictorum conueniantur coram episcopo, uel eius officiali et excipiant de foro, debent ad decanum remitti. De criminalibus uero causis sic a nobis est ordinatum, decanus summatim et de plano, si res ita exigat, poterit de criminalibus inquirere et cognoscere, et presbyteros et clericos propter infamiam uel scandalum, uel aliam causam rationabilem suspendere, et de quibus expedire uiderit, eos capere et detinere, si tamen incarcerari debeant, episcopo debent tradi, de maioribus autem criminibus in forma iudicii, uel per solempnem inquisitionem cognoscere non pertinet ad decanum. De prouentibus autem siue explectis causarum utriusque curie ordinauimus, quod inter episcopum et decanum equaliter diuidantur, et iurabit officialis decani episcopo quod bona fide porcionem suam ei conseruabit et reddet, similiter officialis episcopi iurabit decano quod de prouentibus uidelicet causarum, hominum ciuitatis Autissiodorensis, et locorum que sunt superius nominata medietatem integraliter ei reddet.

Preterea de domo de Monte Autrico et de domo leprosorum Sancti Simeonis diximus quod institutio magistrorum et destitutio, si destituendi fuerit, in domibus illis pertinet ad episcopum, uocato tamen ad hoc decano, minor autem iurisdictio et correctio personarum in eisdem domibus et auditus compotorum super prouentibus et expensis pertinet ad decanum. Non tamen prohibemus episcopo, quin ipse si uelit ex causa, de statu domorum cognoscere et correctionem facere, sine contradictione hoc possit.

In cuius rei perpetuam firmitatem presenti scripture sigillum nostrum fecimus apponi. Actum apud Autissiodorum anno gratie M CC uicesimo quarto mense Septembri.

Item littera de compromissione inter dominum episcopum et decanum super contencione iurisdictionis.

Disagreements between Bishop Henry and his chapter had been growing for several years; see the following document. There is a large round hole in fol. 28, which the scribe wrote around.

22

November 1221

Hervé and Matthew, canons of Auxerre, settle a quarrel between the cathedral chapter and Bishop Henry, who had taken over the jurisdiction of the dean when Dean William died. Both sides of the quarrel had settled on them as arbiters. They rule that when the office of dean is vacant, the bishop can exercise the appropriate jurisdiction.

MANUSCRIPTS: Bishops' cartulary, fol. 29r. Coll. Bourgogne 3, fol. 7r.
EDITION: GC 12, instr. col. 155, no. 81.
SUMMARY: Q 3:392, no. 754.

Item articuli scripti super eadem contencione.

Omnibus presentes litteras inspecturis Herueus et Matheus canonici Autissiodorensis in Domino salutem. Nouerint uniuersi quod cum post[1] mortem bone memorie Willelmi Autissiodorensis decani uacante decanatu, inter uenerabilem patrem et dominum Henricum episcopum[2] et uenerabilos uiros capitulum Autissiodorensis ad quem iurisdictio decanatus ipso uacante deuolui debetur, controuersia emersisset, asserente dicto episcopo ipsam ad eum pertinere, capituloque ad ipsum non ad episcopum pertineret e contrario proponente, tandem in nos duos ab utraque parte super hoc extitit compromissum. Nos igitur auditis utriusque partis rationibus, in primis protestantes quod de iurisdictionem super canonicos maioris ecclesie nichil diffinebamus, finaliter pronunciamus predictam iurisdictionem uacante decanatu ad dictum episcopum pertinere. Actum anno incarnacionis Domini MCC uicesimo primo, mense Nouembris.

Fol. 29v.

Prolacio arbitrii sigillata sigillo abbatis Sancti Dyonisii et magistri Henrici de Virziliaco, episcopi, comitis et comitisse super discordia porte pendentis, porte claustri, et super apertura murorum cunctorum claustro episcopi quod inuenietur in scrinio signato per D.

23

Paris, December 1275

The abbot of St-Denis and the treasurer of Laon settle a quarrel between Erard, bishop of Auxerre, and Count John over a new gate that the count has cut in the city walls of Auxerre. The bishop had said it harmed both him and the nearby

1 The cartulary reads 'post post.'
2 Henry, bishop of Auxerre (1220–35).

house of Notre-Dame-la-Dehors. The count had also closed up a gate by the river, at the bridge, although the bishop had forbidden him to do so. He is ordered to restore the walls and gates to how they had been before.

MANUSCRIPTS: Bishops' cartulary, fols. 29v–30v. Bibl. Auxerre, MS 153, fols. 455r–456v; seventeenth-century copy by Dom Viole.
EDITION: GC 12, instr. cols. 176–8, no. 112.
SUMMARY: Q 3:394, no. 774.

Vniuersis presentes litteras inspecturis M.[1] Dei gratia abbas Sancti Dyonisii in Francia et magister Henricus de Virziliaco, thesaurarius Laudunenis,[2] salutem in Domino. Notum facimus quod cum dicordia esset inter reuerendum patrem E[rardum] Dei gratia Autissiodorensis episcopum[3] ex una parte et illustrem uirum Iohannem comitem Autissiodorensis[4] ex altera super hoc quod dictus episcopus dicebat quod dictus comes perforari fecerat Autissiodorensis muros uille prope clausum ecclesie Beate Marie extra muros ciuitatis,[5] et apperturam tantam fecerat in eisdem, quod patebat aditus intrandi et exeundi uillam per aperturam predictam in preiudicium dicti episcopi et ecclesie Autissiodorensis et contra prohibicionem dicti episcopi seu mandati ipsius, dicto comite in contrarium asserente.

Item super hoc quod dictus episcopus dicebat quod dictus comes seu mandatum ipsius amouerat seu fecerat amoueri, per uiolenciam in preiudicium dicti episcopi et ecclesie Autissiodorensis et contra prohibicionem dicti episcopi uel eius mandati, quasdam portas uersus Yonam subtus domum dicti episcopi pendentes, in muris claustrum suum circuncingentibus, claudentes et apperienes infra claustrum, cum dictus episcopus esset tempore amocionis, et adhuc sit nomine ecclesie sue in possessione habendi in loco predicto portas claudentes et apperientes. Item super hoc quod dictus comes iniuste et in preiudicium predicti episcopi et ecclesie Autissiodorensis per uim suam amouerat, seu amoueri fecerat contra prohibitionem dicti episcopi, uel eius mandati, barellum et ferram cuiusdam alterius porte, que uocatur porta pendens, site et pendentis in muris claustrum ipsius episcopi circuncingentibus, et clauem ipsius ferre asportari fecerat, cum dictus episcopus esset tempore amotionis, et adhuc sit nomine ecclesie sue in possessione habendi in loco predicto dictam

1 He was named Matthew, according to GC.
2 The abbot of St-Denis, outside of Paris, and the treasurer of Laon.
3 Erard, bishop of Auxerre (1270–8).
4 John of Chalon, count of Auxerre through his marriage with the heiress.
5 Notre-Dame-la-Dehors was outside the original Roman walls, which surrounded the cathedral, but inside the city walls erected during the twelfth century.

portam claudentem, apperientem et firmantem, necnon in possessione claudendi, apperiendi et firmandi eandem.

Tandem pro bono pacis in curia domini regis inter partes et ipsis partibus expresse consentientibus, super dictis discordiis taliter extitit ordinatum, uidelicet quod predictus comes apperturam predictam quam fecit seu fieri fecit in muris uille prope dictum clausum, reobturari faciet, et ex toto reduci in pristinum statum, in quo erant antequam facta esset appertura predicta, qui murus sic refectus absque ulla discussione in statu remanebit antiquo, sine preiudicio comitis in possessione, uel in proprietate murorum. De portis autem fuit taliter ordinatum, quod predictus comes portas deuersus Yonam quas fecerat amoueri, restituet et reponet, seu restitui et reponi faciet in loco suo in quo erant tempore amocionis predicte. In altera quoque porta que dicitur porta pendens barellum, ferram et clauem que fecerat amoueri, reponi faciet et restitui in eadem, et reponi in statu in quo erant ante amocionem, ita quod claudi aperiri et firmari poterunt. Que predicta omnia fient, et restituentur per bailluisi et prepositos dicti comitis in statum pristinum, sub forma predicta infra instans festum Beati Hilarii, super discordiis uero dictarum portarum, uidelicet portarum deuersus Yonam, et porte pendentis, electi sunt duo, uidelicet uenerabilis uir Guillelmus archidiaconus Autissiodorensis pro parte dicti episcopi, et Guido de Meso quondam bailliuus Autissiodorensis pro parte dicti comitis, qui predicta porta deuersus Yonam, et barrello et ferra et claue porte pendentis in statu pristino sub forma predicta primitus repositis, tenebunt premissa in manu sua, et dictis portis sine amocione aliqua in statu pristino remanentibus, cognoscent et diligenter inquirent de dictis discordiis quantum ad dictas portas et dictas discordias infra finem instantis parlamenti quod erit post Penthecostem, si in unam possint concordare sententiam, pace uel iudicio terminabunt.

Si uero discordes fuerint, debent infra finem dicti pallamenti tradere nobis abbati predicto tercio arbitro, seu arbitratori a partibus electo, illud in quo essent discordes sufficienter instructum. Et nos dictus abbas solus, uel cum altero predictorum duorum, dictas discordias pace uel iudicio, alte et basse infra dictum finem pallamenti terminabimus, si commode facere potuerimus. Alioquin infra finem immediate subsequentis pallamenti, quod erit in festo Beati Martini yemalis, promiserunt autem dicte partes stare arbitrio, seu ordinationi dictorum arbitrorum si concordare possint, uel dicto, seu ordinationi nostri abbatis predicti, sub forma superius annotata.

Dictus autem episcopus ad preces nostras super hoc quod citauerat dictum comitem coram se super refectione quorundam castrorum mouencium de feodo dicti episcopi, et repositione eorum in bono statu supersedebit ad presens, et uoluit dictus episcopus ad preces nostras, quod prepositi Autissiodorensis excommunicati, auctoritate officialis sui pro fractura claustri ipsius episcopi, si petant absolui, in forma ecclesie absoluantur, et emendam si uoluerit leuare, leuabit de consilio nostri abbatis predicti. Nos autem predictus episcopus et comes predictus et nos Aalydis comitissa Autissiodorensis[6] predicta omnia uolumus et concedimus et in predictis expresse consentimus et sigilla nostra una cum sigillis uenerabilis patris abbatis predicti et uenerabilis uiri magistri Henrici de Virziliaco predicti presentibus litteris apposuimus in testimonium premissorum. Actum Parisiis anno Domini Millesimo CC septuagesimo quinto, die sabbati post festum Beati Nicholay yemalis.

Item in dicto scrinio continetur totus processus de eadem materia.

The scribe understandably decided not to copy all the documents pertaining to what was clearly a long and messy dispute. The walls around the city had originally been put up in the twelfth century.

Fol. 31r.

In scrinio signato per E inuenientur littere regis super equitaciones.

24

Paris, April 1207

Philip II, king of France, yields the right to the regalia of Auxerre during an episcopal vacancy. The cathedral chapter may keep the regalia when there is no bishop.

MANUSCRIPTS: Bibl. Auxerre, MS 142, p. 261, from the original, copied in the early thirteenth century into the 'Gesta' of the bishops. Philip's Register A, fol. 45r (abbreviated). Bishops' cartulary, fol. 31r. Bibl. Auxerre, MS 153, fols. 258v–259r, from the 'Gesta' of the bishops; done by Dom Viole in the seventeenth century. Arch. Yonne G 1832, a nineteenth-century copy, from the MS of the 'Gesta.'

EDITIONS: GC 12, instr. col. 147, no. 65. L.-M. Duru, ed., *Bibliothèque historique de l'Yonne*, 1:460–1; from the MS of the 'Gesta.' *Recueil des actes de Philippe Auguste*, 3:11–13, no. 968. *Gesta*, 2:217, from the MS of the 'Gesta.'

SUMMARIES: Q 3:391, no. 743. Léopold Delisle, *Catalogue des actes de Philippe-Auguste*, p. 235, no. 1021A.

---

6 Adelaide, heiress of Auxerre and wife of Count John.

In nomine sancte et indiuidue trinitatis amen. Ph[ilipus] Dei gratia Francorum rex.[1] Nouerint[2] uniuersi presentes pariter et futuri quod nos intuitu[3] pietatis et[4] ob remedium anime nostre et parentum nostrorum damus et concedimus[5] imperpetuum ecclesie Autissiodorensis[6] quicquid iuris habebamus in regalibus Autissiodorensis uacante sede,[7] ita quod decanus et capitulum eiusdem ecclesie custodient regalia[8] sede uacante et omnes prouentus qui exinde procedent et prebendas si quas interim uacare contigerint[9] ad opus futuri episcopi, saluo seruicio nostro equitationis, exercitus[10] et submonitionis, sicut episcopi Autissiodorenses nobis fecerunt. Quod[11] imperpetuum[12] robur obtineat[13] sigilli nostri auctoritate et regii nominis karactere inferius annotato presentem paginam confirmamus.

Actum Parisius[14] anno Domini MCC sexto, regni[15] uero nostri anno uicesimo septimo.[16] Astantibus in palatio[17] nostro quorum[18] nomina supposita sunt et signa. Dapifero nullo, signum Guidonis buticularii, S. Mathei camerarii, S. Droconis constabularii, data uacante cancellaria per manus fratris Garini.[19]

Item littera duplicata est.
Item in eodem scrinio est littera papalis confirmatoria.[20]

---

1 Philip II, king of France (1180–1223). This whole invocation is missing in the royal register, which starts with 'Notum.'
2 For 'Nouerint – futuri' the royal register reads 'Notum et cetera.'
3 The 'Gesta' MS adds 'diuine.'
4 This word is omitted in the cartulary.
5 The royal register reads 'concedimus et donamus.'
6 The royal register reads 'Altisiodorensis,' here and throughout.
7 The 'Gesta' MS reads 'se.'
8 The royal register adds 'eadem.'
9 The 'Gesta' MS reads 'contigerit.'
10 The 'Gesta' MS reads 'nostre exercitus.'
11 This sentence is omitted in the royal register.
12 The 'Gesta' MS reads 'ut perpetuum.'
13 The cartulary has the words 'presentem paginam' here rather than below.
14 This word is omitted in the royal register.
15 Beginning here, the royal register omits the rest of the text, giving only 'mense Aprili.'
16 The 'Gesta' MS reads 'sexto.'
17 The cartulary reads 'parlamento.'
18 The 'Gesta' MS omits the phrase 'in … quorum.'
19 The 'Gesta' MS reads 'per manum Garini.'
20 The pope's confirmation is printed in Rainer Murauer and Andrea Sommerlechner, eds., *Die Register Innocenz' III*, vol. 10, pp. 123–6, no. 71.

Both the cartulary and the manuscript of the 'Gesta' reproduce a monogram that spells out PHILIPUS, doubtless from the original. According to the *Gesta* of the bishops of Auxerre, one of the first acts of Bishop William of Seignelay, once he was consecrated in 1207, was to persuade King Philip to return the regalia, from which royal officials had been taking the income, and agree not to demand them again in the future. It took a large gift from the bishop to ensure this grant.[21] Although the date is given as 1206, this must be 1207, which until Easter was considered part of 1206. Although the month is not given in the cartulary, it was April, as indicated by the royal register. The king made similar concessions to Bishops William of Nevers and Ponce of Mâcon in the following two years.[22]

This document may be the only one for which the original certainly existed in post-medieval times. According to the seventeenth-century inventory of the bishop's rights (Arch. Yonne G 1592), there existed a parchment original of what must be this document. Fol. 31 of the cartulary has a big hole in it.

25

Paris, 1175

King Louis VII orders that no commune be established at Auxerre. Count Gui of Nevers had tried to establish one, but Bishop William argued that the two previous counts of Nevers had given the bishops privileges that no new institutions would be set up in Auxerre without episcopal assent.

MANUSCRIPTS: Bishops' cartulary, fol. 31v. Coll. Bourgogne 3, fol. 8r.

EDITIONS: GC 12, inst. col. 135, no. 50. Q 2:263–4, no. 245, from Coll. Bourgogne 3 and GC.

SUMMARIES: M. de Brequigny, *Table chronologique des diplômes, chartes, titres et actes imprimés*, vol. 3, p. 506. Achille Luchaire, *Etudes sur les actes de Louis VII*, p. 315, no. 684.

Littera de communia non facienda.

In nomine sancte et individue trinitatis amen, Ludouicus Dei gratia Francorum rex.[1] Notum facimus uniuersis presentibus et futuris quod uerbum motum est a comite Niuernensis de communia facienda Autissiodorensis, a

21 *Gesta*, 2:217. See also Constance Brittain Bouchard, *Spirituality and Administration*, pp. 132–3.

22 *Recueil des actes de Philippe Auguste*, 3:123–4, 139–40, nos. 1052, 1066.

1 Louis VII, king of France (1137–80).

comite uidelicet Guidone,[2] cui rei cum episcopus Autissiodorensis Guillemus[3] dilectus et fidelis noster instanter reclamaret et contradiceret, asserens penes se priuilegia esse tam predicti comitis quam patris sui Willelmi et fratris sui Willelmi[4] quondam comitum Niuernensium in quibus continebatur quod nullam consuetudinem nouam poterant Autissiodero constituere uel introducere, preter eius assensum et uoluntatem, uel successorum suorum episcoporum.[5] Nos eadem priuilegia presentari nobis fecimus ac cum omni diligencia recitari. Ex eorum itaque moti continencia que prenominati comites concesserant et confirmauerant nos quoque ad peticionem iamdicti episcopi amici nostri concessimus. Et ne fieri possit Autissiodorum communia sine ipsius assensu et uoluntate, uel successorum suorum episcoporum presenti pagina confirmamus. Quod ut inconcussum et stabile maneat imperpetuum sigilli nostri auctoritate ac regii nominis subter instructo karactere iussimus communiri.

Actum publice Parisius anno incarnati uerbi MC LXXV, astantibus in palacio nostro quorum nomina supposita sunt et signa. S. comitis Theobaldi dapiferi nostri.[6] S. Guidonis buticularii. S. Radulphi constabularii. S. Reginaldi camerarii. Data vacante cancellaria.

The document ends in a monogram, representing the name Louis. According to the *Gesta* of the bishops of Auxerre, King Louis was originally amenable to the idea of a commune at Auxerre, saying that all cities with communes were his, but he was persuaded to issue this charter after the bishop made him a sizeable gift.[7]

26

Sens, November 1204

King Philip Augustus grants the bishop of Auxerre the procurations he had formerly demanded at Auxerre and Varzy. In return, the bishop frees him from doing homage for the fief of Gien, which the king now holds. If Gien reverts to the bishop, the king will again be able to demand the procurations.

---

2 Gui, count of Nevers (1168–75).

3 William of Toucy, bishop of Auxerre (1167–81).

4 Count Gui was son of Count William III of Nevers (1149–61) and younger brother of Count William IV (1161–8), his predecessor.

5 This is a reference to document 4, in which Count Gui said that he had read and accepted his predecessors' agreements with the bishop of Auxerre.

6 Count Theobold V of Blois (1152–90).

7 *Gesta*, 2:117. See also Constance Brittain Bouchard, *Spirituality and Administration*, pp. 85–6; and Yves Sassier, *Louis VII*, pp. 432–8.

MANUSCRIPTS: Philip's Register A, fol. 37v (abbreviated). Bishops' cartulary, fol. 32r. Bibl. Auxerre, MS 153, fol. 238r; seventeenth-century copy by Dom Viole. Coll. Bourgogne 3, fol. 8r–v. Arch. Yonne G 1832, a nineteenth-century copy, from Philip's register.

EDITIONS: GC 12, instr. col. 147, no. 64. *Recueil des actes de Philippe Auguste*, 2:447–8, no. 860.

SUMMARIES: M. de Brequigny, *Table chronologique des diplômes, chartes, titres et actes imprimés*, 4:361. Léopold Delisle, *Catalogue des actes de Philippe-Auguste*, p. 200, no. 879.[1]

Littera de quittacione procuracionum.

In nomine sancte et indiuidue trinitatis amen. Philipus Dei gratia Francorum rex.[2] Nouerint[3] uniuersi presentes pariter et futuri quod nos de duabus procuracionibus quas episcopus Autissiodorensis nobis debet, unam uidelicet apud Autissiodorum et alteram apud Varziacum,[4] ipsum quitamus, pro eo quod idem episcopus de feodo et homagio[5] Giemi[6] quod ad ipsum pertinebat nos quittat. Nos autem Giemum in dominio nostro tenemus, saluo cereo maioris ecclesie Autissiodorensis, quem reddemus eidem ecclesie Beati Stephani Autissiodorensis sicut antecessores nostri ante nos reddiderunt. Si autem contigerit feodum illum et homagium[7] ad episcopum Autissiodorensem reuerti, nos et heredes nostri procuraciones predictas rehabebimus sicut prius. Quod[8] ut firmum sit et stabile, sigilli auctoritate et regii nominis karactere inferius annotato presentem paginam confirmamus. Actum Senonis, ab incarnacione Domini anno MCC quarto, regni nostri anno uicesimo sexto.[9] Astantibus in palacio nostro quorum nomina supposita sunt et signa. Dapifero nullo. S. Guidonis buticularii. S. Mathei camerarii. S. Droconis constabularii. Data uacante cancellaria.

The king obtained Gien from Hervé of Donzy in return for agreeing to Hervé's marriage with the heiress to Nevers. In a separate document, also issued in 1204, Bishop Hugh of Auxerre freed the king from having to do homage for the

1 Delisle says that this charter is printed in RHGF 18:726, but in fact this is just an excerpt from the *Gesta*, discussing the events surrounding this charter but not reproducing it.

2 Philip II ('Augustus'), king of France (1180–1223). The royal register omits the invocation and begins with 'Notum.'

3 For 'Nouerint … futuri' the royal register reads 'Notum et cetera.'

4 Varzy, 51 km south-southwest of Auxerre.

5 The royal register reads 'hominagio.'

6 Gien, 76 km west-southwest of Auxerre.

7 The royal register reads 'hominagium.'

8 The royal register omits this sentence.

9 The royal register omits the rest of the charter after this point.

fief of Gien in return for being freed from procurations.[10] Léopold Delisle suggests that this document was given in November, because Philip was in Sens in that month in 1204.

According to the *Gesta* of the bishops of Auxerre, these procurations had entailed the requirement that the bishop had to put up and feed the king or any royal official who came to an episcopal residence. The *Gesta* author was laudatory of Bishop Hugh's success in abolishing this requirement, especially since, as he noted, even though the king did not have to do homage for Gien he still had to pay the traditional hundred pounds of wax a year that the castellan of Gien owed the bishop.[11]

Fol. 32v.

In scrinio signato per F inueniuntur littera de moneta Autissiodorensis et totus processus.

27

Paris, 1188

King Philip II attests that Count Peter of Nevers and Countess Agnes have agreed not to change the weight or value of money struck at their mint. If they or their children or grandsons do so, then the money from their mint need not be used in their counties. In return for accepting their money exclusively, the ecclesiastical and secular lords of the region may, this year only, levy a fee of twelve pennies on each house they own.

MANUSCRIPTS: Bishops' cartulary, fol. 32v.[1] Coll. Bourgogne 3, fols. 8v–9r.
EDITIONS: Lebeuf 2:30–1, no. 63. Lebeuf 4:57–8, no. 78. Q 2:383–4, no. 374. *Recueil des actes de Philippe Auguste*, 1:290–1, no. 237, from Lebeuf.
SUMMARY: Léopold Delisle, *Catalogue des actes de Philippe-Auguste*, p. 53, no. 217.

---

10 Q 3:18–19, nos. 36, 38. For the political context, see René de Lespinasse, *Le Nivernais et les comtes de Nevers*, 2:1–26.

11 *Gesta*, pp. 161–3. Philip Augustus ordered his provost in Gien to pay the wax he owed each year to the cathedral; *Recueil des actes de Philippe Auguste*, 2:413, no. 833.

---

1 This document is copied in a later hand than those on the preceding and succeeding pages. It is the last folio of a gathering, and presumably the page was originally left blank.

In nomine sancte et inidiuidue trinitatis amen. Ph[ilipus] Dei gratia Francorum rex.[2] Nouerint uniuersi quod cognatus noster comes Niuernensis,[3] ad consilium et consensum episcoporum, abbatum et baronum comitatus Niuernensis, monetam fecit ad quatuor denarios de fino argento et sexdecim solidos et octo denarios de pondere in marca Trecensi, quam comes et uxor sua Agnes comitissa[4] iurauerunt perpetuo de cetero in iamdicto pondere et legalitate fideliter conseruandam, quam etiam iurabit filius comitis uel filia, et filii filiorum uel filiarum successiue in posterum, ut duret imperpetuum. Si uero comes uel filius suus uel filia aut filius filii uel filie monetam ipsam de supradicto pondere et ualore in aliquo defraudarent uel fraudari sustinerent, ecclesiastice persone uel barones terre sue monetam suam deinceps non tenerentur recipere, sed monetam quam uellent in terra sua sine occasione mitterent, et episcopi Autissiodorensis et Niuernensis de comite et terra sua et heredibus suis iustitiam facerent.

Si autem fabricatores monete predictum pondus et ualorem minuere presumerent, de ipsis iustitia districta fieret, nec eis fauore aliquo aut gratia pateretur. Et ut nulla possit in moneta ipsa fieri diminutio uel falsitas, frequentius probabitur a cambitoribus et discretis uiris in cognitione argenti et ponderis, et ecclesiastice persone uel barones eam, quandocumque uoluerint, probari facient.

Pro perpetuitate uero ipsius monete et pro uia Iherosolymitana, placuit personis ecclesiasticis et baronibus terre comitis ut de singulis domibus que proprium habent mansionarum duodecim denarios hoc tantum anno accipiet per ciuitates et castella, burgos et uillas in quibus moneta Niuernensis debitum cursum habet. Ne uero beneficium duodecim denariorum quod comite sponte hoc tantum anno impenditur, ecclesiis uel baronibus in consequentiam trahatur quod nunquam fuerat nec amodo erit, litteras nostras eis patentes tradidimus, tam de monete perpetuitate quam de indempnitate, pro beneficio comiti semel gratis impenso.

Quod ut in posterum ratum illibatumque permaneat, presentem paginam sigilli nostri auctoritate ac regii nominis karactere inferius annotato precipimus confirmari. Actum Parisius anno ab incarnatione Domini MC LXXXVIII, regni nostri anno nono, astantibus in palacio nostro quorum nomina supposita sunt et signa. S. comitis Theobaldi dapiferi nostri.[5] S. Guidonis buticularii. S. Mathei camerarii. S. Radulphi constabularii. Data uacante cancellaria.

2 Philip II ('Augustus'), king of France (1180–1223).

3 Peter of Courtenay (d. 1219), count of Nevers and Auxerre, was the king's cousin.

4 Agnes was the heiress of Nevers after her brother's death in 1181. Her husband, Peter of Courtney, became count when he married her in 1184.

5 Count Theobold V of Blois (1152–90).

Inuenientur totus processus in eodem scrinio.

Again, the scribe only felt it necessary to copy the final royal document that settled a doubtless prolonged case.

Fol. 33r.

In scrinio signato per G inuenientur littere de institutione prioris Sancti Amatoris.

28

Auxerre, December 1163

Bishop Alain of Auxerre submits the church of St-Amâtre of Auxerre to the canons of St-Satur of Bourges; they will be governed by the Augustinian rule. The bishop specifies that in the episcopal vineyards, where the church of St-Amâtre had collected a tithe, he and his successors shall pay twelve measures of wine a year, ten of red and two of white.

MANUSCRIPTS: Bishops' cartulary, fol. 33r. Bibl. Auxerre, MS 153, fol. 142r; seventeenth-century copy by Dom Viole. Coll. Bourgogne 3, fol. 9r–v.
EDITIONS: GC 12, instr. col. 127, no. 39. Q 2:142, no. 131.

Ad episcopalis officii discretionem perinet loca religiosa, non solum tutari et conseruare uerum etiam ipsam religionam in meliorem statum promouere. Inde est quo ego Alanus Dei gratia Autissiodorensis dictus episcopus[1] ecclesiam Beati Amatoris ex officio michi, iniuncto et apostolice auctoritatis mandato, cum illis possessionibus quas canonici regulares tunc tenebant ecclesie Sancti Saturi imperpetuum concedo, saluis institutionibus que sunt inter ecclesiam Sancti Amatoris et Beati Stephani et ea condicione ut per episcopum prior ibi de donis illa constitutur et ibidem iuxta consuetudinem et disciplinam prenominate ecclesie uiuat et cum fratribus suis, adiuuante gratia Domini, ordinem Beati Augustini teneat et cum fuerit constitutus nisi per episcopum non amoueatur.

Ne qua uero deinceps inter episcopum et canonicos controuersie oriatur occasio, constitutum est meo et corum assensu, ut de uineis episcopi in quibus canonici decimam requirebant, episcopus singulis annis duodecim modios

1 Alain, bishop of Auxerre (1152–67).

persoluat, decem de rubeo et duos de albo. In terra uero que Cunemine dicitur Episcopi, quotiens culta fuerit, canonici decimam habeant. Facta est autem hec constitutio in octauis Beati Stephani, in capitulo Autissiodorensi, Guidone preposito, Rainaudo archidiacono, Radulpho thesaurario, Stephano cantore presentibus et assencientibus sub assensu etiam totius capituli, anno ab incarnacione Domini MCC LXIII,[2] Domino Alexandro III summo pontifice, Ludouico rege Francorum, Willelmo iuniore comite Niuernensis.[3]

Item littera papalis confirmatoria in eodem scrinio.

The church of St-Amâtre was located just south of Auxerre, in the old Gallo-Roman cemetery on Montartre, where the see's earliest bishops were buried, including Amator.

29

April 1208

Andreas, abbot of St-Satur of Bourges, attests that the canons of St-Amâtre have given Bishop William the annual payment of twelve measures of wine that he had owed them. In return the bishop gives them land at Murat he had acquired from the knight Itier Bornus.

MANUSCRIPTS: Bishops' cartulary, fol. 33r–v. Bibl. Auxerre, MS 153, fol. 294r; seventeenth-century copy by Dom Viole. Coll. Bourgogne 3, fol. 9v.
EDITIONS: Lebeuf 2:37, no. 78. Lebeuf 4:69, no. 103.
SUMMARY: Q 3:416, no. 949.

Item alia littera de permutacione uini quod canonici Sancti Amatoris habebant in domo episcopi.

Andreas Dei permissione dictus abbas et uniuersis ecclesie Beati Satori conuentus omnibus ad quos litere presentes peruenerint, in Domino salutem. Nouerint uniuersi presentes pariter et futuri quod dilecti fratres et canonici nostri Sancti Amatoris Autissiodorensis de assensu et uoluntate nostra

2 The date should read 1163, not 1263. This is the kind of slip it would be easy for a thirteenth-century scribe to make.

3 Pope Alexander III (1159–81); King Louis VII of France (1137–80); and Count William IV of Nevers (1161–8).

quittauerunt imperpetuum uenerabili patri Willelmo Autissiodorensi episcopo[1] et successoribus suis decem modios uini rubei et duos albi, quos idem episcopus memoratus canonicis nostris annuatim soluere tenebatur, sicut in autentico bone memorie Alani quondam Autissiodorensis episcopi continetur.[2] Prenominatus uero episcopus in recompensationem quittationis istius dedit et concessit imperpetuum canonicis nostris Sancti Amatoris terram in territorio de Moreto[3] sitam, quam acquisiuit ab Iterio Borno milite, et quamdam portionem clausi sui domui dictorum canonicorum contiguam, ab omni censu liberam et immunem, saluis et integris per omnia aliis articulis qui in prelibato autentico continentur.

Vt autem quittatio dicta de assensu nostro facta, perpetuam obtineat firmitatem, presentem cartam scribi fecimus sigillorum nostrorum munimine roboratam. Actum anno Domini Millesimo CC octauo, mense Aprili.

The canons of St-Amâtre were dependent on St-Satur of Bourges. See the preceding document.

30

October 1208

William, bishop of Auxerre, attests that the burgher Peter of Chablis has, from his own resources, built a drawbridge on the bridge piles in the river, which belong to the bishop. The bishop grants him and his heirs in perpetuity half the tolls from the bridge, keeping the other half.

MANUSCRIPTS: Bishops' cartulary, fol. 33v. Coll. Bourgogne 3, fols. 9v–10r.

Willelmus Dei gratia Autissiodorensis episcopus,[1] omnibus presentes litteras inspecturis in Domino salutem. Vniuersitatem uestram scire uolumus quod Petrus de Chableis[2] burgensis Autissiodorensis, de assensu nostro et instudato, super duas pilas pontis Autissiodorensis que in terra et aqua nostra site sunt, cum sumptibus suis edificauit tornum ad naues superius trabendas. Nos autem propter sumptos quos ibi fecerat ei donauimus et heredibus eius imperpetuum medietatem emolumenti quod de torno illo proueniet, reliquam

1 William of Seignelay, bishop of Auxerre (1207–20).
2 This is a reference to document 28, issued by Bishop Alain of Auxerre (1152–67).
3 Murat, near Billy, 37 km south-southwest of Auxerre.

1 William of Seignelay, bishop of Auxerre (1207–20).
2 Chablis, 13 km east of Auxerre.

medietatem nobis retinentes. Ipse uero et heredes ipsius successores quecunque torno fuerint norra de suo facient et omnia in eo reparanda de suo reparabunt. Preterea Petrus uel heres suus non poterit extra manum suam ponere portionem torni que eum contingit. Quod si forte facere uelleret, cum a nobis eam habeat, nobis potius eam retinemus si uellerimus habere. Quod ut stabile sit et ratum, presentem cartam sigillo nostro sub cirographo fecimus roborari. Actum anno Domini M CC VIII, mense Octobri.

Although this is clearly a separate document from the preceding, the cartulary scribe copied it directly afterwards, with no rubric, although it does begin a new line and has a paragraph marker in the margin. It has not been previously printed.

31

1213

Archdeacon Hugh of Auxerre notes that his office is supposed to provide a lector for the cathedral but is unable to do so because of insufficient funds. Bishop William has now established a prebend to pay for the lector, and the archdeacon agrees that from now on bishops will be able to choose the lector.

MANUSCRIPTS: Bishops' cartulary, fols. 33v–34r. Coll. Bourgogne 3, fol. 10r.
EDITION: GC 12, instr. cols. 151–2, no. 74 (abbreviated).
SUMMARY: Q 3:392, no. 749.

Item littera super institutione lectorie in eodem scrinio.

Hugo Autissiodorensis archidiaconus omnibus presentes litteras inspecturis, in Domino salutem. Nouerint uniuersi presentes pariter et futuri quod cum ad officium dignitatis archidiaconi spectaret ecclesie nostre prouidere lectorem, qui totum legendi officium ordinaret, nec inuenirem propter reddituum paucitatem, qui honus[1] uellet subire lectoris, quoniam laborem stipendia non sequebantur condigna, unde ecclesie seruicium non modicum turbabatur, uenerabilis pater et dominus meus Willelmus episcopus[2] noster eidem officio, et succentorie pariter fructus prebende unius integros de assensu capituli imperpetuum assignauit, et ego ei suisque successoribus in posterum cessi et concessi benigne ius instituendi lectorem.

Quod ut stabile firmumque permaneat, presentem cartam notari feci et sigilli mei impressione muniri. Actum anno Domini MCC tercio decimo.

1 The classical Latin is 'onus.'
2 William of Seignelay, bishop of Auxerre (1207–20).

See also document 33, in which the pope had approved episcopal authority over the lector in 1208.

32

November 1249

Bishop Gui of Auxerre notes that there is at present no one who can act in the bishop's absence when he is out of town on official business. Accordingly, Gui establishes that the schoolmaster, who is supported by the bishop, shall henceforth serve as the bishop's chaplain, assisting in the mass, and shall act for him when he is absent. The schoolmaster shall get an additional ten pounds a year for this service. The office of schoolmaster is currently vacant.

MANUSCRIPTS: Bishops' cartulary, fol. 34r–v. Bibl. Auxerre, MS 153, fols. 403v–404r; seventeenth-century copy by Dom Viole. Coll. Bourgogne 3, fol. 10r–v.
EDITION: GC 12, instr. cols. 167–8, no. 100.
SUMMARY: Q 3:393, no. 766.

Item littere de scolastica in eodem scrinio.

Omnibus presentes litteras inspecturas, Guido diuina miseracione episcopus Autissiodorensis,[1] salutem in Domino. Cum nos tam causa uisitandi episcopatum Autissiodorensis quam aliis iustis causis contingat ab Autissiodorensi ciuitate frequencius procul esse, nec in ecclesia Autissiodorensis fuerit hactenus aliquis qui ex officio suo uices absentis pontificis agere teneatur, propter quod possunt nonnulla animarum pericula prouenire. Nos super hoc salubre consilium apponere cupientes, uacante scolastica ecclesie Autissiodorensis ad nostram collationem spectante, statuimus quod scolasticus Autissiodorensis sit capellanus episcopi et teneatur assistere et seruire episcopo Autissiodorensi quando celebrabit sollempniter in maiori ecclesia, et alibi si presens sit, et episcopum contigerit sollempniter celebrare, et in aliis horis similiter quando diuinum officium celebrabit. Statuimus etiam quod absente episcopo in officiis ad episcopum pertinentibus supleat uices eius, sicut in exclusione penitencium ab ecclesia in capite ieiuniorum, et in reconciliacione eorundem in die cene et in similibus. Statuimus etiam quod illis diebus in quibus consuetum est episcopum si presens est diuinum officium celebrare, si persone ecclesie Autissiodorensis absentes fuerint, uel dictum officium celebrare noluerint uel nequiuerint, ipse loco episcopi teneatur celebrare, nisi iustum habeat impedimentum uel iuxta de causa absens fuerit, quo casu ad ebdomadarium pertinebit.

1 Gui of Mello, bishop of Auxerre (1247–70).

Preter hec statuimus quod in institucione sua tenebitur iurare episcopo, quod ad ordines sacerdotii promouebitur infra annum, iurabit etiam quod in ecclesia Autissiodorensi residentiam faciet personalem per nonem menses, nisi uocatus fuerit ab episcopo, uel ab eodem episcopo alicubi destinatus, seu etiam a capitulo pro negotiis ecclesie alicubi destinatus, ita tamen quod missus a capitulo infra dies quindecim reuertatur, et tunc quantum ad iuramentum pro residenti habebitur uel nisi in peregrinacione profectus fuerit ultra mare, uel ad sedem apostolicam, uel ad Sanctum Iacobum iurabit nichilominus quod scolas ad suam collationem pertinentes, bona fide gratis conferet personis, sub quibus crediderit auditores posse proficere et debere. Tenebitur etiam audire confessiones loco episcopi, cum ad ipsum uenire contigerit confitentes.

Et quoniam dicto officio honus[2] solito maius extra iuxta presentis statuti tenorem duximus imponendum, ut eius maiori labore beneficium consequatur, statuimus quod idem capellanus, ultra redditus quos percipere consueuit racione scolastice, decem libras Turonenses percipiat annis singulis imperpetuum in festo Beati Andree apostoli in decima de Saciaco, que spectat ad ecclesiam de Betriaco,[3] uacantem et ad collacionem nostram spectantem. Dicta autem scolastica et capellania ad collacionem episcopi pertinent et semper pertinebunt. Scolasticus uero et capellanus erit homo ligius episcopi et fidelitatem faciet, salua tamen fidelitate quam debet capitulo tanquam canonicus. Nos uero H decanus totumque capitulum Autissiodorensis presenti statuto consentimus et quantum in nobis est approbamus.

In cuius rei testimonium et munimen, nos Guido predictus episcopus et nos H decanus et capitulum Autissiodorensis sigilla nostra presentibus duximus apponenda. Actum anno Domini MCC quadragesimo nono, die Martis propter festum Beati Martini hyemalis.

The bishop had provided the revenues for the schoolmaster since 1208; see the following document.

33

Rome, 23 January 1208

Pope Innocent III notes that the archdeacon of Auxerre has the right to confer the offices of lector and schoolmaster, but his revenues are insufficient.

---

2 The classical Latin is 'onus.'

3 Sacy, 24 km southeast of Auxerre, and Bétry, 20 km southeast of Auxerre.

Therefore the pope confirms that the bishop of Auxerre may take over these offices and provide an appropriate income for those who hold them.

MANUSCRIPTS: Bishops' cartulary, fols. 34v–35r.[1] Bibl. Auxerre, MS 153, fol. 291r; seventeenth-century copy by Dom Viole. Coll. Bourgogne 3, fols. 10v–11r.

EDITIONS: PL 215:1301, no. 196, dated 1207; abbreviated. Rainer Murauer and Andrea Sommerlechner, eds., *Die Register Innocenz' III*, vol. 10, pp. 346–7, no. 196 (abbreviated).

SUMMARY: August Potthast, *Regesta pontificum Romanorum*, 1:280, no. 3279.

Item littera papalis de lectoria et scolastica in eodem scrinio.

Innocencius seruus seruorum Dei[2] uenerabili fratri Altissiodorensis episcopo,[3] salutem et apostolicam benedictionem. Ex parte tua fuit propositum coram nobis quod cum archidiaconus tuus officia duo, lectoriam uidelicet et scolastriam, in ecclesia tua potestatem habeat conferendi, quia non reperiuntur qui eadem uelint recipere cum redditus non habeant competentes, idem collacionem ipsorum ad ius episcopale deuenire consentit, pro eo quod tu ecclesie utilitatem attendens proposuisti predictis officiis congruos redditus assignare. Verumque id sine auctoritate sedis apostolice robur obtinere non putas, nobis humiliter suplicasti ut collacionem predictorum officiorum tibi et successoribus tuis concedere dignaremur. Nos igitur benigne tuis precibus annuentes, tibi et successoribus tuis auctoritate presentium indulgemus ut si archidiaconi tui consensus accesserit, predicta officia personis ydoneis libere conferatis, postquam curaueris ad eadem competentes redditus deputare. Nulli ergo omnino hominum liceat hanc paginam nostre concessionis infringere uel ei ausu temerario contraire. Si quis autem hoc attemptare presumpserit indignacionem omnipotentis Dei et Beatorum Petri et Pauli apostolorum eius se nouerit incursurum.

Datum Rome apud Sanctum Petrum, x kalendas Februarii, pontificatus nostri anno decimo.

The increased authority of the pope is demonstrated by the bishop's need to have this new arrangement officially approved.

1 A later marginal hand dates this document 1210.

2 Pope Innocent III (1198–1216).

3 William of Seignelay, bishop of Auxerre (1207–20).

34

November 1247

William of Mello, lord of St-Bris, and Droco of Mello, lord of Loches, attest that the knight Gui of 'Ortum' has declared himself the liegeman of the bishop of Auxerre and agrees that he holds his house from him.

MANUSCRIPTS: Bishops' cartulary, fol. 35r. Bibl. Auxerre, MS 153, fol. 399r; seventeenth-century copy by Dom Viole. Coll. Bourgogne 3, fol. 11r.
EDITION: GC 12, instr. cols. 162–3, no. 93.

Item alia littera de castello de Ortis sub sigillo archidiaconi Senonensi in eodem scrinio.

Ego Guillermus de Melloto dominus Sancti Prisci et ego Droco de Melloto dominus Locharum.[1] Notum facimus uniuersis presentes litteras inspecturis quod in nostra presencia constitutus Guido de Orto miles recognouit se tenere a reuerendo patre Dei gratia Autissiodorensis episcopo[2] domum suam de Orto, cum omnibus appendiciis et pertinenciis dicte domus, et homo suus ligius est de dicta domo et de appendiciis et pertinenciis supradictis, prout ea in allodio possidebat et tenebat, et eandem domum reddibilem et iurabilem tenet ab episcopo supradicto.

In cuius rei testimonium presentes litteras sigillis nostris ad petitionem domini Guidonis duximus roborandas. Actum anno Domini MCCXL septimo, mense Nouembri.

Lords William and Droco were brothers, and William was the father of Bishop Gui, who had taken office just a few months earlier.[3] The family of the lords of Mello, which is in the Ile-de-France, near Senlis, appear to have come to the Auxerrois with Peter of Courtenay. 'Ortum' is not identified.

35

Sens, 27 October 1249

Gilo, archbishop of Sens, attests that the knight Gui of 'Ortum' has recognized that he holds his house at Ortum in fief from Bishop Gui of Auxerre, to whom

1 St-Bris, 10 km southeast of Auxerre; and Loches, in the valley of the Loire.
2 Gui of Mello, bishop of Auxerre (1247–70).
3 Q 3:80–1, 244–5, nos. 177, 519, 521. *Gesta*, 2: 293.

he owes liege homage. All that he holds there is enumerated. The bishop in return gives Gui eighty pounds.

MANUSCRIPTS: Bishops' cartulary, fol. 35v. Bibl. Auxerre, MS 153, fol. 400r; seventeenth-century copy by Dom Viole. Coll. Bourgogne 3, fol. 11r (abbreviated).

EDITION: GC 12, instr. cols. 165–6, no. 98.

Item alia littera de castello de Ortis sub sigillo curie archiepiscopi Senonensis in eodem scrinio.

Gilo Dei gratia Senonensis archiepiscopus,[1] omnibus presentes litteras inspecturis, salutem in Domino. Noverint uniuersi quod in nostra presencia constitutus Guido de Orto miles recognouit se recepisse et tenet in feodum et homagium ligium pre omnibus hominibus a uenerabili fratre Guidone Autissiodorensis episcopo[2] domum suam de Orto, iurabilem et reddibilem episcopo predicto et successoribus suis Autissiodorensibus episcopis, ad magnam uim et ad paruam, cum omnibus pertinentiis dicte domus, uidelicet prata sita circa domum predictam, et insulas, et saliceta, et terram arabilem de Champo Chardon, et censum quem tenet in ualle de Beone et in Ioinchiis, et terram arabilem de Campo Polin,[3] et denarios, et auenam que debentur eidem de uineis de Vlmofendu, et censum et auenam in quibus partitur cum episcopo Autissiodorensi, de uineis et domibus Sancti Geruasii, et tam homines quam feminas, et omnes uineas que dictus G[uido] miles habet Autissiodori, et omnia alia quecumque ibidem tenet, excepta uinea de Campo Polin, et tali modo debet idem G[uido] miles et heredes sui imperpetuum tenere ab episcopo Autissiodorensi qui pro tempore fuerit domum et pertinentias predictas, et quicquid acquisierint in futurum circa domum predictam quod non sit de alterius feodo, et ad omnia tenenda et adimplenda obligauit predictus miles heredes suos specialiter et expresse.

Preterea dictus G[uido] miles res pertinentes ad domum predictam facere ualere tenetur sexaginta libras terre annuatim. Quod si aliquis in domo uel rebus predictis ratione feodi, uel alio quocunque modo aliquid in posterum reclamaret, dictus miles et heredes sui quos ad hoc obligauit tenentur dictum feodum dicto episcopo et suis successoribus garentire, et pro hiis faciendis dedit dictus episcopus predicto militi octoginta libras Turonenses, de quibus recognouit sibi a dicto episcopo in pecunia numerata plenarie satisfactum.

1 Gilo, archbishop of Sens (1244–54). He was the brother of his predecessor, Walter. See Vincent Tabbagh, *Diocèse de Sens*, pp. 109–13.

2 Gui of Mello, bishop of Auxerre (1247–70).

3 These places are not identified. They are presumably names of fields around Ortum.

In cuius rei testimonium et munimen ad petitionem predicti militis presentes litteras sigilli nostri munimine fecimus roborari. Datum Senonis apud Sanctum Paulum super Vennam,[4] anno Domini MCC XL nono, in uigilia apostolorum Simonis et Iude, mense Octobri.

Item alia littera super eodem sub sigillo Guillermi de Melloto domini Sancti Prisci.[5]

Item alia littera super eodem sub sigillo Droconis de Melloto domini Locharium et de Medogne.[6]

This is the same case as the preceding.

36

1208

Manasses, bishop of Orléans, settles a quarrel between the bishop of Auxerre and the abbess of St-Julien, over a tannery. The two sides had asked him to reach an agreement, along with the heads of the houses of St-Pierre and Notre-Dame-la-Dehors. Manasses rules in favour of the bishop.

MANUSCRIPT: Bishops' cartulary, fol. 36r.
EDITION: GC 12, instr. col. 148, no. 67.
SUMMARY: Q 3:391, no. 745.

Item littere de domibus de tanneria Autissiodorensis.

M[anasses] Dei permissione Aurelianensis episcopus,[1] omnibus presentes litteras inspecturis, in Domino salutem. Vniuersitatem uestram scire uolumus quod cum mota fuisset querela inter uenerabilem patrem Autissiodorensis episcopum[2] et dilectam in Christo abbatissam Sancti Iuliani Autissiodorensis[3] super quibusdem domibus dę tanneria Autissiodorensis, quas dicebat episcopus

---

4 St-Paul of Sens.

5 St-Bris, 10 km southeast of Auxerre.

6 Loches, in the valley of the Loire; and Mayenne, in Normandy. Droco had acquired Mayenne through marriage with the heiress; Léopold Delisle, *Catalogue des actes de Philippe-Auguste*, p. 521, n. 1.

---

1 Manasses, brother of Bishop William of Seignelay, was bishop of Orléans (1207–21).

2 William of Seignelay, bishop of Auxerre (1207–20).

3 Heluise, abbess of St-Julien of Auxerre.

super aquam suam extentas fuisse et antiquas metas excedere sine conscientia et mandato suo, abbatissa uero dicebat domos illas esse de censiua sua et ob hoc dominis illarum domorum guaranciam portabat. Tandem conuenerunt et firmiter promiserunt, abbatissa cum litteris suis apertis et episcopus in uerbo sacerdotis, quod super ista querela inquisitioni nostre consentirent et eam firmiter tenerent. Nos autem ut super hoc certificati inquisitionem nostram certius et iure partis utriusque integro remanente proferre possemus iniunximus cum assensu partium, dilectis nostris A. abbati Sancti Petri and magistro R. priori Sancte Marie extra muros Autissiodorensis,[4] ut loco et uice nostri diligenter inquirerent de domibus illis, que et quot et quantum occupauerant de aqua episcopi.

Qui diligenter inquisita ueritate ad nos reportarunt quod omnes ille domus metas antiquas excedebant et de aqua episcopi occupauerant secundum magis et minus, preter domum Roberti Coille Dasne et domum Sancti Mariani et domum Balbini, que tres metas antiquas non excedunt. Vnde et nos partibus conuocatis et presentibus pronunciamus quod in quibuscunque domibus illis inuentum est excrementum, excrementum illud uel penitus amoueatur uel domini dominorum tantum faciant erga dominum episcopum quod uelit et tolerit excrementa illa remanere. Actum anno Domini MCC octauo.

The bishop and the abbess of St-Julien had long quarrelled over their respective rights. A decade earlier, under the previous bishop, it had taken a papal mandate to settle their disagreements.[5] See also the following document.

37

1207

Abbess Heluise of St-Julien of Auxerre confirms that she has ended her quarrel with the bishop of Auxerre over a tannery, as mediated by the bishop of Orléans

MANUSCRIPTS: Bishops' cartulary, fol. 36r–v. Coll. Bourgogne 3, fol. 11r.

Item alia littera super eodem.

Heluisia humilis abbatissa Sancti Iuliani Autissiodorensis uniuersis presentem paginam inspecturis, salutem in salutis auctore. Notum facimus uniuersis presentem paginam inspecturis quod quicquid uenerabilis pater M[anasses]

4 The abbot of St-Pierre and the prior of Notre-Dame-la-Dehors, both in Auxerre.

5 Arch. Yonne H 1741.

Aurelianensis episcopus[1] per composicionem ordinauerit super querela que uertebatur inter uenerabilem patrem nostrum W[illelmum] Autissiodorensis episcopum[2] et nos, super excrementis domorum de tannaria Autissiodorensis, ratum habemus et hec debite stabilitatis firmitatem obtineat presentes litteras patentes fecimus et sigilli nostri munimine roborauimus. Actum anno gracie MCC septimo.

This document has not been printed before. See also the preceding document.

38

May 1251

The canons of St-Marien inform the bishop that they have elected Stephen, previously abbot of St-Paul of Sens, as their new abbot. They ask the bishop to accept him.

MANUSCRIPT: Bishops' cartulary, fol. 36v.
EDITION: GC 12, instr. col. 168, no. 101.
SUMMARY: Q 3:393, no. 767.

Item littere de obediencia abbatis Sancti Mariani.

Reuerendo patri ac domino suo karissimo G[uido] Dei gratia Autissiodorensis episcopo,[1] humiles eius filii frater G. prior et conuentus ecclesie Sancti Mariani Autissiodorensis, salutem et obedienciam cum omni reuerencia et honore. Nuper ecclesia nostra uacante et die ad eligendum nobis prefixa, nos ipsa die inuocata prius spiritus sancti gratia, omnibusque rite peractis que secundum nostrum ordinem in electione debent fieri uel requiri, uirum religiosum Stephanum tunc abbatem Sancti Pauli Senonensis postulantes, nominauimus et elegimus canonice et concorditer in abbatem ecclesie nostre et pastorem, unde paternitati uestre humiliter suplicamus quatinus ipsum in uestra gratia recommandatum habentes, ad curam monasterii admitatis. Valeatis in Domino Iesu Christo. Datum die Veneris ante festum Beati Peregrini, anno Domini MCC quinquagesimo primo.

1 Manasses, bishop of Orléans (1207–21), brother of Bishop William of Seignelay.
2 William of Seignelay, bishop of Auxerre (1207–20).

1 Gui of Mello, bishop of Auxerre (1247–70).

St-Marien was a Premonstratensian house. It is interesting that the cartulary scribe characterized the canons' request that the bishop receive their newly elected abbot as 'obedience.' The feast of Saint Peregrinus, like those of most of Auxerre's semi-legendary early bishops, fell in May.

Fol. 37r.

In scrinio signato per H inuenientur littere de franchisia Appoigniaci.

39

August 1276

Bishop Erard of Auxerre makes an agreement with the men and women of Appoigny, les Bries, and Bailly. They have not been paying the appropriate tithes on their agricultural produce, which they promise now to do. The bishop in return frees them from having to pay main-morte. He also frees them from certain tailles, in return for an annual payment.

MANUSCRIPT: Bishops' cartulary, fols. 37r–41r.
EDITION: Estienne Perard, ed., *Recueil de plusieures pièces curieuses servant à l'histoire de Bourgogne*, pp. 533–7.[1]

In nomine patris et filii et spiritus sancti amen. Vniuersis presentes litteras inspecturis. Nos Erardus miseracione diuina Autissiodorensis episcopus[2] et nos Adam Garangier, Perrinetus Garengier, Laurencius dictus Sapiens, Petrus Dauid, Humbeletus Gibauz, Radulphus Manpilez, Stephanus Li Bograz, Guido Gibauz, Stephanus Loois, Stephanus Li Vecruz, Iohannes de Heuaco, Odo Gaillardi, Guillelmus piscator, Petrus piscator, Iohannes piscator, Garnerus piscator, Iohannes Barde, Rocelinus Marius, Rocelinus Garengier, Huguenetus filius defuncte Iacobe preposite, Iohannes Sapientis, Guido de Floriaco, Stephanus Sapientis, Regnaldus Fossars, Garnerus Moine, Iohannes filius defuncti Ferroti, Regnaldus Succor, Stephanus clericus, Girardus Robarche, Vincencius Sapientis, Perrinetus Sapientis, Doetus Carnifex, Robinus Li Boiterre, Iohannes Chaois, Gila, Veltera Droconis, Iohannes Dementis, Girardus Dementis, Colinus dou Bourgeaul, Dorus Le Veichaz, Iohannes Gombadi,

1 Although based on the cartulary, this edition suggests a very hasty transcription, with many slips and misreadings, such as 'sicut' for 'sed' or 'similiter' for 'seruandum.' I have not found it worthwhile to enumerate the differences between his edition and mine.

2 Bishop Erard of Auxerre (1270–8).

Humbertus de Virgulto, Guilotus Carnifex, Iohannes de Bellomagno, Iohannes Chenoiche, Petrus Menauz, Petrus Pucelle, Iohannes Coiserat, Dioynus Li Coifiers, Stephanus Garengiers, Adam filius Petri Dauid, Regnaldus Coipet, Diuinus Amaurici de Esbria, Petrus Bociaus, Iohannes Guidonis de Balliaco, homines dicti domini episcopi nomine ecclesie Autissiodorensis, ceterique homines et femine de Appoigniaco, de Esbria et de Bailliaco[3] homines ipsius domini episcopi nomine ecclesie Autissiodorensis, salutem in Domino. Notum facimus quod cum nos homines predicti rectam et integram decimam fructurum et prouentuum terrarum et prediorum nostrorum infra fines decimacionis de Appoigniaco de Esbria et de Bailliaco existencium, quam rectam decimam ad dictum episcopum Autissiodorensis nomine ecclesie sue Autissiodorensis recognoscimus pertinere, minus sufficienter non absque animarum nostrarum periculo hactenus soluerimus. Tandem saniori religiosorum uirorum et aliorum bonorum ducti consilio salubriter attendentes quod nichil prodest si totum mundum lucretur anime autem sue detrimentum paciatur, et quod ex diuturnitate temporis peccatum non minutur sed augetur.

Volentes animabus nostris consulere in hoc casu, publice recognoscimus pro nobis heredibus successoribus et posteris nostris, nos ac heredes et successores nostros quoscunque ex nunc in antea teneri domino Autissiodorensis episcopo suisque successoribus nomine ecclesie Autissiodorensis ex causis predictis ad rectam et integram decimam fructuum et prouentuum nostrorum omni inferius nominatorum et promittimus ex nunc in antea et soluere tenemur singulis annis dicto domino episcopo uel eius mandato suisque successoribus nomine ecclesie Autissiodorensis imperpetuum plenarie et integraliter decimam partem bladi, uini, leguminum, ceparum, aliorum canabium,[4] et omnium aliorum fructuum nostrorum, exceptis inferius nominatis, scilicet de decem unum uel unam sub modis inferius nominatis, uidelicet quod omnium fructuum nostrorum excepta decima uini in terra ubi crescent integre decimam partem dictorum fructuum collectoribus, a domino episcopo uel eius mandato deputando sine fraude soluere tenebimur, uocatis collectoribus supradictis per tres uices aliquo sufficienti interuallo a se distantes alta uoce ad uidendum numerum rerum decimandarum, et ad recipiendum decimam de eisdem.

Ita tamen quod si dicti collectores non uenirent sic uocati seu accederent ad uidendum res decimandas seu ad capiendum decimam de eisdem, quod ex tunc sine messacere quilibet nostrum in terra ubi crescent fructus predicti posset rectam decimam dimittere sub testimonium messorum, uel gerbas ligantium

3 Appoigny, 10 km north-northwest of Auxerre; les Bries, 7 km north-northwest of Auxerre; and Bailly, a now-disappeared hamlet in the commune of Appoigny, according to Maximilien Quantin, *Dictionnaire topographique du département de l'Yonne*, p. 7.

4 The manuscript reads 'canabilini.'

seu aliorum fide dignorum ibidem existencium cum iuramento etiam eorumdem, si dominus episcopus uellet super hoc ab eis exigere iuramentum. Et hac diligencia sit adhibita, extunc non posset aliquis nostrum occasionari a domino episcopo uel eius mandato de minoritate decime sic dimisse nisi de dolo uel fraude posset legitime couinci.

De nutrimentis uero animalium, agnis, porciculis, uitulis et huiusmodi necnon de lana et alia minuta decima de qua in presentibus expressa non sit mentio, poterit idem dominus episcopus et successores eius integram et rectam decimam, uidelicet de decem unum uel unam si tot existant capita exigere et leuare, prout de rebus aliis superius est expressum, alioquin exiget et leuabit prout extitit retroactis temporibus usitatum, uidelicet de agno obolum, de porciculo obolum, de uitulo denarium, et de lana pro rata. Aliis nutrimentis animalium, fructibus naturalibus, necnon ortolanis, porcis, feno, salicetis sileribus de quibus usque nunc, nos dicti homines soluere decimam non consueuimus prorsus exceptis.

Ita tamen quod de terris, uineis, et aliis possessionibus decimialibus nullam poterimus in salicetum uel pratum redigere uel sileretum nisi terra, uinea, uel possessio huiusmodi propter sui sterilitatem et incommoditatem ad salicetum uel pratum commodior seu utilior uideretur, quas terras, uineas, seu possessiones alias adhuc absque consensu domini episcopi Autissiodorensis uel eius mandati ad salicetum uel pratum redigere non poterimius.

Decimam uero uini soluemus in hunc modum, scilicet quod omnes et singuli de Appoigniaco omnia uina nostra decimacionis de Appoigniaco apud Appoigniacum facere tenebimur. Et nos de Esbria apud Esbriam et nos de Bailliaco apud Bailliacum. Et uindemiis completis dominus episcopus uel eius mandatum decimam capiet in cellariis nostris in doliis et in caudis. Quando uero aliquis nostrorum habebit decem dolia uel decem caudas uini, electis duobus uel duabus de dictis decem doliis uel caudis ab illo qui soluet decimam. Dominus episcopus habebit de decem doliis unum uel de decem caudis unam, et de aliis residuis de numero decem poterit exigere, capere et leuare, quod uel quam maluerit pro decima supradicta.

Si autem minus essent quam decem dolia uel decem caude, mandatum domini episcopi poterit capere[5] decimam si uelit de quolibet dolio seu de qualibet cauda, uel integram decimam de altero doliorum uel caudarum quo uel qua maluerit. Ita tamen quod dictam decimam leuabit annis singulis infra hyemale festum Beati Martini uel infra octabus dicti festi prout maluerit, de unus uero in magnis tonnis repositis, capiet dominus episcopus si uelit decimam de qualiter tonna prout de illis qui habebunt minus quam decem dolia uel decem caudas est

5 The cartulary reads 'cape.'

superius ordinatum, ubi autem dominus episcopus dolium plenum uino uel caudam plenam pro decima capiet pro ligno dolii septem solidos et pro ligno caude quatuor solidos et dimidium decimam soluenti persoluet. Item si dominus episcopus malet capere decimam uini in uineis seu racemis quam in uino, capiet in hunc modum. In introitibus uille de Appoigniaco, de Esbria et de Bailliaco, dominus episcopus faciet fieri ciconellas seu portas introitus uille claudentes ad quas de decem quadrigatas unam capiet, quam maluerit, quam tenebitur soluere decimam quadrigam apud Appoigniacum ad domum seu ad domos domini episcopi. Quadrigam uero uindemie mandatum domini episcopi curialiter tenebitur expedire et quarnto celerius commode poterit siue incommode dominorum.

Item nos de Esbria de decem quadrigatis unam quam maluerit dominus episcopus uel eius mandatum soluere tenebimur et quadrigare apud Appoigniacum ad domum uel ad domos dicti domini episcopi. Quadriga uero uindemie mandatum dicti domini episcopi tenebitur expedire prout superius est expressum. Nos uero de Bailliaco de decem quadrigatis unam quam maluerit dominus episcopus uel eius mandatum soluere tenebimur et quadrigare apud Appoigniacum ad domum uel ad domos domini episcopi sicut illi de Appoigniacum et de Esbria. Si uero minus quam decem quadrigatas habuerit aliquis nostrorum de Appoigniacum uel de Esbria seu de Bailliaco soluere tenebitur rectam decimam secundum quantitatem uini uel uindemie. Item si contingeret quod dominus episcopus capiendo unam quadrigatam integram plus quam rectam decimam caperet. Item dominus episcopus uel eius mandatum uinum uel uindemiam seu denarios quod mallet de tribus istis illi a quo plus recepisset restitueret ad estimacionem domini episcopi uel eius mandati, factam tamen secundum quod committitur uinum uel uindemia debere estimatum pro exigencia temporis, et uindemie bonitate.

Si autem aliquis nostrum dictarum uillarum de Appoignum, de Esbria et de Bailliaco uinum suum uel uina sua uendiderit antequam decimata fuerint, et requisierit decimatorem quod decimam suam de uino capiat uel pretium in denariis pro dicta decima iuxta precium uenditionis dictorum uinorum, tenebitur decimator capere decimam predictam in uino uel in pecunia secundum quod uenditum fuerit prout maluerit decimator, illa die uel in crastino diei qua super hoc fuerit requisitus. Item si aliquis nostrum uendidit suam uindemiam antequam soluerut decimam, tenebitur uendicionem significare decimatori antequam dictam uindemiam uenditam delibetur a emptori, et soluere dicto decimatori de toto precio dicte uendicionis de quibuslibet decem denariis unum denarium, uel decimam partem dicte uindemie si maluerit decimator.

Volumus etiam et consentimus expresse nos predicti homines de Appoigniaco, de Esbria et de Bailliaco et concedimus unanimiter et de consensu communi quod quocunque modo uoluerit dominus episcopus uidelicet in racemis uel uino decimam capere possit, etiam si uendatur uinum antequam decimetur ut predictum est, et hoc semper sit in electione et optione uel uoluntate dicti domini episcopi ut dictum est, nec aliquo cursu temporibus seu aliqua presumptione sibi possit auferri quin eo modo quo maluerit capiat decimam libere in racemis uel in uino pro sue libito uoluntatis. Item uolumus quod si aliquis nostrum de Appoigniacum uel Esbria uel de Bailliaco in soluenda decima tam uini quam bladi et omnium aliorum fructuum fraudem adhibuerit, recelando uel occultando fructus aut partem eorum uel minus soluendo, seu alias fraudem commitendo, quod totum illud quod recelauerit sit domini episcopi et esse debeat et cadat in commissum si de hoc possit legitime committi. Saluo tamen domino episcopo iure decime in eo quod non fuerint recelatum seu eciam occupatum, et nichilominus ita delinquens tenebitur soluere domino episcopo uel eius mandato quinque solidos pro emenda. Hoc eciam addito quod si decimator uoluerit quilibet nostrum iuramentum super sacrosancta prestare tenebitur, saluis premissis quod decimam recte et integre soluent nec fraudem aliquam commiserit in eadem.

Rursus cum idem dominus episcopus habeat et predecessores sui episcopi Autissiodorensis habuerunt ab antiquissimis temporibus bannum uini in uilla de Appoigniaco annis singulis per unum mensem integrum, ita quod eodem mense durante nemo potest uel debet ibi uinum uendere ad tabernam preterquam dominus episcopus. Nos prospiciantes quod idem dominus episcopus et successores sui habent et haberent tempus breuius et recisius quam expediret eisdem ad uendendum uina sua et quod ex augmento decime supradicte quantitas uini maior, solito amodo accesceret eisdem uolumus, consentimus et concedimus spontanei, non coacti, pro nobis, heredibus et successoribus nostris et pro tota posteritate nostra quod ad augmentum dicti banni amodo singulis annis dictus dominus episcopus et successores sui habeant sex ebdomadas ad uendendum seu explectandum uina sua, uidelicet quindecim dies incipientes currere a crastino Pasche usque ad quindecim dies complete, et postea quatuor ebdomadas, incipientes currere octo diebus intrante Augusto elapsis et quod nullus in dicta uilla possit uinum uendere ad tabernam uel alio modo quamdiu durabit dictum bannum nisi uendat in grosso modium caudam uel dolium uini uel plus commorantibus extra uillam, uel illis de uilla, dum tamen ducerent extra uillam.

Nos autem supradictus episcopus attendentes quod inter nostras temporalium sollicitudines illa debet esse precipua per quam ecclesie Autissiodorensis utilitatibus prouidemus, et quietam nostris subditis preparamus, affectantes eciam a nostris subditis diligi[6] pocius quam timeri, attendentes eciam curalitatem seu

6 The cartulary reads 'dirigi.'

curalitates quam uel quas fecerunt nobis homines nostri de Appoigniaco, de Esbria et de Bailliaco in modo soluendi decimam, necnon in augmentacionem banni prout superius est expressum, de gratia speciali accedente ad hoc consensu dilectorum filiorum decani et capituli Autissiodorensis ecclesie quamdam consuetudinem que uulgaliter appellatur manus mortua, quam in predictis nostris hominibus de Appoigniaco, de Esbria et de Baailliaco habebamus ipsius et eorum heredibus, successoribus et posteris in posterum perpetuo remittimus et quittamus, subo modo et forma inferius annotatis, uidelicet quod bona omnia mobilia et immobilia predictorum hominum nostrorum in predicta uilla de Appoigniaco et in uilla de Esbria et de Balliaco decedencium que ad nos ante quittacionem istam ratione manus mortue deuenire solebant ex nunc in antea per legitimam excasuram ad propinquiorem seu propinquiores[7] de genere taliter decedencium sine difficultate et pertubacione aliqua a nobis uel successoribus nostris eis pacienda seu eciam inferenda et absque ullo interuentu pecunie libere deuenient et quiete. Itam tamen quod si aliqui de predictis hominibus nostris nati uel manentes apud Appoigniacum seu apud Esbriam uel Bailliacum a predictis locis uel uillis recesserint et se transtulerint ad aliam uillam ubi habemus manum mortuam, ibidemque mansionarii decesserint sine herede de proprio corpore existente in propria potestate, ipsi erunt de manu mortua nostra quantum ad bona que habebunt in omni loco ubi habemus manum mortuam sicut alii homines nostri ibidem manentes et decedentes, sed alia bona sua que possidebunt tempore mortis sue apud Appoigniacum uel Esbriam seu Bailliacum transibunt per legitmam excasuram ad propinquiorem seu propinquiores de parentela sua ubicunque fuerint manentes. Si uero eis sic recedentibus uel heredibus eorumdem apud Appoigniacum uel Esbriam seu Bailliacum in iusticia et dominio nostro redire placuerit et ibidem manentes decesserint, predictam franchisiam et libertatem obtinebunt et habebunt integre, quantum ad illa bona que habebunt apud Appoigniacum uel apud Esbriam seu apud Bailliacum in iusticia et dominio nostro, sed illa bona que haberent tempore mortis sue in loco ubi habemus manum mortuam, si sine herede existente in patria potestate decederent ut dictum est, nobis quiete et libere remanerent. Si autem excasuram aliquam seu exchaetam euenire contigerit que ab aliquo qui se heredem legitimum probare potuerit non fuerit requisita, eam reseruabimus in manu nostra per annum et diem, et si infra annum et diem quis apparuerit sub cuiuscunque dominio existat et se heredem legitimum illius a quo uenerit dicta excasura uel exchaeta probauerit, dictam excasuram seu exchaetam sine difficultate qualibet et absque ullo interuentu pecunie, libere et integraliter ei deliberare tenebitur. Si uero nullus comparuerit heres legitimus descendentis

7 The cartulary reads 'proprinquiorem seu proprinquiores.'

completis anno et die predictis, dicta excasura nobis quitta et libera remanebit, nisi sit minor annis uel absens ex iusta et racionabili causa sine culpa sua, quam causam absens probare tenebitur. Si ad dictam excasuram uoluerit admitti, item tailliam quam predictis hominibus nostris de Appoigniaco, de Esbria et de Bailliaco possumus facere alte et basse ad uoluntatem nostram de gratia speciali, accedente ad hoc consensu predictorum decani et capituli Auttisiodorensis ecclesie, temperamus in hunc modum, uidelicet quod dicti homines de Appoigniaco, de Esbria et de Baailliaco loco dicte taillie et eciam alterius taillie, que taillia de Marciaco nuncupatur, singulis annis nobis reddent et soluere tenebuntur octies uiginti libras Turonenses tantum modo in quocunque statu dicta uilla de Appoigniaco fuerit, siue ius nostrum in dicta uilla de Appoigniaco per aliquem contrarium a nobis seu successoribus nostris celebratum seu celebrandus augmentatum fuerit seu eciam diminutum.

Quas octies uiginti libras Turonenses nobis soluent predicti homines in hunc modum, quod singulis annis eligentur tres uiri probi et idonei de uilla de Appoigniaco ex parte hominum de Appoigniaco et tres alii de eadem uilla ex parte nostra uel mandati nostri qui iurati in presencia nostra uel mandati nostri consideratis uiribus et facultatibus hominum de Appoigniaco, de Esbria et de Baalliaco cuilibet iuxta facultates suas in presencia nostra uel mandati nostri congruam porcionem de dicta summa assignabunt persoluendam, et per se uel per alios fidedignos leuabunt seu leuari facient dictam summam cuilibet assignatam, presente mandato nostro et gagiante auctoritate nostra si necesse fuerit quousque de dicta summa octies uiginti librarum ad plenum nobis fuerit satisfactum. Ita tamen quod si dicti homines de Appoigniaco discordes essent in eligendo tres uiros ydoneos ut dictum est quod illi tres qui erunt electi ex parte nostra uel mandati nostri de dicta summa octies uiginti librarum poterunt assignare cuilibet iuxta facultates suas congruam porcionem et leuari seu leuari facere prout superius est expressum. Item uolumus quod si aliquis de uilla de Appoigniaco, de Esbria seu de Baaliaco recedat a dicta uilla de Appoigniaco uel de Esbria seu de Baalliaco causa inauendi alibi, quod ille qui sic recedet quandiu manebit extra uillam de Appoigniaco uel de Esbria uel de Baalliaco medietatem taillie assignare de summa octies uiginti libras Turonenses predictis uel assignande iuxta facultates suas si presens et manentes in uilla quoddam extra uilla de Appoigniaco uel Esbria seu Baaliaco soluere teneatur, nisi causu matrimonii aliquis recederet, in quo casu uolumus quod sine taillia recedat, quem si forte postea durante uel finito matrimonio cum apud Appoigniaco, Esbriam et Baaliacum reuerti contigerit ad talliam integram quandiu[8] manebit

8 The cartulary here adds 'ibi,' above the line. Perhaps the scribe meant to strike out the 'ibi' two words further on, but he did not do so.

ibi sicut alii iuxta facultates suas teneatur. Pro qua medietate taillie persoluenda, ille qui sic recederet domum suam si quam habeat in uilla de Appoigniaco uel de Esbria seu de Baaliaco sufficientem aut aliam possessionem suam sufficientem si domum non habeat specialiter obligat et onerat, et quandiu extra uillam de Appoigniaco uel de Esbria seu de Baalliaco fuerit esse uult obligatam. Si uero sic recedentem reuerti contigeret ad uillam de Appoigniaco uel de Esbria seu de Baalliaco, tunc sicut antea totam tailliam sibi assignatam uel assignandam iuxta facultates suas soluere teneretur. Fiet autem per eos qui prenominati et electi fuerint ut dictum est annis singulis predicta taillia predictarum octies uiginti librarum infra octabas Sancti Remigii et soluentur nobis de predicta summa centum libre Turonensis infra festum purificacionis Beate Marie uirginis, residuum uero scilicet sexaginto libre Turonensis soluentur infra Pascha immediate sequens.

Item de terciis quas hactenus soluerunt dicti homines de Appoigniaco, de Esbria seu de Bailliaco uolumus quod ipsi nomine tercie ex nunc in antea pro arpento tantummodo soluere teneantur panem ad ualorem unius denarii et pro dimidio arpento panem ad ualorem unius oboli, et pro quarto arpenti panem ad ualorem dimidii oboli. Item de coustumis talem graciam eisdem facere uolumus quod de quolibet arpento, quilibet terram tenens ad coustumam teneatur soluere duos bichetos et dimidium auene et duodecim denarios et obolum pro dimidio arpento, unum bichetum et quartum bicheti cum sex denariis et dimidio obolo, et sic destendendo. Considerata quantitate terre quam aliquis tenuerit, ad coustumam saluis nobis et successoribus nostris coustumis, integris super domos et ortos de quibus nullam facimus graciam seu remissionem. In personis autem et rebus omnibus mobilibus et immobilibus dictorum hominum de Appoigniaco, de Esbria et de Bailliaco necnon in personis heredum successorum et omnium postrerorum eorumdem hominum de Apoigniaco, de Esbria et de Bailliaco omnimodam iusticiam magnam et paruam, census, minagium, roagium, linagium, corueyas chaluaratam, seruicia consueta, necnon prestaciones et omnia alia iura corporalia et incorporalia personalia et realia que et quas nos et predecessores nostri hacetenus habuimus et habere potuimus, prout habuimus et habere consueuimus in omnibus bonis et rebus ipsorum que non sunt per presentem cartam remissa, quittata, diminuta uel immutata, integre, specialiter et expresse, nobis salua in omnibus et per omnia retinemus.

Pro omnibus autem et singulis supradictis firmiter obseruandis et tenendis et specialiter pro recta decima annis singulis prout superius dictum est persoluenda, et specialiter pro medietate taillie persoluenda, si aliquem nostrum uel posterum nostrorum a predicta uilla de Appoigniaco, de Esbria et de Baalliaco recedere contingeret prout superius est expressum, nos homines et femine de Appoigniaco, de Esbria et de Baalliaco obligamus dicto domino nostro

Autissiodorensis episcopo et eius successoribus omnes terras, uineas et predia de quarum et quorum ue fructibus et prouentibus rectam decimam soluere promisimus prout superius est expressum, premissa etiam omnia et singula pro nobis et heredibus nostris per iuramenta ad sancta Dei euuangelia corporaliter prestita, integre et inuiolabiliter implere tenere et obseruare promittimus et contra premissa uel aliquod de premissis per nos uel per alios imposterum et imperpetuum non uenire. Et ad hoc seruandum, tenendum, perficiendum integraliter et iurandum, heredes et[9] successores et quoscunque posteros nostros astringimus et obligamus expresse. Ita uidelicet quod nullus hereditatem alicuius nostrum in totum uel in partem adhuc ualeat, nisi de herede in heredem is qui eam adire uoluerit super hiis omnibus et singulis supradictis corporale prestiterit iuramentum. Volumus insuper nos predicti homines et femine quod si in predictis omnibus uel aliquo predictorum deficeremus in toto uel in parte, uel contra premissa seu aliquod de premissis attemptaremus, reuerendus in Christo pater G[ilo] Dei gratia Senonensis archiepiscopus[10] et successores sui archiepiscopi Senonensis qui pro tempore fuerint in nos heredesque nostros et successores ubique[11] contigerit nos transferre, quo ad hec nos iuridictionem ipsius supponendo excommunicacionis sentenciam promulgare et promulgatam faceret inuiolabiliter obseruari, iuris ordine non obseruato quousque esset dicto domino nostro episcopo Autissiodorensis et successoribus suis episcopis Autissiodorensis de omnibus et singulis predictis et de omnibus dampnis et interesse propter uel a se facto plenarie satisfactum super quibus diuersis interesse uolumus quod credatur dicto domino episcopo Autissiodorensis uel eius successoribus per simplex uerbum sine alio probatione onere super hoc adhibendo. Rogamus etiam supradictum reuerendum patrem Senonensis archiepiscopum quia sigillum proprium non habemus ut sigillum suum presentibus apponat, una cum sigillis predicti domini Autissiodorensis episcopi et uenerabilium uirorum decani et capituli Autissiodorensis in testimonio premissorum.

Et nos predictus Gilo[12] miseracione diuina Senonensis archiepiscopus ad preces et instanciam dictorum hominum et feminarum sigillum nostrum una cum sigillis uenerabilis fratris nostri Erardi Dei gratia Autissiodorensis episcopi et decani et capituli Autissiodorensis predictorum presentibus litteris duximus apponendum.

Nos uero Erardus eadem miseracione episcopus, decanus et capitulum Autissiodorensis predicti sigilla nostra una cum sigillo predicti reuerendi patris

9 The cartulary reads 'et et.'

10 Gilo II, archbishop of Sens (1274–92). He was nephew of Archbishop Gilo I; Vincent Tabbagh, *Diocèse de Sens*, pp. 120–2.

11 The cartulary reads 'uibique.'

12 The scribe originally left a blank for the archbishop's name, added later.

Senonensis archiepiscopi presentibus litteris apposuimus in testimonio ueritatis. Anno domini Millesimo CC septuagesimo sexto, mense Augusto, die sabbati post festum Beati Bartholomei apostoli.

This long agreement was summarized by the author of the *Gesta.* The bishop issued a charter to his chapter, reassuring them that this agreement would not be to their detriment.[13] It is striking to see peasants, both men and women, successfully negotiating for a new arrangement of dues with their episcopal landlord. Folio 41v is blank, suggesting that the scribe grew weary with copying this long document, left plenty of space, and moved ahead before coming back to finish it.

Fol. 42r.

Item in eodem scrinio littera Iohannis et Milonis de Autissiodoro militum de uendicione censum quos habebant apud Appoigniacum.

Item littera Milonis de Autissiodoro militis de permutatione quicquid habebant apud Appoigniacum ad molendinum de Bofant.

Item littera de confirmacionis de permutatione predicta ab Agnete uxore domini Milonis.

Item littera de uendicione molendini de Bofant.

Item littera quod omnia que habet Milo de Autissiodoro miles apud Appoigniaum obligata sunt episcopo pro vi libris Turonensis.

Item plures littere de sentenciis latis contra Gaillardum et plures aliis de Appoigniacum.

Item littera de homagio et recognicione Guidonis Bailledart.

Item alia littera Guidonis Bailledart de recognicione iuris episcopi apud Baalliacum et Appoigniacum in bicheto banno poto et mensuris.

Item due littere de Petranis de Gurgiaco.[1]

Item littera comitis Sacricezaus[2] quod dedit episcopo Autissiodorensis quicquuid habebat in decimis uini et bladi apud Appoigniacum.

Item tres littere de conquestibus factis ab episcopo apud Charbuiacum.[3]

---

13 *Gesta*, 2:341. Q 3:349–50, no. 691.

---

1 Gurgy, 8 km north of Auxerre.

2 The count of Sancerre.

3 Charbuy, 9 km northwest of Auxerre.

Item due littere de usagio concesso hominibus de Appoigniaco a Theobaldo de Barro in nemoribus de Chaulon et de Arcia[4] ad omnia necessaria.
Item littera de emptione census de Lindriaco.[5]

Fol. 42v.

In scrinio signato per I inuenientur littere super constitutione seu diuisione archidiaconatuum et plures alie.

40

Lyon, 23 October 1249

Pope Innocent IV confirms the division of the archdeaconry of Auxerre into two. With the increase in the city's population, there was too much work for just one archdeacon.

MANUSCRIPTS: Bishops' cartulary, fols. 42v–43r. Coll. Bourgogne 3, fols. 11v–12r.
EDITION: GC 12, instr. cols. 166–7, no. 99 (abbreviated).
SUMMARIES: Q 3:393, no. 765. Q 3:400, no. 829, mistakenly dated 1204 and attributed to Innocent III. August Potthast, *Regesta pontificum Romanorum*, 2:1145, no. 13841. Ernest Petit, *Histoire des ducs de Bourgogne de la race capétienne*, 4:379, no. 2652.

Innocencius episcopus seruus seruorum Dei.[6] Venerabili fratri episcopo Autissiodorensis salutem[7] et apostolicam benedicionem. Ea que ab ecclesiarum prelatis presentium nostra fretis auctoritate pro animarum salute ac ipsarum ecclesiarum utilitatibus prouidere, statuimus libenter apostolico munimine roboramus ne cuiusquam tenientas illa presumat contriire uel turbare.

Cum igitur olim te nobis insinuante tantam esse in tua dyocese populi multitudinem quod uis poterat per solum archidiaconum Autissiodorensis ecclesie, cum unicus duntaxat esset, in ea uisuari pro tempore et per hoc nunnulla posse animarum pericula prouenire, nos tuis suplicacionibus inclinati, super hoc utiliter prouidere uolentes, diuidendi archidiaconatus ipsius ecclesie in tres archidiaconatus, dummodo ad id archidiaconi qui tunc erat ac maioris et sanioris partis capituli Autissiodorensis assensus accederet, necnon et deputati per te

4 Arcy, 26 km southeast of Auxerre.
5 Lindry, 11 km west of Auxerre.
6 Pope Innocent IV (1243–54).
7 Gui of Mello, bishop of Auxerre (1247–70).

ipsum in augmentum archidiaconatus huiusmodi, postquam iam recepti de mandato apostolico in prefata ecclesia prebendas fuerint affetuti, prebendam integram proximo tunc uacaturam in ea, et compescendi contradictores per censuram ecclesiasticam, tibi per nostras litteras sub certa forma concesserimus facultatem. Tu auctoritate litterarum ipsarum de assensu decani, archidiaconi, et capituli Autissiodorensis et aliorum proborum uirorum consilio, predictum archidiaconatum in duos diuidens, statuisti quod prebenda uacatura proximo iuxta earundem litterarum continenciam, in ecclesia supradicta hoc modo cedat in augmentum archidiaconatuum eorumdem, uidelicet quod capitulum Autissiodorensis prebendam eandem percipiet integre, ac pro ea maiori archidiacono preter distributionem quam percipere consueuit tanquam canonicus, aliam distributionem integram minori uero archidiacono, excepta distributione quam percipiet racione prebende sue, medietatem alterius distributionis integre assignare tenebitur, postquam prebenda uacauerit supradicta.

Preter hec a maiori archidiaconatui de Nonnaxo et minori archidiaconatui de Triguiaco ecclesiis tue dyocesis uacantibus, et spectantibus ad collationem tuam cum oneribus et emolumentis suis, saluo in omnibus in utraque iure episcopali annexis, retenta sibi nichilominus potestate permutandi dictas ecclesias archidiaconatibus ipsis, cum aliis ecclesiis ad tuam collationem spectantibus, cum eas uacare contigerit, uel etiam cum aliis ecclesiis de consensu patronorum ipsarum que commodiores predictis archidiaconis uidebuntur, si de tua et ipsorum archidiaconorum processerint uoluntate.

Statuisti etiam quod iidem archidiaconi in institucione sua teneantur iurare, quod per nonaginta dies in Autissiodorensi ecclesia prout eiusdem canonici faciunt, et in uisitando archidiaconatu suo per totidem alios dies, et in ecclesia parochiali annexa archidiaconatui per sexaginta dies facient residenciam personalem, quodque infra annum institucionis sue ad sacerdotii ordinem se facient promoueri, qui si ab episcopo qui pro tempore fuerit uel capitulo Autissiodorensis uocati fuerint, uel alicubi destinati, seu causa peregrinacionis partes transmarinas adierint, uel apostolorum Petri et Pauli, siue Iacobi limina uisitauerint, quandiu fuerint in ipsorum episcopi et capituli obsequiis, aut in huiusmodi pergrinacionibus constituti, pro residentibus habebuntur.

Ita tamen quod distribuciones non habebunt, nisi sicut alii canonici in similibus casibus percipiunt uel percipient in futurum, et quod nec episcopus, nec capitulum possint remittere iuramenta huiusmodi, nec contra premissa in aliquo dispensare. Adiecisti preterea, statuendo quod minor archidiaconus post quatuor personas ab antiquo in Autissiodorensi ecclesia constitutas persona existat, et post easdem quatuor personas in omnibus tam in choro quam in capitulo habeatur, idemque minor archidiaconus sit homo ligius tuus et episcoporum Autissiodorensium qui pro tempore fuerint, sicut alie persone Autissiodorensis ecclesie sepedicte, ac post fidelitatem episcopo prestitam, salua ea fidelitate capitulo tenebitur exhibere. Archidiaconatus uero minoris siue maioris collatio semper ad episcopum pertinebit, memoratam quoque residenciam non tenebuntur facere archidiaconi supradicti, nisi cum secundum ecclesie consuetudinem percipere poterunt fructus prebendarum suarum, et tunc demum prius iuramento prestito, quantum ad residenciam astringentur, prout in tuis et ipsorum decani, archidiaconi, et capituli litteris inde factis plenius continetur. Nos igitur tuis et ipsorum decani et capituli archidiaconi precibus inclinati, premissa sicut proinde facta sunt, auctoritate apostolica confirmamus, et presentis scripti patrocinio communimus, prouiso quod dilectis filiis Gaufrido Chauderoim et Conradino nato dilecti filii Iacobi Papie ciuis Ianuensis canonicis Autissiodorensibus per confirmacionem huiusmodi nullum preiudicium generetur.

Nulli ergo omnino hominum liceat hanc paginam nostre confirmacionis infringere uel ei ausu temerario contraire. Si quis autem hoc attemptare presumpserit indignacionem omnipotentis Dei et beatorum Petri et Pauli apostolorum eius se nouerit incursurum. Datum Lugdunensem x kalendas Nouembris, pontificatus nostri anno septimo.

This document is sometimes mistakenly attributed to Innocent III, probably because it seems close in content to document 33.

41

Viterbo, 8 June 1266

Pope Clement IV has heard that many of the canons of Auxerre absent themselves from the cathedral on major feast days. Instead they invite others to take their place. He orders that anyone who is not normally part of the chapter shall not eat on that day.

MANUSCRIPT: Bishops' cartulary, fol. 43v.

Item alia littera quod canonici Autissiodorensis non possunt comedere unus cum alio in decem festiuitatibus.

Clemens episcopus seruus seruorum Dei[1] uenerabili fratri episcopo Autissiodorensis[2] et dilectis filiis capitulo Autissiodorensis, salutem et apostolicam benedictionem.

1 Pope Clement IV (1265–8).

2 Gui of Mello, bishop of Auxerre (1247–70).

Cum a nobis petitur quod iustum est et honestum tam uigor equitatis quam ordo exigit racionis ut id per sollicitudinem officii nostri ad debitum perducatur effectum. Sane peticio uestra nobis exhibita continebat quod nos proinde attendentes quod canonici Autissiodorensis ecclesie in natiuitatis, epiphanie, resurrectionis et ascensum dominice, penthecostis, assumpcionis et purificacionis Beate Marie uirginis, omnium sanctorum, natalis Beati Stephani prothomartiris, et inuencionis corporis eius festiuitatibus[3] se absentabant ab eadem ecclesia, eo forsitam pretextu quod iuxta ipsius ecclesie consuetudinem unus alium et eciam forenses ad comuna inuitabant, ad quod eorum facultates minime suppetebant, propter quod dicta ecclesia in hoc modo festiuitatibus debitis obsequiis fraudabatur. Deliberacione prouida statuistis ut aliquis canonicus uel persona predicte ecclesie cum alio canonico nisi forte maneret cum eo in eodem hospicio uel esset commensalis ipsius non comedat in festiuitatibus superdictis.

Nos igitur uestris supplicacionibus inclinati quod super hoc proinde factum est ratum habentes et firmum, id auctoritate apostolica confirmamus et presentis scripti patrocinio dicto munimus. Nulli ergo omnino hominum liceat hanc paginam nostre confirmacionis infringere uel ei ausu temerario contraire. Si quis autem hoc attemptare presumpserit indignacionem omnipotentis Dei et beatorum Petri et Pauli apostolorum eius se nonerit incursurum. Datum Viterbii, vi Idus Iunii, pontificatus nostri anno secundo.

This document has not been previously printed or indeed noted. The pope was indeed in Viterbo on this date.

Fol. 44r.

Item due littere super decimis acquirendis et quod dominus possit habere partem decimarum.

Item littera contra usurarios quod dominus possit eos compellere ad desistendum.

Item littera papalis quod episcopus non teneatur ad prouisionem.

Item due littere de salagio ad archiepiscopum utiles.

Item quedam littera siunalis legati contra Templarios.

Item quedam littera episcopi B. contra archidiaconum de institucione archipresbitorum et officio foraneo discuriente.

---

3 Christmas, Epiphany, Easter, Ascension, Pentecost, the Assumption and the Purification of the Virgin, All Saints, and the birth date and the day of the discovery of the relics of Saint Stephen, the cathedral's patron saint.

Fol 44v.

In scrinio signato per K inuenientur littere quod Guido comes Niuernensis dedit episcopo Autissiodorensis quitquid habebat apud capellam Sancti Andree et plures alie.

42

Sens, 1173

Count Gui of Nevers makes gifts to the bishop of Auxerre for the soul of his father and brother. He gives whatever he has at La Chapelle-St-André, including men and tenements.

MANUSCRIPTS: Bishops' cartulary, fol. 44v. Coll. Bourgogne 3, fol. 12v (abbreviated). BnF MS fr. 18692, pp. 385–6, from the cartulary. Arch. Yonne G 1592, fol. 193r, from the preceding.
EDITION: GC 12, instr. col. 133, no. 46.

Notum sit omnibus presentibus et posteris quod ego Guido comes Niuernensis[1] pro Dei amore et remedio animarum patris et fratris mei W[illelmi][2] et mee donaui et concessi domino W[illelmo] Autissiodorensis episcopo[3] et aliis successoribus episcopis ecclesie Autissiodorensis quicquid habebam in uilla que Capella Sancti Andree nominatur[4] et in potestates eiusdem uille, siue in hominibus siue in casamentis siue alio quocumque dominio, iure perpetuo possidendum. Quod ut ratum permaneat et inconcussum et ne quis deinceps super hec calumpniam ullam inferat, sigilli mei impressione muniui.

Huius rei testes sunt, Nariotus de Tuciaco,[5] Gauterius Berardi, Damianus,[6] Girardus Grossus, Stephanus de Landa, Gaufridus abbas de Rochiis,[7] Odo abbas Sancti Petri,[8] Guido de Porta, Gilo de Tornecello, Petrus de Cinthum, Fornerius de Droya,[9] Thomas notarius, Radulphus clericus episcopi. Actum est hoc Senonensem, anno ab incarnacione Domini MC LXXIII.

---

1 Gui, count of Nevers (1168–75).
2 Count Gui had been preceded as count by his father William III (1149–61) and older brother William IV (1161–8).
3 William of Toucy, bishop of Auxerre (1167–81).
4 La Chapelle-St-André, 48 km south-southwest of Auxerre
5 Narjod II of Toucy (d. 1192); Toucy is 22 km southwest of Auxerre.
6 These two men also witnessed document 4.
7 Geoffrey II, abbot of Les Roches (1168–91).
8 Odo, abbot of St-Pierre of Auxerre.
9 Druyes, 27 km south-southwest of Auxerre.

The biographer of Bishop William said that the count made this gift out of gratitude for the bishop's assistance in having a sentence of excommunication lifted.[10]

43

June 1239

Odo, lord of Châtillon-en-Bazois, gives the bishop of Auxerre whatever he has at Varzy, especially vineyards, and his house at 'Cepens.' He will hold it all in fief from the bishop. The bishop in return gives him four hundred pounds.

MANUSCRIPTS: Bishops' cartulary, fols. 44v–45r. Coll. Bourgogne 3, fol. 12v (abbreviated).

Item littere de domino Castellionis pro feodo de Cepense et de Varziaco.

Ego Odo dominus de Castellione in Bazois.[1] Notum facio uniuersis presentes litteras inspecturis quod quicquid habebam apud Varziacum[2] in iusticia uenerabilis patris Autissiodorensis episcopi[3] extra uillam, tam terris quam uineis, ac eciam uineis quas Porteria femina mea possidebat apud dictam uillam de Varziaco que estimata fuerunt ad ualorem uiginti quinque librarum annui redditus, et domum meam de Cepense[4] cum triginta quinque libris annui redditus circa eandem domum secundum taracionem que consueuit fieri in assignacione redditurum que omnia tenebam et nulla nomine feodi propter predictam tanquam domino tenebai, uolui assignare et tenere in feodum a predicto episcopo, ita quod ego et successores mei qui pro tempore fuerint domini Castellionis in Bazois teneamus eidem et successoribus suis imposteri substituendis facere homagium de predictis, nec ego nec successor meus dominus Castellionis poterit supradicta uel aliqua de supradictis uendere, alienare uel dare, sed in manu mea ego et heredes mei tenemur tenere omnia supradicta alioquin libera et quita episcopatum autem remanient.

Predictus siquidem episcopus pro supradicto feodo et dicto homagio eidem facto, prout superius est expressum, dedit nobis quatercentum libros Turonensis de quibus nobis est plenarie satisfactum. Cum autem concederem de decima

10 *Gesta*, 2:119.

1 Châtillon-en-Bazois, 36 km east of Nevers and 80 km south of Auxerre.

2 Varzy, 51 km south-southwest of Auxerre.

3 Bernard, bishop of Auxerre (1235–45).

4 This place is not identified.

supradictarum uinearum non soluenda uolui quod teneor soluere dicto episcopo et successoribus eius decimam numeratam uinearum supradictarum, et heredes meos teneri ad soluendem eadem decime ubicunque unium earum duci contigerit uel portari. Item si contra predicta me uel heredes meos quod absit uenire contigerit, uolui et concessi et heredes meos obligaui quod in nos et terram nostram sententiam excommunicationis et interdicti predictus episcopus et successores sui possint promulgare donec fit eidem plenarie satisfactum. Si uero aliquis turabaret uel impediret supradictum ius episcopi et successorum suorum qui uti posset in supradictis rebus tanquam dominus feodi, tenemur ego et heredes mei omnem turbacionem inquietacionem et impedimentum remouere alioquam supradicta omnia que habeo apud Varziaco quitta et libera supradictis episcopo et successoribus suis remanebunt, ac eisdem centum libras Turonensis soluere tenebor et similiter heredes mei qui pro tempore fuerint quitare supradicta et centum libras soluere, si turbacio inquietacio uel impedimentum aliquod de rebus supradictis factum fuerit tenebuntur.

Ita tamen quod pacificato et liberato feodo et satisfacio episcopo dictas centum libras et res supradictas apud Varziaco sitas michi uel heredibus meis restituet episcopo qui pro tempore fuerit, nulla michi nec heredibus meis restitucione de fructibus perceptis nisi de sua speciali gratia facienda. Hec uero omnia supradicta prestito iuramento promisi ad implemenda et fideliter obseruanda. Actum anno Domini MCC XXX nono, mense Iunio.

Item littera alia de eodem sub sigillo Eduensis episcopi.
Item alia littera de eodem sub sigillo comitis Niuernensis et Forensis.
Item alia littera de eodem sub sigillo archiepiscopi Senonensis.

This document has not been previously printed.

44

July 1245

Andreas, prior of the Hospitallers, settles the quarrel he had had with Bishop Bernard of Auxerre, recently deceased, over a gift the lord of Lormes had made to the Hospitallers, which the bishop had refused to confirm, as the property had been held in fief from him. Andreas and the brothers now give the bishopric sixty-five solidi a year.

MANUSCRIPTS: Bishops' cartulary, fol. 45r. Bibl. Auxerre, MS 153, fol. 378r; seventeenth-century copy by Dom Viole. Arch. Yonne G 1708.

EDITION: GC 12, instr. col. 161, no. 89 (abbreviated).

Vniuersis presentes litteras inspecturis, frater Andreas Polius sancte domus Hospitallis Iherusalem prior humilis in Francia, salutem in Domino. Vniuersitati uestre notum facimus quod cum coram reuerendo patre B[ernardo][1] quondam Autissiodorensis episcopo diutius laborauerimus, ad hoc ut ipse laudaret elemosinam a defuncto Hugone quondam domino Vlmi[2] nobis et domui nostre factam apud Pleseium iuxta Arbusam,[3] in terris, nemoribus, hominibus, iusticiis et rebus aliis de feodo episcopi Autissiodorensis mouentibus. Nos pensata utilitate domus nostre, de fratrum nostrorum consilio et assensu, pro dicta laudacione nobis facienda sexaginta quinque solidos Turonenses quos percipiebamus annuatim in natiuitate Beati Iohannis Baptiste, in censibus de feodo ipsius episcopi mouentibus, extra cruces Saciaci,[4] reuerendo patri R[enaudo][5] Autissiodorensis episcopo eiusque successoribus concedimus et imperpetuum quittamus, promittentes quod contra dictam quittacionem per nos uel per alium non ueniemus in futurum.

In cuius rei memoriam, testimonium et munimen, presentes litteras sigilli nostri munimine duximus roborandas. Actum anno Domini MCC XLV, mense Iulio.

45

October 1232

Henry, bishop of Auxerre, recalls that his predecessor, Bishop Hugh of Noyers, had given Raynald, son of the provost of Mailly, forty pounds for the fief of Sacy, held from the bishop. Now Bishop Henry has seen that Raynald's son William is very poor, so he gives him twenty pounds for the same fief.

MANUSCRIPTS: Bishops' cartulary, fol. 45v. Arch. Yonne G 1708.

Henricus Dei gratia Autissiodorensis episcopus,[1] omnibus presentes litteras inspecturis, in Domino salutem. Notum facimus uniuersis quod cum bone memorie Hugo predecessor noster quondam Autissiodorensis episcopus[2] mutuo

---

1 Bernard, bishop of Auxerre (1235–45).
2 Lormes, 60 km south-southeast of Auxerre.
3 These places are not identified.
4 Sacy, 24 km southeast of Auxerre. See also document 48.
5 Raynald, bishop of Auxerre (1245–7).

---

1 Henry, bishop of Auxerre (1220–35).
2 Hugh of Noyers, bishop of Auxerre (1183–1206).

dedisset Regnaudo filio Iteri prepositi de Mailliaco[3] quadraginta libras Pruuinensis super feodum de Saciaco,[4] quod idem Regnaudus tenebat ab episcopo Autissiodorensis, nos uidentes Vuillelmum filium dicti Regnaudi ad quem iure hereditario dictum feodum deuenit paupertate grauari, eiusque paupertati compacientes, dicto Vuillelmo mutuo dedimus uiginta libras Parisiensis super feodum memoratum. Ita quod dictum feodum redimere poterit quoniam uoluerit de quadraginta libris Pruuinensis et uiginta libris Parisiensis supradictis.

In cuius rei memoriam et testimonium presentes litteras sigilli nostri munimine fecimus roborari. Datum anno Domini M CC XXX II, mense Octobri.

This document has not been previously printed. Both Bishop Hugh and Bishop Henry seem to have given money to assure that the fief of Sacy be held from them. See also the following document.

46

23 March 1236

The abbot of Châtel-Censoir attests that one of his canons, Raynald of Choiseul, and his mother Richaldis have sold Bishop Bernard of Auxerre all they had at Sacy for one hundred pounds. They will guarantee this against all, especially Raynald's sister Agnes.

MANUSCRIPTS: Bishops' cartulary, fol. 45v. Arch. Yonne G 1708.

Omnibus presentes litteras inspecturis, B. Castri Censorii[1] dictus abbas, salutem in Domino. Noueritis quod in nostra presencia constituti Regnaudus de Chosial[2] canonicus ecclesie nostre et mater eius Richaldis recognouerunt se uendidisse uenerabili patri B[ernardo] Autissiodorensis episcopo[3] ea que habebant apud Saciacum[4] et circa, que omnia de feodo ipsius erant ut dicebant, pro centum libras Turonensis. Et hanc uendicionem promiserunt fide prestita garentire aduersus omnes et maxime aduersus Agnetam, sororem dicti Renaudi.

---

3 Mailly-le-Château, 23 km south of Auxerre.

4 Sacy, 24 km southeast of Auxerre.

---

1 Châtel-Censoir, 30 km south-southeast of Auxerre.

2 Choiseul, in Champagne, 30 km northeast of Langres.

3 Bernard, bishop of Auxerre (1235–45).

4 Sacy, 24 km southeast of Auxerre.

In cuius rei testimonium ad petitionem illorum presentem paginam sigilli mei munimine roboramus. Actum anno gratie MCC XXXV, decimo kalendas Aprilis.

This document has not been previously printed. The date is 1236 in 'new style.' See also document 49, done at the same time.

47

Auxerre, January 1243

The archdeacon and cantor of Auxerre attest that Elizabeth of Sacy has given the bishop of Auxerre everything she has at Sacy. The bishop in return gives her one hundred pounds.

MANUSCRIPTS: Bishops' cartulary, fol. 45v. Arch. Yonne G 1708.

Omnibus presentes litteras inspecturis, H archidiaconus et Ph[ilipus] cantor Autissiodorensis, salutem in Domino. Notum facimus uniuersis quod in nostra presencia constituta Elizabet de Saciaco[1] filia defuncte Margarite rendidit reuerendo patri ac domino Dei gratia Autissiodorensis episcopo[2] quicquid ipsa apud Saciacum uel circa habebat et possidebat, siue in terris, pratis, uineis, censibus, hominibus, iusticiis, redditibus siue quibuscumque rebus aliis quocumque nomine censeantur, pro centum libras Turonensis, de quibus coram nobis se tenuit pro pagata recognoscens per suum iuramentum coram nobis corporaliter prestitum se quatuordecim annos habere, sui iuris esse, nec uoto religionis aliquo astuttam esse.

Iurauit etiam eadem Elizabeht quod prefatam uendicionem non circoimenta non ui nec metu inducta, maximo cum deliberacione sponte et proinde faciebat et quod contra eandem uendicionem per se uel per alios non ueniet in futurum. Et ut pepetui roboris obtineat firmitate presentes litteras ad peticionem dicte Elizabeht sigillis nostris sigillari. Actum Autissiodorensem anno Domini MCC XL II, mense Ianuarii.

This document has not been previously printed. The year is 1243 in 'new style.' See also the preceding documents on Sacy.

1 Sacy, 24 km southeast of Auxerre.
2 Bernard of Sully, bishop of Auxerre (1235–45).

48

August 1235

The dean of Auxerre, the archdeacon of Nevers, the abbot of St-Pierre of Auxerre, and the cantor of Auxerre attest that John, son of the late knight Artald of Sacy, has sold Bishop Bernard of Auxerre whatever he has 'outside the crosses' at Sacy, for thirty pounds.

MANUSCRIPT: Bishops' cartulary, fol. 46r.

Omnibus presentes litteras inspecturis, R. decanus Autissiodorensis, archidiaconus Niuernensis, abbas Sancti Petri, et R. cantor Autissiodorensis, salutem in Domino. Nouerint uniuersi quod in nostra constitutus presencia Iohannes filius defuncti Aurardi de Saciaco[1] militis recognouit se uendidisse uenerabili patri B[ernardo] Autissiodorensis episcopo[2] pro triginta libras Turonensis quicquid ipse habebat extra cruces de Saciaco,[3] in decimis, terciis, censibus et iusticiis, et rebus aliis quibuscunque que ab ipso episcopo ibidem tenere se in feodum recognouit, fide corporaliter prestita. Promittens quod contra hanc uendicionem per se uel per alium non remet in futurum, sed eam dicto episcopo eiusque successoribus erga omnes garentiet bona fide.

In cuius rei memoriam et testimonium ad peticionem dicti episcopi et Iohannis sigilla nostra duximus presentibus apponenda. Actum anno Domini MCC XXXV, mense Augusto.

This document has not been previously printed. Bishop Bernard seemed to be consolidating his holdings at Sacy; see the preceding documents.

49

March 1236

The abbot of St-Germain, the abbot of St-Pierre of Auxerre, the archdeacon of Morin, and the official of the dean's curia attest that Raynald of Choiseul and his mother, Richaldis, have sold their property at Sacy to Bishop Bernard of Auxerre, for one hundred pounds. They will guarantee it against all claimants, especially Raynald's sister Agnes.

---

1 Sacy, 24 km southeast of Auxerre.

2 Bernard, bishop of Auxerre (1235–45).

3 For another mention of the crosses at Sacy, see document 44.

MANUSCRIPT: Bishops' cartulary, fol. 46r.
EDITION: GC 12, instr. col. 159, no. 86.

Omnibus presentes litteras inspecturis, R. abbas Sancti Germani,[1] B. abbas Sancti Petri Autissiodorensis,[2] archidiaconus Morinensis, et I. officialis curie decani canonici Autissiodorensis, [salutem in Domino. Noueritis quod in nostra presentia constitutus Regnaudus de Chosial[3] canonicus ecclesie Castri Censorii][4] et nobilis mulier Richaldis mater eiusdem, uendiderunt uenerendo patri B[ernardo] Autissiodorensis episcopo[5] pro centum libris Autissiodorensis monete quitquid ipsi habebant et possidebant apud Saciacum[6] et circa, tam in terris, pratis, uineis, censiuis, iusticiis, domibus, quam in rebus aliis quibuscunque que omnia erant de feodo ipsius episcopi ut dicebant, fide corporali prestita, promittentes quod contra dictam uendicionem per se uel per alium non uenient in futurum, sed eandem uendicionem dicto episcopo eiusque successoribus bona fide garentient erga omnes et precipue erga Agnetem sororem prefati Regnaudi. Recognouerunt etiam coram nobis dicti Regnaudus et mater eius quod de dicta pecunia sibi fuerat plenarie satisfattum.

In cuiius rei memoriam et testimonium ad peticionem dictorum Regnaudi et Richaldis matris eius sigilla nostra presentibus duximus apponenda. Actum anno gratie MCC XXX quinto, mense Martio.

See also document 46, done at the same time. The year is 1236 in 'new style.'

Fol. 46r

Item littera de inuadiacione feodi de Saciaco quod Hugo quondam Autissiodorensis episcopus accepit mutuo a Regnaudo filio Iterii de Mailliaco pro quadraginta librorum Pruuienensis et H. subsequens episcopus a Guillelmo predicti R. filio pro triginta libras pariter.

Item littera sub sigillo R. Sancti Germani et H. Beatri Petri Autissiodorensis abbatium quod Guillelmus de Mailliaco armiger recepit mutuo a reuerendo

1 Raynald, abbot of St-Germain of Auxerre (1226–38). The editors of GC mistakenly identify him with Raynald of Choiseul, due to the lacuna in the cartulary.

2 Bartholomew, abbot of St-Pierre of Auxerre.

3 Raynald of Choiseul was a canon of Château-Censoir, 30 km south-southeast of Auxerre.

4 This phrase is missing in the cartulary, doubtless due to a slip by the scribe. I have provided it on the basis of document 46.

5 Bernard, bishop of Auxerre (1235–45).

6 Sacy, 24 km southeast of Auxerre.

patro H. Autissiodorensis episcopo super feodo suo de Saciaco nonaginta libris Turonensis.[1]

Item littera sub sigillis decani et abbatis Sancti Petri Autissiodorensis quod Regnaudus de Malliaco clericus obligauit pro sexaginta libris Turonensis quicquid habebant apud Saciacum.

Fol. 46v

Item alia littera sub sigillis R. Sancti Germani H. Sancti Petri abbatum, R. decani et H. archidiaconi Autissiodorensis, et Hugo de Latticiaco miles et nobilis mulier Nazaria uxor eius obligauerunt erga uenerabilem patrem B. Autissiodorensis episcopum medietatem omnium que habebant apud Saciacum pro ducentis libris Turonensis.

50

7 June 1263

Lady Agnes, widow of Robert of Chevannes, recognizes as a fief, held from Droco of Mello, property she had inherited at Villiers-le-Sec. Droco had held it in fief from the bishop of Auxerre.

MANUSCRIPT: Bishops' cartulary, fol. 46v.

Item due littere de feodo de Villers.

Omnibus presentes litteras inspecturis, frater Iohannes dictus abbas monasterii Escharleyacum Cisterciensis ordinis et Iohannes decanus Christianitatis de Curtiginiaco,[2] salutem in Domino. Notum facimus uniuersis quod coram nobis constituta nobilis mulier Agnes relicta Roberti de Cheuannis[3] militis publice recognouit se recepisse in legium feudum a nobili uiro Drocone de Melloto milite, domino Sancti Prisci et Castri Canini,[4] quandam uillam sitam prope Varziacum[5] que uocatur Villers li Ses[6] mouentem de capite et hereditate ipsius Agnetis ut dicebat cum pertinenciis[7] dicte uille, quam uillam cum pertinenciis

1 This document would have confirmed document 45.

2 John, abbot of the Cistercian house of Escharlis, and John, dean of Courtenay.

3 Chevannes, 8 km southwest of Auxerre.

4 St-Bris, 10 km southeast of Auxerre, and Château-Chinon, 86 km south-southeast of Auxerre.

5 Varzy, 51 km south-southwest of Auxerre.

6 Villiers-le-Sec, 46 km south-southwest of Auxerre.

7 The cartulary reads 'pertinencis.'

eiusdem dictus Droco tenet in ligium feudium a reuerendo patre episcopo Autissiodorense, prout dicta domina coram nobis asseruit et sicut in litteris dicti Droconis plenius uidimus contineri.

In cuius rei testimonium ad requisicionem dicte Agnetis presentes litteras sigillorum nostrorum munimine duximus roborandas. Datum anno Domini MCC LXIII, septimo mense Iunio.

This document has not been previously printed. See also the following document.

51

July 1267

The abbots of St-Marien and St-Pierre of Auxerre and the presiding officials of the bishop's and the dean's curias attest that Agnes, widow of Robert of Chevannes, does homage to the bishop for what she inherited at Villiers-le-Sec.

MANUSCRIPT: Bishops' cartulary, fol. 46v.

Vniuersis presentes litteras inspecturis, G. abbas Sancti Mariani Autissiodorensis, B. abbas Sancti Petri Autissiodorensis, officialis curie Autissiodorensis et officialis curie decani Autissiodorensis, salutem in Domino. Notum facimus quod in nostra presencia constituta Agnes relicta Roberti de Chauannis[1] publice recognouit se recepisse in feodum ligium a reuerendo patri G[uido] Dei gratia episcopo Autissiodorensis[2] quandam uillam sitam prope Varziacum que uocatur Vilers le Sec,[3] mouentem de capite et hereditate ipsius Agnetis ut dicebat cum pertinenciis dicte uille, et se fecisse homagium episcopo supradicto, confitens etiam publice et recognoscens quod tam ipsa qui heredes sui qui predictam uillam tenebunt dicto episcopo et eius successoribus episcopis debent facere homagium ligium et tenentur. Promisit insuper dicta Agnes se garentizare eidem episcopo et successoribus suis episcopis Autissiodorensis dictum homagium erga omnes qui super hoc ius aliquod reclamarent.

1 Chevannes, 8 km southwest of Auxerre.

2 Gui of Mello, bishop of Auxerre (1247–70).

3 Villiers-le-Sec, 46 km south-southwest of Auxerre, and Varzy, 51 km south-southwest of Auxerre.

In cuius rei testimonium ad peticionem dicte Agnetis presentibus litteris sigilla nostra duximus apponenda. Datum anno Domini Millesimo CC sexagesimo septimo, mense Iulio.

Agnes had recognized Villiers as a fief four years earlier; see the previous document. Then, however, she had held it from Droco of Mello, who held it from the bishop; now she holds it directly from the bishop. This document has not been previously printed.

52

June 1248

The bishop of Autun attests that Droco of Mello and his wife, Heluidis, have sold the burgh of 'Conches' near Varzy to the dean and chapter of Auxerre for seventy pounds. It includes everything that the late lord Hugh of Lormes had had there. They guarantee it against all claimants and promise that their son Droinus will agree. The bishops of Autun, Langres, Auxerre, and Nevers will be able to excommunicate Droco and Heluidis and their heirs if they do not keep the agreement.

MANUSCRIPTS: Bishops' cartulary, fol. 47r–v. Coll. Bourgogne 3, fols. 12v–13r (abbreviated).

Omnibus presentes litteras inspecturis, A[nsellus] Dei gratia Eduensis episcopus,[1] salutem in Domino. Notum facimus quod in presencia mandati nostri ad hoc specialiter destinati, uidelicet dilecti soccu et senescalli mei Guillermi de Gissiaco canonici Eduensis, nobilis uir Droco de Melloto, dominus Espissie, Castri Canini, et Vlmi,[2] et Heluidis uxor eius recognouerunt se uendidisse uenerabili uiro decano et capitulo Autissiodorensis burgum de Conchiis iuxta Varziacum[3] cum omni iure, iusticia, dominio et omnibus pertinenciis eiusdem burgi, et quitquod hunc tenent uel possident ibidem et apud Varziacum, tam in hominibus iustitiis, feudis, pedagio, furno, dominio, redditibus quam rebus aliis quibuscumque, et quitquid habeat tenebat et possidebat in locis predictis nobilis uir Hugo quondam dominus Vlmi tempore mortis sue in omnibus et singulis rebus predictis, et etiam aliis quibuscunque, promittentes

1 Anselm, bishop of Autun (1245–53).

2 Epoisses, 58 km southeast of Auxerre, Château-Chinon, 86 km south-southeast of Auxerre, and Lormes, 60 km south-southeast of Auxerre.

3 Varzy, 51 km south-southwest of Auxerre.

per iuramentum coram predicto mandato nostro corporaliter prestitum se omnes et singules res predictas renditas garantizaturos erga omnes qui in rebus predictis uel in aliqua ipsarum aliquid reclamareret. Et ad rectam garanciam ferendum se et heredes suos specialiter et expresse obligarunt.

Si uero contingeret quod dicti decanus et capitulum res predictas transferent in alium, predicti Droco et uxor eius et heredes ipsorum tenerentur ei ad quem res predictas transferri contingeret, a dictis decano et capitulo eandem garenciam fere super rebus predictis, ad quam dictis decano et capitulo tenentur per idem iuramentum, promittentes quod contra dictam rendicionem per se uel per alium non uenient in futurum, hec possessorem seu possessores rerum predictarum super hiis in aliquo molestabunt. Et insuper promiserunt dicti Droco et uxor eius quod dictam rendictionem a Droino filio ipsorum gratis laudari facient et concedi cum ipsi uel alter eorum uel ipse Droynus ex parte dictorum decani et capituli uel illius in quem dicti decanus et capitulum res predictas transferrent, si eas transferri contingeret fuerint requista.

Recognouerunt etiam dicti Droco et uxor eius coram dicto mandato nostro quod de toto predicto uendicionis antedicte, uidelicet de septingentis libris Turonensis, sibi fuerat in pecunia numerata plenarie satisfactum a decano et capitulo supradictis, et ipsos de dicte rendicionis precio quittauerunt. Prefacta uero Heluidis per item iuramentum coram eodem mandato recognouit quod dictam uendicionem faciebat spontanea, non coacta seu in aliquo circimenta, renuncians expresse ac specialiter quantum ad omnis et singula predicta omni iuris auxilio et omni priuilegio quod sibi posset prodesse et obesse dictis decano et capitulo, nec illi in quem dicti decanus et capitulum res predictas transferrent si eas transferri contingeret ab eisdem.

Pro hiis autem omnibus et singulis rebus uenditis et pro omnibus et singulis conuencionibus supradictis tenendis, obligauerunt et in responsionem dederunt dicti Droco et uxor eius prefatis decano et capitulo et illi in quem res predictas transferrent, si eas transferri contingeret, quicquid ab episcopo Autissiodorensis apud Hondant uel alibi tenent in feodum, uolentes et concedentes quod si dicti decanus et capitulum seu alius uel alii in quem uel in quos ipsi decanus et capitulum transferrent res predictas, si eas transferri contingeret, aliqua dampna incurrerent uel expensis facerent occasione destitus garencie super rebus predictis, uel aliqua ipsarum uel super aliqua de conuencionibus antedictis non seruata, quod ipsi decanus et capitulum uel ille seu illi in quem uel in quos dicti decanus et capitulum transferrent res predictas, si eas transferri contingeret, haberent recursum ad omnes res ipsorum Droconis et uxoris eius siue heredum ipsorum que mouent de feudo episcopi Autisiodorensis, et ipsas res absque contradicione aliqua tenerent et fructus suos facerent, donec eis de dampnis et expensis hiis uel factis esset plenarie satisfactum. Ita tamen quod ab seruicium quod dictus feudus requirit ipsi et heredes ipsorum nichilominus teneantur.

Voluerunt etiam et concesserunt prefati Droco et uxor eius et heredes suos ad hoc expresse ac specialiter obligauunt quod pro residuo feudi teneantur integraliter seruire episcopo Autissiodorensis et reddere ecclesie Autissidorensis annualiter quinquaginta libras cere, sicut pro toto feodo antedictam uendicionem tenebantur. Episcopus uero Autissiodorensis de cuius feudo res predicte uendite mouent sicut dicti Droco et uxor eius coram dicto mandato recognouerunt dictam uendicionem ratam et gratam hiis ipsam concessit laudauit et etiam approbauit. Quantum autem ad omnia et singula predictorum tenenda complenda et firmiter obseruanda, dicti Droco et uxor eius per predictum iuramentum se specialiter obligauunt et se iuridicioni nostre et successorum nostrorum et uenerabilum patrum Lingonensis Autissiodorensis et Niuernensis episcoporum[4] qui pro tempore fuerint quantum ad hec subdiderunt ubicunque maneant uel existant, uolentes et concedentes quod si ipsi uel heredes eorum in predictis uel in aliquo predictorum deficerunt, nos et successores nostri et uenerabiles patres predicti Lingonensis Autissiodorensis et Niuerensis episcopi excommunicamus in ipsos et heredes ipsorum et in terram ipsorum interdicti sentenciam proferemus. Et nos in testimonium predictorum sigillum nostrum presentibus duximus apponendis. Datum anno Domini MCC XL octauo, mense Iunio.

Item alia littera consimilis sub sigillo episcopi Lingonensis.
Item alia consimilis sub sigillo episcopi Autissiodorensis.
Item alia littera de eodem sub sigillo episcopi Niuernensis.

A month later Droco and Heluidis were preparing to leave for the Holy Land, so it is possible that this sale was intended to raise the money they needed.[5] The late Hugh of Lormes mentioned here is most likely the same as the one of document 56. This document has not been previously printed. See also the following.

53

June 1248

The dean and chapter of Auxerre have bought the villa of 'Conches' from Droco of Mello and his wife. It had been held in fief from the bishop of Auxerre and was bought with his consent. They now give it to the bishop in exchange for a grange at their villa of Chichery.

---

4 Bishops Gui of Langres (1249–57), Gui of Auxerre (1247–70), and Robert of Nevers (1240–52).

5 *Le premier cartulaire de l'abbaye cistercienne de Pontigny (XIIe–XIIIe siecles)*, ed. Martine Garrigues, p. 270, no. 193.

MANUSCRIPT: Bishops' cartulary, fols. 47v–48r.
EDITION: GC 12, instr. col. 164, no. 96 (abbreviated).

Item littera de eodem de permutacione capituli ad episcopum.

Omnibus presentes litteras inspecturis, H decanus totumque capitulum Autissiodorensis, salutem in Domino. Nouerint uniuersi quod cum nos emissemus a uiro nobili Drocone de Melloto domino Espossie, Castri Canini, et Vlmi[1] et Heluidi uxore eius, laudente et consentiente uenerabili patre nostro Guidone Dei gratia Autissiodorensis episcopo,[2] burgum de Conchiis iuxta Varziacum[3] et omnia que ipsi habebant tenebant et possidebant apud Varziacum, sicut in litteris predictorum Droconis et uxoris eius et uenerabilium patrum Lingonensis et Niuernensis episcoporum, et etiam in litteris predicti patris Guidonis episcopi Autissiodorensis, de cuius feodo omnia predicta a nobis empta dinoscuntur mouere, plenius continetur.

Tandem nos attendentes utilitatem tam predicti patris Guidonis Dei gratia Autissiodorensis episcopi et successorum eius, quam nostram, eo quod predicta a nobis empta, iuxta et intra Varziacum sita utiliora uidebantur predicto patri et successoribus suis, quam nobis cum et idem pater aliquos redditus haberet iuxta nos, nobis utiliores. Talem cum ipso comutationem duximus faciendam, uidelicet quod nos omnia predicta a nobis empta predicto patri et successoribus eius dedimus et concessimus imperpetuum possidenda, pro granchia sua de Chicheriaco[4] uilla nostra, et terris et pratis et censu eidem granchie appendentibus, que eodem tempore quo dicta commutacio inter nos et ipsum facta fuit, ad admodiationem tenebat maior de Chicheriaco ab eodem, et pro triginta et quatuor libris Turonensibus singulis annis a nobis in teloneo suo de Autissiodoro percipiendis. Voluit etiam et concessit idem G[uido] episcopus et successores suos ad hec specialiter obligauit quod quicumque tenuerit dictum teloneum soluat nobis annuatim predictas triginta quatuor libras Turonenses, uidelicet ad festum Sancti Remigii decem et septem libras Turonenses, et ad Pascha decem et septem libras Turonenses. Si uero illum uel illos qui dictum teloneum a dicto episcopo uel a successoribus suis tenerent in solutione dicte pecunie quacumque occasione in dictis terminis uel in aliquo eorum deficere contingeret, obligauit se dictus episcopus et successores suos ad dictam pecuniam dictis terminis nobis integre persoluendam.

---

1 Epoisses, 58 km southeast of Auxerre, Château-Chinon, 86 km south-southeast of Auxerre, and Lormes, 60 km south-southeast of Auxerre.

2 Gui of Mello, bishop of Auxerre (1247–70).

3 Varzy, 51 km south-southwest of Auxerre.

4 Chichery, 12 km north-northwest of Auxerre.

Hec autem omnia predicta sub predictis conuentionibus. Idem pater pro commutacione rerum a nobis emptarum superius expressarum dedit nobis et quittauit imperpetuum possidenda, nisi ipse uel successores eius nomine episcopatus redditus emerent, qui secundum arbitrium quatuor personarum ecclesie Autissiodorensis que pro tempore erunt, capitulo Autissiodorensi eque uel magis utiles uideantur, quos redditus a predicto G[uidone] episcopo uel a successoribus eius emptos, capitulum Autissiodorense loco predictorum reddituum imperpetuum possidebit. Et tunc omnia predicta que per commutationem inter nos et ipsum factam tenebamus, ad episcopatum libere reuertentur.

Quod ut ratum et firmum permaneat, presentibus litteris sigillum nostrum apposimus. Actum anno Domini MCCXL octauo, mense Iunio.

This was given at the same time as the preceding document. After all the complicated agreements concerning the chapter's acquisition of 'Conches,' they found it more useful to give it to the bishop in exchange for something else.

54

April 1239

Archbishop Walter of Sens attests to the end of a quarrel between Bishop Bernard of Auxerre and the knight Raynald Chomez. Raynald had been a burgher of Varzy, dependent on the bishop, and yet he became a knight, which the bishop believed harmed his rights. Raynald now promises to pay the same tithes and other customary dues he had paid as a burgher. In addition, he says that he will treat everything he has at Villiers-le-Sec as a fief held from the bishop and will do homage for it.

MANUSCRIPT: Bishops' cartulary, fol. 48v.

Item littere de burgense de Varziaco facto milite qui emendauit.

Galterius Dei gratia Senonensis archiepiscopus,[1] omnibus presentes litteras inspecturis, salutem in Domino. Nouerint uniuersi quod in nostra presencia constitutus Regnaudus dictus Chomez miles recognouit quod cum contencio uerteretur inter ipsum ex una parte et uenerabilem fratrem episcopum Autissiodorensis[2] ex altera, super eo quod item Regnaudus quondam burgensis

1 Walter, archbishop of Sens (1223–41). For Walter, see Vincent Tabbagh, *Diocèse de Sens*, pp. 104–9.

2 Bernard, bishop of Auxerre (1235–45).

ipsius episcopi de Varziaco[3] in preiudicium eiusdem et iurisdicionis sue factus erat miles, ut dicebat idem episcopus, tandem dictus Regnaudus super hoc emendam fecit episcopo supradicto. Promittens se eidem episcopo et successoribus eius integre soluere constrictos census decimas et alias consuetudines possessionum, eo modo quo soluerat quando erat burgensis. Preterea dictus Regnaudus totam terram suam quam possidet apud Villare Siccum[4] uersus Varziacum prope Sanctum Petrum de Montibus,[5] uidelicet terras, prata, census, iusticiam et quitquid ibidem noscitur habere, que a nullo dicebat se in feodum tenere, assignauit in feodum prenominato episcopo et successoribus suis, et recognouit quod eiusdem episcopo homagium fecerat de omnibus supradictis. Promisit etiam idem Regnaudus quod ipse quadraginta libras ponet in emptione quoniam commode poterit in augmentatione feodi prenotati. Quantum ad hoc se supponens iuridicioni prefati episcopi ubicunque mansionarius fuerit, ita quod si ipsum Regnaudum in aliqua predictarum pactionum contingerit defecisse, idem episcopus in eundem Regnaudum possit excommunicacionis sentenciam promulgare.

In cuius rei testimonium et memoriam presentes litteras ad peticionem partium sine preiudicio alterius, sigilli nostri munimine fecimus roborari. Actum anno Domini MCC tricesimo nono, mense Aprili.

This document has not been previously printed. See also the following document, given at about the same time.

55

December 1239

Nicholas of 'Alta Villa,' a knight and royal bailiff, attests to the end of the quarrel between the knight Raynald Chomez and the bishop of Auxerre. Raynald recognizes that he was wrong to become a knight, as he harmed the bishop's rights, and now promises to pay all the dues he had paid as the bishop's burgher. He also will do homage to the bishop for everything he has at Villiers-le-Sec, which will become a fief.

MANUSCRIPTS: Bishops' cartulary, fols. 48v–49r. Coll. Bourgogne 3, fol. 13r.

---

3 Varzy, 51 km south-southwest of Auxerre.

4 Villiers-le-Sec, 46 km south-southwest of Auxerre.

5 St-Pierre-du-Mont, 44 km south-southwest of Auxerre.

Omnibus presentes litteras inspecturis, Nicholaus de Alto Villari miles, domini regis balliuus, salutem. Notum facimus uniuersis quod in nostra presencia constitutus Regnaudus dictus Chomoz miles recognouit quod cum contencio uerteretur inter ipsum ex una parte et uenerabilem patrem Autissiodorensis episcopum[1] ex altera, super hoc quod idem Regnaudus quondam burgensis ipsius episcopi de Varziaco[2] in preiudicium ipsius episcopi et iuridicionis sue factus est miles, ut dicebat idem episcopus, tandem dictus R[egnaudus] super hoc reatum suum confitens, fecit emendam episcopo supradicto. Promisit eciam dictus R[egnaudus] integre soluere predicto episcopo et successoribus consuetos, census, decimas et alias consuetudines quascunque burgenses supradicti castri soluere consueuunt, et ad hoc idem Regnaudus heredes suos obligari et teneri. Preterea dictus Regnaudus totam terram suam si quam possidet apud Villaria prope Sanctum Petrum de Montibus,[3] uidelicet terras, prata, uineas, homines, iusticiam et quitquid ibidem que a nullo in feodum dicebat se tenere, assignauit in feodum prenominato episcopo et sucessoribus suis et recognouit eidem episcopo de preditiis rebus homagium se fecisse. Promittensque ipse sexaginta libras Turonenses ponet in emptione in augmentacione feodi prenotati.

In cuius rei testimonium et munimen, presentes litteras sigilli nostri caractere dignum duximus roborandas. Actum anno Domini MCC trecesimo nono, mense Decembri.

For this case see also the preceding document; this charter has not been previously printed.

Fol. 49r

Item alia littera de uendicione molinarum apud Varziaco.
Item littera de quitacione nemoris de Hennois et de Codreto.

56

May 1226

Hugh, lord of Lormes, attests to the end of a quarrel between Bishop Henry of Auxerre and Simon of Châtelet. Simon had claimed a share of the tithes of

1 Bernard, bishop of Auxerre (1235–45).

2 Varzy, 51 km south-southwest of Auxerre.

3 Villiers-le-Sec, 46 km south-southwest of Auxerre, and St-Pierre-du-Mont, 44 km south-southwest of Auxerre.

Varzy, which he now gives up. He will make sure none of his brothers, sisters, nephews, or nieces make a similar claim.

MANUSCRIPT: Bishops' cartulary, fol. 49r.

Ego Hugo dominus de Vlmo.[1] Notum facio omnibus presentes litteras inspecturis quod cum inter reuerendum patrem Henricum Autissiodorensis episcopum[2] et Simonem de Chatelai esset contencio super tercia parte decimarum de Varziaco[3] quam a predicto episcopo petebat dictus Simon. Tandem interuenientibus amicis fuit compositum in hunc modum, quod dictus Simon in presencia mea constitutus quittauit penitus episcopo et ecclesie Autissiodorensis quitquid iuris habebat uel poterat habere, uel debebat in decimis de Varziaco ex quacunque causa. Et sacramento corporaliter prestito ab eodem promisit quod de cetero nec per se nec per alium petit aliquid in dictis decimis nec reclamabit, nec procurabit episcopum Autissiodorensis uel ecclesiam Autissiodorensis super dictis decimis molestari, sed garantizabit dictas decimas et deffendet contra omnes. Promisit etiam per dictum sacramentum quod dictas decimas et dictam quittacionem concederi et laudari faciet a suis fratribus et sororibus, nepotibus et neptibus, et contra ipsos et alios dictas decimas et quittacionem dictam garantizabit et deffendet, et super hiis predictis per omnia obserandis sacramento prestito renunciauit omni iuri rei uel persone colenti, pro qua quidem quictacione et defensione reuerendus pater prefatus episcopus Autissiodorensis promisit se satisfacturum de sexaginta libris forte Niuernensis prenominato Simoni et de una marcha argenti uxor eiusdem Simonis.

In cuius rei testimonium presentes litteras ad peticionem predictorum sigilli mei apposicione roboraui. Actum anno Domini MCC XXVI, mense Maio.

This document has not been previously printed. For Hugh of Lormes, see also document 52.

57

Viterbo, 13 February 1258

Pope Alexander IV has heard that men subject to the bishop of Auxerre have been moving to other jurisdictions, and the lords of those jurisdictions have refused to acknowledge that the men are the bishop's without a duel to prove it. The pope forbids such a battle, as it is against the canons.

---

1 Lormes, 60 km south-southeast of Auxerre.

2 Henry, bishop of Auxerre (1220–35).

3 Varzy, 51 km south-southwest of Auxerre.

MANUSCRIPTS: Bishops' cartulary, fol. 49r–v. Paris, BnF MS lat. 17048, p. 113.
EDITIONS: GC 12, instr. col. 126, no. 37 (abbreviated); dated 1162. Lebeuf 2:59–60, no. 118 (abbreviated), from the cartulary; dated 1250. Lebeuf 4:112, no. 193 (abbreviated). Q 2:163, no. 148 (abbreviated); dated 1163–4, from GC.
SUMMARY: August Potthast, *Regesta pontificum Romanorum inde ab a. post Christum natum MCXCVIII ad a. MCCCIV*, 2:1403, no. 17183.

Item littera papalis de probacione hominium de corpore per testes.

Alexander episcopus seruus seruorum Dei,[1] uenerabili fratri episcopo Autissiodorensis,[2] salutem et apostolicam benedictionem. Iustis petencium desideriis dignum est nos facilem prebere consensum et uota que a rationis tramite non discordant effectu prosequente complere. Ex parte siquidem tua fuit propositum coram nobis quod cum contingat interdum aliquos hominum tuorum de corpore se a tuo dominio subtrahendo ad loca transferri alterius iuridictionis subiecta, locorum ipsorum rectores et domini prefatos homines non eos te repetente uolunt restituere nisi per duellum probes eos tuos homines extitisse, in tuum preiudicium non modicum et grauamen. Quare nobis humiliter supplicasti ut cum ex hec tam tu quam ecclesia tua grauem sustineatis pluries lesionem prouidere super hoc indempnitati tue ac ipsius ecclesie paterna sollicitudine curaremus. Cum igitur monomachia sacris sit canonibus interdicta, nos tuis supplicationibus inclinati ut contra predictos testibus instrumentis et aliis probacionibus legitimis uti libere ualeas, auctoritate tibi presencium indulgemus.

Nulli ergo omnino hominum liceat hanc paginam nostre concessionis infringere uel ei ausu temerario contraire. Si quis autem hoc attemptare presumpserit indignacionem omnipotentis Dei et beatorum Petri et Pauli apostolorum eius se nouerit incursurum. Datum Viterbii idibus Februarii, pontificatus nostri anno quarto.

Although most printed editions have assumed the pope was Alexander II or III, the pope was almost certainly Alexander IV. He was in Viterbo on 13 February 1258, which is the correct date. Potthast's summary identifies him correctly.

58

May 1267

Droco of Mello attests that he holds Villiers-le-Sec in fief from the bishop of Auxerre.

1 Pope Alexander IV (1254–61).
2 Gui of Mello, bishop of Auxerre (1247–70).

MANUSCRIPTS: Bishops' cartulary, fol. 49v. BnF MS fr. 18692, p. 435, from the cartulary. Arch. Yonne G 1592, fol. 214v, from the preceding. Coll. Bourgogne 3, fol. 13r (abbreviated).

Item littera de feodo de Villari Sicco.

Je Dreus de Mello, sires de Saint Briz et de Chastiau Chiegnon,[1] fais a scauoir[2] a touz ces qui uerront ces presentes leittres que je tiens de monseigneur l'euesque d'Aucuerre[3] quique il soit en fie lige la uille de Viller le Sec de lez Varzi[4] ou toutes les appertenances de celle uille. Et en tesmoign de ceste chose j'ai fait sceller ces presentes leittres en mon scel. Ce fut fait en l'an de l'incarnacion nostre seigneur mil deus cenz LXVII ou mois de Mai.

This document in Old French has not been previously printed. Droco was a nephew of the current bishop.

59

1216

Yolendis, countess of Auxerre, has been received as the bishop's vassal for Mailly-le-Château, Coulanges-sur-Yonne, and Bétry. Nonetheless, her husband Peter will continue to be the bishop's man for these fiefs during his lifetime.

MANUSCRIPTS: Bishops' cartulary, fols. 49v–50r. Coll. Bourgogne 3, fol. 13r (abbreviated).

EDITION: GC 12, instr. col. 154, no. 78.

SUMMARY: Q 3:392, no. 752.

Item littera Yolendis de recognicione feodi de Colengiis.

Ego Yolendis comitissa Autissiodorensis.[1] Notum facio uniuersis quod dominus et pater meus Willelmus Dei gratia Autissiodorensis episcopus[2] ad petitionem Ph[ilippi] filii mei comitis Niuernensis, domino et uiro meo Petro

1 St-Bris, 10 km southeast of Auxerre, and Château-Chinon, 86 km south-southeast of Auxerre.
2 The cartulary reads 'ssauoir.'
3 Gui of Mello, bishop of Auxerre (1247–70).
4 Villiers-le-Sec, 46 km south-southwest of Auxerre, was just a short distance from Varzy, 51 km south-southwest of Auxerre.

1 Yolendis, countess of Auxerre through her marriage to Peter of Courtenay.
2 William of Seignelay, bishop of Auxerre (1207–20).

comite Autissiodorensis[3] presente petente et consentiente, me recepit in feminam de Mailliaco castro, Colengiis super Yonam et Betriaco[4] cum eorum pertinenciis, in omnibus tam de dotaligo meo quam de omni iure quod ego in dicta terra habeo et quod Philippus filius meus in dicta terra habebat quamdiu uixero, saluo tamen in omnibus iure episcopatus Autissiodorensis et quorumlibet aliorum qui in dicta terra ius habunt, salua etiam uita P[etri] comitis uiri mei qui super hoc remanet homo dicti episcopi. Actum anno Domini MCC sexto X.

This is the same document as number 7, apparently copied into the cartulary a second time by mistake; it is also possible that the bishopric had two separate copies of the charter and kept them in different boxes. The differences between this version and document 7 are very minor ones of spelling.

60

1189

Siguin of Tournelle and Hugh of Glanon settle the quarrel between Bishop Hugh of Auxerre and Hugh of Lormes. After he dies, the agreement is confirmed by his wife, the sister of Siguin of Tournelle and Hugh of Glanon.

MANUSCRIPTS: Bishops' cartulary, fol. 50r. Bibl. Auxerre, MS 155, p. 69, dated 1275; seventeenth-century copy by Dom Viole.[1] Coll. Bourgogne 3, fol. 13v (abbreviated).

EDITION: GC 12, instr. col. 178, no. 113; dated 1275.

Item littera H. de Vlmo super homagio de Vlmo.

Ego Siguinus de Tournella Castri Canini dominus[2] et ego Hugo dominus Glenne,[3] notum uolumus fieri tam presentibus quam futuris quod cum diu controuersia extitisset inter dominum Hugonem Autissiodorensis episcopum et Hugonem de Vlmo[4] super homagio episcopo Autissiodorensis a domino Vlmi

3 Peter of Courtenay, count of Nevers and Auxerre (1184–1219).

4 Mailly-le-Château, 23 km south of Auxerre; Coulanges-sur-Yonne, 30 km south of Auxerre; and Bétry, 20 km southeast of Auxerre.

1 Viole notes in a marginal comment that GC's date of 1275 cannot be right.

2 Château-Chinon, 86 km south-southeast of Auxerre.

3 Glanon, 34 km south-southeast of Dijon.

4 Lormes, 60 km south-southeast of Auxerre. Men named Hugh were also lords of Lormes in the thirteenth century; see documents 52 and 56.

prestando. Tandem mediante concordia inter eos statutunt est et concessum quod dominus Vlmi ligium debet prestare hominium episcopo Autissiodorensis, salua fidelitate quam comiti debet Niuernensis. Et quod singulis annis reddere tenetur ecclesie Beati Stephani cereum, L librarum cere. Mortuo Hugone de Vlmo facta est hec eadem conuentio inter dominum episcopum et sororem nostram prefati H[ugonis] relictam, concedente filio suo Hugone quod quam cito terram suam in manu sua teneret ligium prestaret hominium Autissiodorensis episcopo, salua fidelitate comitis Niuernensis, et quod singulis annis cereum reddet sicut statutum est. Nos uero pro bono pacis concessimus quod si idem Hugo ab conuencione ista resilire presumeret, nullum ei super hec prestaremus auxilium sed conuencionem ita fuisse factam testificaremus. Ad maiorem autem huius rei noticiam presenti carte sigilla nostra apposuimus. Actum est hoc anno incarnati uerbi MCC LXXXIX.

Although the document is clearly dated 1289, this is most likely an error for 1189. Bishop Hugh of Noyers (1183–1206) was bishop of Auxerre on that date, but there was no Bishop Hugh in the thirteenth century after him. The GC editors changed the name of the bishop from Hugh to Erard (without noting that they had done so) to correspond with their mistaken date of 1275. The editors seem to have read the third X for a V and ignored the IX that followed.

Siguin of Tournelle is most likely the son of the Siguin of Tournelle who witnessed an agreement between the count of Nevers and the bishop of Auxerre in 1145; see document 1.

Fol. 50v.

In scrinio signato per L inuenientur littere Heruei comitis de feodo et tradicione castellorum, uidelicet Sancti Saluatoris, Conade, Castri Noui et plures alie.[1]

61

22 June 1209

Hervé, count of Nevers, preparing to leave on the Albigensian Crusade, settles his quarrel with Bishop William. He agrees that he will have to yield the castles of St-Sauveur and Châteauneuf to the bishop whenever the latter wants.

1 The scribe was clearly not copying the boxes' contents in alphabetical order.

Although the bishop also asserted his right to Cosne, he agrees not to demand it of Hervé during his lifetime.

MANUSCRIPTS: Bishops' cartulary, fol. 50v. BnF MS fr. 18692, pp. 77–8; abbreviated. Arch. Yonne G 1592, fol. 44r–v; abbreviated. Coll. Bourgogne 3, fol. 13v; abbreviated.

EDITION: GC 12, instr. col. 149, no. 69.

SUMMARY: Q 3:391, no. 747.

Herueus comes Niuernensis[2] omnibus presentes litteras inspecturis, salutem in Domino. Nouerint uniuersi quod cum controuersia uerteretur inter uenerabilem patrem et dominum meum Willelmum Autissiodorensis episcopum[3] ex una parte et me ex altera super domibus et munitionibus castrorum meorum uidelicet Sancti Saluatoris, Conade, Castri Noui[4] quas episcopus dicebat sibi debere tradi ad suum beneplacitum secundum quod in carta eius continebatur. Tandem in hanc formam composicionis uenimus quod nos recognouimus domos et munitiones Sancti Saluatoris et Castri Noui tradendas esse episcopo sicut in carta eius exprimitur et ei tradi precepimus. De domo uero et municione Conade ad preces meas et quorumdam amicorum tam suorum quam meorum sustinuit dominus episcopus. Et promisit quod non peteret tradicionem earum sibi fieri in uita mea nec me super eis traheret in causa, salua carta domini episcopi et saluo omni iure suo et successorum suorum post mortem meam, saluo etiam iure meo et heredum meorum.

Hoc autem factum est saluis omnibus querelis suis et meis et saluis litteris ad dominum Remensis et coniudices suos de communi assensu partium impetratis usque ad reditum meum a peregrinacione Albigensi, saluo etiam eo quod auctoritate dictarum litterarum uel eciam aliarum me non poterit conuenire super tradicione domus et munitionis Conade sibi facienda in uita mea querelis de mutatione monete et de rachatacione terre remanentibus in eo statu in quo erant tempore facte compositionis. Tempus autem quod effluxerit a die composicionis usque ad redditum meum a dicta peregrinacione neque sibi contra me neque michi contra ipsum proderit ad prescribendum. Datum anno Domini Millesimo CC nono, mense Iunio, decimo kalendas Iulii.

2 Hervé IV of Donzy (d. 1222) became count of Nevers in 1199 by marrying the heiress.

3 William of Seignelay, bishop of Auxerre (1207–20).

4 St-Sauveur, 35 km southwest of Auxerre, Cosne, 65 km southwest of Auxerre, and Châteauneuf, 64 km south-southwest of Auxerre.

62

Vermenton, 10 February 1211

Count Peter of Auxerre and Tonnerre recognizes that Countess Mathilda of Tonnerre had held Mailly and Bétry in fief from the bishop of Auxerre. Peter now receives these castles in fief from Bishop William.

MANUSCRIPT: Bishops' cartulary, fols. 50v–51r.
EDITION: GC 12, instr. col. 150, no. 71; abbreviated.
SUMMARY: Q 3:391, no. 748.

Item littera Petri comitis Autissiodorensis et Tornodorensis de feodo Mailliaci et Betriaci et de tradicione dictorum castellorum.

Ego Petrus comes Autissiodorensis et Tornodorensis,[1] notum facio uniuersis quod cum michi tam per cartas autenticas antecessorum meorum comitum quam per litteras Mathildis comitisse quondam Tornodorensis[2] in quibus expresse continebatur quod ipsa Mailliacum castrum[3] in feodum tenuit a bone memorie Hugone quondam Autissiodorensis episcopo,[4] necnon et per testimonia multorum bonorum uirorum et fidedignorum et per communem famam terre michi constitisset quod Mailliacum et Betriacum[5] cum pertinenciis suis sunt de feodo episcopi Autissiodorensis, accessi ad dominum meum Willelmum Autissiodorensis episcopum[6] et Mailliacum et Betriacum cum pertinenciis ab ipso in feodum cepi et de ipsis eidem publice et sollempniter homagium manuale feci, iuramento a me eidem corporaliter prestito quod nunquam per me faciam nec fieri procurabo, nec ut fiat consentiam nec si factum fuerit ratum habebo, nec auxilium aut consilium uel fauorem alicui impendam super dicto feodo episcopum impetenti, quominus Autissiodorensis episcopi feodum illud pacifice et quiete obtineant. Ita autem Malliacum et Betriacum teneo ab Autissiodorensis episcopo quod ad eius beneplacitum ei et successoribus eius ea tradentur. Ita tamen quod eo discedente michi uel ministerialibus meis cum integritate restituentur.

---

1 Peter of Courtenay, count of Nevers and Auxerre (1184–1219).
2 Mathilda, widow of Count Gui of Nevers, held the title of dowager countess of Tonnerre. Her charter does not survive.
3 Mailly-le-Château, 23 km south of Auxerre.
4 Hugh of Noyers, bishop of Auxerre (1183–1206).
5 Bétry, 20 km southeast of Auxerre.
6 William of Seignelay, bishop of Auxerre (1207–20).

Quod ut ratum ac stabile permaneat, presentem paginam feci annotari et sigilli mei munimine roborari. Actum publice apud Vermentum,[7] anno incarnacionis dominice MCC decimo, mense Februariio, quarto idus eiusdem mensis.

Count Peter initially claimed that Mailly and Bétry were held in fief from the countess of Champagne, not from the bishop of Auxerre. Indeed, in 1210 he asserted this to the pope, having already announced that knowledgeable men had told him Mathilda had long held from the counts and countesses of Champagne.[8] Although Peter here said that Mailly had always been held in fief from the bishop, three years later he said that he had in fact always held it from the counts of Champagne, and had only said differently under threat of excommunication.[9] The beginning of the year 1211 in 'new style' was considered 1210. See also the following document.

63

Vermenton, 9 February 1211

Count Peter of Auxerre and Tonnerre recognizes that Countess Mathilda of Tonnerre had held Mailly and Bétry in fief from the bishop of Auxerre. Peter now receives these castles in fief from Bishop William.

MANUSCRIPT: Bishops' cartulary, fol. 51r.

Ego Petrus comes Autissiodorensis et Tornodorensis,[1] notum facio uniuersis quod cum michi tam per cartas autenticas antecessorum meorum comitum quam per litteras Matildis quondam comitisse Tornodorensis in quibus expresse continetur quod ipsa Mailliacum castrum in feodum tenuit a bone memorie Hugone[2] quondam Autissiodorensis episcopo necnon et per testimonium multorum bonorum uirorum et fidedignorum et per communem famam terre michi constitisset quod Mailliacum et Betriacum cum pertinenciis suis ab ipso in feodum cepi, et de ipsis eidem publice et sollempniter homagium manuale feci, iuramento a me corporaliter eidem prestito quod nunquam per me faciam nec fieri procurabo nec

7 Vermenton, 19 km southeast of Auxerre.

8 *Gesta*, p. 249. *The Cartulary of Countess Blanche of Champagne*, ed. Theodore Evergates, pp. 33–6, nos. 1, 4. See also Yves Sassier, *Recherches sur le pouvoir comtal en Auxerrois*, p. 199.

9 *The Cartulary of Countess Blanche*, ed. Evergates, pp. 34–5, no. 2.

1 Peter of Courtenay, count of Nevers and Auxerre (1184–1219).

2 The cartulary reads 'mememorie Huogne.'

ut fiat consentiam nec si factum fuerit ratum habebo, nec auxilium aut consilium uel fauorem alicui impendam super dicto feodo episcopum impetenti, quominus Autissiodorensis episcopi feodum illud pacifice obtineant et quiete. Ita autem Malliacum et Betriacum teneo ab Autissiodorensis episcopo quod ad eius beneplacitum ei et successoribus suis ea tradentur. Ita tamen quod eo discedente michi uel ministerialibus meis cum integritate restituentur.

Quod ut ratum ac stabile permaneat presentem paginam feci annotari et sigilli mei munimine roborari. Actum publice apud Vermenton,[3] anno incarnacionis dominice MCC X, mense Februarii, quinto idus eiusdem mensis.

This is the same as document 62, identical except for a few minor spelling differences and the date. Presumably it was issued twice, on two successive days. See above for the people and places.

64

Vermenton, 10 February 1211

Manasses, bishop of Orléans, Droco of Mello, and the latter's son William attest that Count Peter of Auxerre received Mailly and Bétry in fief from Bishop William of Auxerre.

MANUSCRIPTS: Bishops' cartulary, fol. 51v. BnF MS fr. 18692, pp. 98–9, from the cartulary. Arch. Yonne G 1592, fol. 56r, from the preceding.

Item littera confirmatoria de eodem sub sigillo Manasse episcopi Aurelianensis Droconis de Melloto et Willelmi eiusdem Droconis filii.

Manasses Dei gratia Aurelianensis episcopus,[1] Droco de Melloto[2] et Willelmus eiusdem Droconis filius, omnibus presentes litteras inspecturis, in Domino salutem. Nouerint uniuersi presentes pariter et futuri quod nobilis uir Petrus comes Autissiodorensis nobis presentibus apud Vermentonem[3] accessit ad uenerabilem patrem et dominum suum Vuillelmum Autissiodorensis episcopum[4] et ab eo cepit in feodum Mailliacum et Betriacum[5] cum petinenciis eorum, et de dicto

3 Vermenton, 19 km southeast of Auxerre.

1 Manasses, brother of Bishop William of Seignelay, was bishop of Orléans (1207–21).
2 Droco of Mello (d. 1218) was royal constable.
3 Vermenton, 19 km southeast of Auxerre.
4 William of Seignelay, bishop of Auxerre (1207–20).
5 Mailly-le-Château, 23 km south of Auxerre, and Bétry, 20 km southeast of Auxerre.

feodo fecit prefato episcopo homagium manuale, prestito eidem corporaliter iuramento quod nec per se faciet nec fieri procurabit, nec ut fiat consentiet nec si factum fuerit ratum habebit, nec auxilium aut consilium uel fauorem alicui impendet super dicto feodo episcopum impetenti, quominus Autissiodorensis episcopi feodum illud pacifice obtineant et quiete. Ita autem Mailliacum et Betriacum tenet idem comes ab Autissiodorensis episcopo, quod ad eius beneplacitum episcopo et successoribus eius ea tradentur. Ita tamen quod eo discedente comiti uel ministerialibus eius cum integritate restituentur.

Nos autem ad peticionem comitis memorati presentes litteras in testimonium fecimus annotari et sigillorum nostrorum munimine roboratas, sepedicto episcopo tradi. Actum publice apud Vermentonem anno dominice incarnacionis MCC X, mense Februarii, iiii idus eiusdem mensis.

This document, not previously printed, was given at the same time that Count Peter agreed that he held Mailly and Bétry in fief from the bishop of Auxerre (documents 62–3).

65

Paris, July 1215

Count Peter of Nevers does homage for Coulanges-sur-Yonne to the bishop of Auxerre. He recognizes before King Philip that the tithes of Coulanges belong to the bishop.

MANUSCRIPTS: Bishops' cartulary, fol. 51v. BnF MS fr. 18692, pp. 523–4, from the cartulary. Arch. Yonne G 1592, fol. 252r–v.

EDITIONS: GC 12, instr. col. 153, no. 76; abbreviated. Lebeuf 4:77, no. 126; abbreviated.

SUMMARY: Q 3:392, no. 750.

Item littera eiusdem Petri de recognicione homagii de Colenges super Yonam.

Ego Petrus comes Niuernensis,[1] notum facio uniuersis ad quos littere presentes peruenerint quod ego uillam de Colenges super Yonam[2] cum pertinenciis suis teneo de episcopo Autissiodorensis[3] in feodum et homagium, tali modo quod post decessum meum ille qui tenebit uillam de Colenges eam tenebit ab

1 Peter of Courtenay, count of Nevers and Auxerre (1184–1219).

2 Coulanges-sur-Yonne, 30 km south of Auxerre.

3 William of Seignelay, bishop of Auxerre (1207–20).

episcopo Autissiodorensis et eius successoribus ad tale ligium homagium ad quale feodus apportat. Preterea in presencia karissimi domini mei Philippi regis Francie[4] recognoui quod decima predicte uille et territorii est episcopi Autissiodorensis, et ad eum pertinet et successores eius episcopos Autissiodorensis et eam predicto episcopo et successoribus eius teneor conseruare.

Quod ut perpetuam et incontussam obtineat stabilitatem, sigilli mei munimine presens scriptum procepi confirmari. Actum Parisius anno incarnati uerbi MCC X quinto, mense Iulio.[5]

Fol. 51v.

Item littera regis super eadem recognicione.

66

10 February 1211

Peter, bishop of Paris, William, the archdeacon of Paris, and Robert of Courtenay attest that Peter, count of Auxerre, has done homage to Bishop William of Auxerre for Mailly and Bétry.

MANUSCRIPT: Bishops' cartulary, fol. 52r.

Item littera Petri comitis Autissiodorensis et Tornodorensis de feodo Mailliaci et Betriaci.

P[etrus] Dei gratia episcopus et Willelmus archidiaconus Parisiensis[1] et Robertus de Curtiniaco, uniuersis ad quod presentes littere peruenerint, in Domino salutem. Nouerint uniuersi quod Petrus comes Autissiodorensis[2] nobis presentibus accedens ad uenerabilem patrem et dominum suum Willelmum

---

4 Philip II ('Augustus'), king of France (1180–1223).

5 Yves Sassier interprets this date as 5 July 1210; *Recherches sur le pouvoir comtal en Auxerrois*, p. 216, n. 197. This seems unlikely, as dates of the month were still being given by reference to the kalends, nones, and ides at the time. In addition, in July 1210 Peter was complaining to the pope that he had never done homage to the bishop of Auxerre for other fiefs; he would therefore be unlikely to do homage for Coulanges.

---

1 Bishop Peter (1208–19) and Archdeacon William of Paris.

2 Peter of Courtenay (d. 1219). He had become count of Nevers, Auxerre, and Tonnerre by marriage, and even after his first wife died he retained title to Auxerre.

Autissidorensis episcopum[3] Mailliacum castrum et forterciciam Betriaci[4] que de castellaria Mailliaci esse dignoscitur cum pertinenciis suis ab episcopo cepit in feodum et de ipsis eidem publice et sollempniter homagium manuale fecit, iuramento ei ab eodem corporaliter prestito quod nonquam per se faciet nec fieri procurabit nec ut fiat consentiet, nec si factum fuerit ratum habebit nec consilium aut auxilium uel fauorem alicui impendet super dictis feodis episcopum impetenti pro posse suo, quominus episcopi Autissiodorensis feoda illa pacifice obtinent. Ita autem predictum castrum Mailliaci et fortericiam Betriaci que est de castellaria Mailliaci confessus est se tenere ab Autissiodorensis episcopo quod in omnibus negociis suis eidem et successoribus suis ea reddentur. Ita tamen quod eo recedente dicto comiti uel heredibus suis in ea integritate qua ei tradita fuerint restituentur.

In omnis rei memoriam presentes litteras ad peticionem dicti comitis fecimus sigillari. Actum publice apud Vermentonem,[5] anno dominice incarnacionis MCCX, mense Februarii, quarto idus eiusdem mensi.

This document, not previously printed, was issued at the same time as Count Peter's own charters recognizing that he held these castles in fief from the bishop (documents 62–3). Robert of Courtenay was his nephew.

67

Billy, August 1214

Manasses, bishop of Orléans, settles the quarrel between Bishop William of Auxerre, with his chapter, and Count Hervé of Nevers with Countess Mathilda over the fortress of Murat. Murat will be held in fief from the bishop, as a supplement to the fief of Donzy, which Hervé already holds. The land and village of Oisy, and everything the count and countess have there, belong to the cathedral chapter. The count and countess, however, will have everything located at Billy, except for tithes. They agree to defend the chapter's interests against Narjod of Toucy, if he returns from Constantinople.

MANUSCRIPT: Bishops' cartulary, fols. 52r–53r.
EDITION: GC 12, instr. cols. 152–3, no. 75.

3 William of Seignelay, bishop of Auxerre (1207–20).
4 Mailly-le-Château, 23 km south of Auxerre, and Bétry, 20 km southeast of Auxerre.
5 Vermenton, 19 km southeast of Auxerre.

Item littera prolacionis arbitrii Manasses inter Willelmum episcopum Autissiodorensis et Herueum comitem Niuernensis de forterícia de Murato.

Manasses Dei gratia Aurelianensis episcopus,[1] omnibus presentes litteras inspecturis, salutem in Domino. Que pro bono pacis inter aliquos statuntur firma neccesse est stabilitate gaudere, et ne interim recidiue scrupulus dissensionis emergat, litterarum beneficio ad perpetuam noticiam posterorum transmitti. Eapropter omnibus tam presentibus quam futuris notum fieri uolumus quod cum inter uenerabilem Willelmum uidelicet episcopum,[2] Villelmum decanum, et capitulum Autissiodorensis ex una parte et nobilem uirum Herueum comitem et uxor eius Matildim comitissam Niuernensis[3] ex altera orta esset dissensio super fortericia de Murat iuxta Billiacum,[4] quam prefati episcopus decanus et capitulum in proprio fundo ecclesie sue pro parte edificare dicebant, et ex ea episcopatui ipsi capitulo hominibus et uillis eorum et rebus ecclesie dampnum non modicum imminere, necnon super hominibus, possessionibus, redditibus, iustitiis, garenis, et super aliis que inter ipsos apud partes illas, scilicet apud Billiacum et Oisiacum[5] emerserant. Tandem hinc inde firmiter promiserunt et sub pena quingentarum librarum se astrinxerunt, quod super illis sequerentur dictum nostrum, haut et bas, prout dicitur in uulgari, quicquid pro bono pacis inter eos statuere curaremus.

Nos igitur omni studio laborantes, et cura ut ea que statueremus de partium amicabili conniuencia faceremus, prehabito in subscriptis articulis eorum consensu, dictum nostrum formauimus et protulimus in hunc modum. Quod fortericia siue castrum de Murat ab episcopo Autissiodorensi et successoribus eius episcopis, utpote a dominis feodi perpetuo teneatur in augmentum feodi de Donziaco,[6] sub hoc tenore, quod reddi debeat et tradi episcopis Autissiodorensibus ad eorum beneplacitum, ita tamen quod ipsis discedentibus restituatur comiti uel ministerialibus eius cum omni integritate.

Item statuimus per dictum nostrum quod quicquid habebat comes siue comitissa in uilla, siue in territorio Oisiaci in hominibus, talliis, questis, redditibus, terris, pratis, consuetudinibus, nundinis, iustitia magna et parua, et in omnibus aliis ut breuiter dicamus in omni iure uniuersaliter, totum sit capituli Autissiodorensis pleno iure imperpetuum possidendum. Insuper et nemus quod dicitur foresta Oisiaci cum iustitia eius et custodia, et omni iure. Nemus quoque de Paruo Faiteo cum iusticia custodia similiter et omni iure, quicquid autem

1 Manasses, bishop of Orléans (1207–21) and brother of Bishop William.
2 William of Seignelay, bishop of Auxerre (1207–20).
3 Hervé of Donzy became count of Nevers in 1199 by marrying Mathilda, the heiress.
4 Murat, near Billy (37 km south-southwest of Auxerre).
5 Oisy, 3 km east of Billy.
6 Donzy, 58 km southwest of Auxerre.

habebat capitulum antedictum uel habere se dicebat in fundo in quo constructa est fortericia supradicta.

Item quicquid habebat in potestate Billiaci siue in hominibus, siue in consuetudinibus, siue in censibus, uel etiam in aliis temporalibus, totum sit comitis et comitisse iure perpetuo, preter terragia et decimas que remanebunt capitulo memorato, sicut ea consueuit habere, de quibus tamen diximus et statuimus, quod capitulum terras suas que sunt ad terragium in potestate Billiaci, nec accipere poterit ad carrucas suas, nec eas auferre hominibus comitis qui eas colunt, sed penes comitem seu comitissam erit potestas dandi eas hominibus suis ad excolendum, saluo terragio et decima capituli supradicti, et eo etiam prouiso quod non comittantur dari ad excolendum, taliter quod inde capitulum damnificetur predictum.

Item statuimus per dictum nostrum, quod omnes homines et femine quos habebat capitulum apud Charmetum uillare Pruneti, Sorgiacum, siue Dorneciacum[7] iure perpetuo sint comitis et comitisse, et pretera quitquid habebat capitulum in nemoribus de Clausello, de Festo, di Montemedio, et in aliis nemoribus siue pasnagiis apud Billiacum, preter nemora pretaxata, scilicet de foresta Oisiaci et de Paruo Faiteo, que pleno iure ut predictum est, erunt capituli sepefati. Itam diximus et statuimus quod nullus [hominum][8] siue feminarum Autissiodorensis ecclesie retineri possit, aut recipi in munitione de Murat, neque in potestate Billiaci, nec aliquis uel aliqua de hominibus eiusdem ecclesie in potestate Oisiaci comorantibus similiter recipi possit aut retineri in tota terra comitis seu comitisse ubicunque.

Illud quoque preter eundum non censuimus, sed dicto nostro adiecimus et diximus quod si nobilis uir Nariodus frater nobilis uiri Iterii de Tociaco[9] qui in partibus Constantinopolitanis existit, rediret, et super hiis capitulo molestiam aliquam inferre uellet, uel etiam quilibet alius, comes siue comitissa ea garentire tenebitur capitulo antedicto, et ei refarcire omnia dampna et grauamina, que propter hoc sustineret, et per omnia ipsum conseruare indempne. Hec sicut superius expressa sunt de consensu partium pro bono pacis diximus, et statuimus inter eos, ipsi uero benigne et gratanter dictum nostrum spontanei receperunt et gratum habuerunt et ratum. Comes quoque iuxta dicti nostri tenorem forteritiam de Murat prelibatam recepit coram nobis incontinenti publice ab episcopo Autissiodorensis predicto in augmentum feodi de Donziaco et de ipso

7 Charmois, 2 km northeast of Billy. The other places are not identified.

8 This word is missing in the cartulary.

9 Toucy, 22 km southwest of Auxerre. Narjod (d. 1217) and Itier III (d. 1218) of Toucy were among the most powerful lords of the Auxerrois; Constance Brittain Bouchard, *Sword, Miter, and Cloister*, pp. 372–5.

fecit ei specialiter homagium manuale. Actum publice apud Billiacum, anno Domini MCC quartodecimo, mense Augusto.

Bishop Manasses, Bishop William's brother, often issued charters on his behalf. The *Gesta* account of Bishop William described this agreement approvingly.[10]

Fol. 53r.

Item littera Heruei comitis de compromissione facta in Manassem episcopum Aurelianensis de Murato.[1]
Item littera Heruei predicti de feodo et homagio facto domino episcopo de Murat.
Item littera Matildis comitisse Niuernensis super approbacione homagii facti domino episcopo de Murat.
Item alia comitis Niuernensis de compromissio in episcopum Aurelianensis.
Item alie tres littere de feodo Mailliaci et Betriaci.

Fol. 53v.

In scrinio signato per M inuenientur littere de feodo de Petrafricta de Montputois et de Lineriis. Item et plures alie.

68

January 1253

Hugh, lord of Charny, and his wife, Mabilla, attest that they hold in fief from the bishop of Auxerre whatever they have at Pierrefitte and nearby villas. The property came from Mabilla.

MANUSCRIPTS: Bishops' cartulary, fol. 53v. Coll. Bourgogne 3, fol. 14r (abbreviated).
EDITION: GC 12, instr. col. 169, no. 102; abbreviated.
SUMMARY: Q 3:393, no. 768.

---

10 *Gesta*, 2:245. For this case, see also Yves Sassier, *Recherches sur le pouvoir comtal en Auxerrois*, p. 137.

---

1 This 1214 document survives as an original, Arch. Yonne G 1846. Count Hervé and Countess Mathilda confirmed the agreement over Murat reached by Bishop Manasses. It survived because it was preserved in the archives of the cathedral chapter rather than that of the bishop.

Vniuersis presentes litteras inspecturis, H[ugo] dominus Charniaci[2] et Mabilla uxor eius, salutem in domino. Notum facimus quod nos tenemus in feodum et homagium ligium a reuerendo patre G[uidone] Dei gratia episcopo Autissiodorensis[3] nomine episcopatus Autissiodorensis uillam nostram que uocatur Petraficta et partem illam quam habemus in uilla de Montbutois et quicquid habemus in uilla de Arci iuxta Petramfictam,[4] et in nemoribus, et quidquid habemus in uilla de Lineriis[5] et in molendinis de Planchiis, et in censu de Valenta,[6] et in omnibus pertinenciis et appendiciis uillarum, et locorum omnium predictorum, promittentes per iuramentum nostrum corporaliter prestitum quod predicta omnia predicto domino episcopo et successoribus suis episcopis Autissiodorensibus garantizabimus, et deffendemus contra omnes sine aliquo feodo uel retrofeodo, et ad hec omnia firmiter tenenda et inuiolabiliter obseruanda nos et heredes nostros obligamus specialiter et expresse.

Ego uero Mabilla uxor dicti Hugonis, de cuius capite mouent omnia que superius sunt expressa, predicta omnia feci laudaui uolui et concessi, non coacta, non circouenta, non seducta, sed spontanea uoluntate, promittens per idem iuramentum quod contra predicta uel aliqua predictorum per me uel per alium non ueniam in futurum.

In cuius rei testimonium et munimen presentes litteras sigillorum nostrorum munimine fecimus roborari. Actum anno Domini MCCL secundo, mense Ianuario.

January 1252 is 1253 in 'new style.'

69

August 1275

Robert, bishop of Nevers, attests that William of Mello has confirmed what he holds in fief from the bishop of Auxerre at Oudan. He owes the bishop fifty pounds of wax a year to illuminate the cathedral and recognizes that he needs to carry new bishops on the day of their enthronement.

MANUSCRIPTS: Bishops' cartlary, fols. 53v–54r. Coll. Bourgogne 3, fol. 14r. Arch. Yonne G 1592, fol. 192v.

---

2 Charny, 38 km west-northwest of Auxerre.

3 Gui of Mello, bishop of Auxerre (1247–70).

4 Pierrefitte, 22 km south-southwest of Auxerre, and Montputois, 20 km south-southwest of Auxerre. 'Arci' no longer exists.

5 Leugny, 19 km southwest of Auxerre.

6 Vallan, 7 km south-southwest of Auxerre.

Item littera de feodo Odanti.

A touz ceus qui uerront ces presentes leittres, Robers par la grace de Dieu euesques de Neuers,[1] salut en nostre Seigneur. Sanchent tuit que deuant nous presens Guillelmes de Mello damoiseaus sires d'Espoisse[2] recognut qu'il tenoit de l'euesque d'Auceurre[3] et de l'eglise d'Auceurre en fie Odant[4] et toute la terre de celui leu et les apparuentes et qu'il en estoit en la foy de l'euesque d'Auceurre, et que pour reison de celui fie il est tenuz a rendre touz les ans au tresorier et au sougretain d'Auceurre cinquante liures de cire pour le luminaire de l'eglise d'Auceurre. Et si recognut en nostre presente que pour raison de celui fie il est tenuz a porter l'euesque d'Auceurre en sa nouelle intronizacion auean les autres qui sont ad ce tenus.

Et an tesmoing de ces choses nous auons mis nostre scel en ces leittres. Ce fut fait en l'an de l'incarnacion nostre seigneur M CC sexante et quinze, ou mois d'Aoust.

This document, written in Old French, has not been previously printed.

70

March 1259

Matthew of Gurgy, with his brothers Milo and Peter and mother, Isabella, had asserted that his late father had received one hundred solidi a year as a fief from the bishop of Auxerre. The bishop denies this, but the parties agree that a field at Gurgy which Matthew had had as allodial property shall be held from the bishop in liege homage. The bishop will pay Matthew and his heirs one hundred solidi a year in recognition of this fief.

MANUSCRIPT: Bishops' cartulary, fol. 54r.

Item littera de feodo de Gurgiaco.

Omnibus presentes litteras inspecturis, I[ohannes] Sancti Germani Autissiodorensis et H. Sancti Petri Autissiodorensis humilis abbas,[1] salutem in

---

1 Robert II, bishop of Nevers (1262–75).

2 Epoisses, 58 km southeast of Auxerre.

3 Erard of Lézinnes, bishop of Auxerre (1270–8).

4 Oudan, 52 km south-southwest of Auxerre.

---

1 Abbot John of St-Germain (1243–77) and the abbot of St-Pierre of Auxerre.

Domino. Notum facimus quod in nostra presencia constitutus Matheus de Gurgiaco[2] miles recognouit quod cum domina Ysabellis, relicta Bastardi de Gurgiaco militis, Milo, Petrus ac idem Matherus de Gurgiaco fratres milites, filii dictorum Bastardi et Ysabellis, peterent a reuerendo patre Guidone Dei gratia Autissiodorensis episcopo[3] centum solidos Turonensis annui redditus quos dictum Bastardum habuisse et recepisse ab antecessoribus suis dicti reuerendi patris in feodo tenuisse dicebant in redditibus de Appoigniaco,[4] dicto reuerendo patre G dicente se non esse certum penitus de premissis.

Tandem de assensu uenerabilorum uirorum G decani et capituli Autissiodorensis fuit inter dictum reuerendum patrem et dictos fratres taliter concordatum, quod predicti Milo et Matherus accepunt a dicto reuerendo patre in feodum et ligium homagium ad augmentationem predicti feodi campum fratrum de quercu situm in parrochia de Gurgiaco qui erat de alodio ut dicebat idem Matherus. Recognouit etiam idem Matherus coram nobis quod ipse et dictus Milo promiserunt pro se et heredibus suis et ad hoc se et heredes obligauerunt quod ipsi et heredes sui simili modo dictum campum accipient et tenebunt imperpetuum feodum a dicto reuerendo patre et successoribus suis episcopis Autissiodorensis. Et dictus reuerendus pater et successores sui episcopi Autissiodorensis dictis Miloni et Mathero et heredibus suis soluere tenebuntur annis singulis centum solidos Turonensis annui redditus ad festum Sancti Andree apostoli de redditibus suis de Appoigniaco, in quibus centum solidis dictus Milo habebit et percipiet sextam partem quodam uixerit dicta Ysabellis mater sua. Post decessum uero ipsius Ysabellis idem Milo uel heredes sui terciam partem habebunt et percipient in centum solidis supradictis. Item recognouit coram nobis predictus Matherus quod ipse et dictus Milo tenentur dicto reuerendo patri et eius successoribus episcopis Autissiodorensis dictum campum in feodum ligium garentire.

In cuius rei testimonium et munimen ad peticionem dicti Matheri presentes litteras sigillis nostris fecimus sigillari. Actum anno Domini MCC quinquegesimo ottauo, mense Martio.

This document has not been previously printed. The year is 1259 in 'new style.'

2 Gurgy, 8 km north of Auxerre.

3 Gui of Mello, bishop of Auxerre (1247–70).

4 Appoigny, 10 km north-northwest of Auxerre.

71

October 1226

Wigo, count of Nevers and Forez, and his wife Mathilda recall that the late count Hervé had intended to establish a chapel at Entrains. They now establish the chapel, with an annual income for the chaplain.

MANUSCRIPT: Bishops' cartulary, fol. 54v.

EDITIONS: Lebeuf 2:48, no. 105, from the cartulary. Lebeuf 4:93, no. 156.

Item littera de fundatorum capelle de Interanniis.

Ego G[uigo] comes Niuernensis et Forensis et M[atildis] comitissa Niuernensis et Forensis uxor mea[1] omnibus notum facimus quod cum bone memorie H[erueus] quondam comes Niuerensis[2] in extrema uoluntate et ante uoluisset et precepisset quandam capellam apud Interannem[3] construi et redditum annum competentem assignari capellano, qui in ea diuinum officium imperpetuum celebraret, nos uotum eius exequi cupientes, cum effectu capellam ipsam construximus et quindecim libras annui redditus in dicta capella assignauimus, unde uolumus quod si quod absit heredes defuncti Guidonis Sancti Pauli[4] aut illi ad quos terra de Interanne deuenerit contra dicti redditus assignationem ire uellent, nos aut heredes aut successores nostri in eadem capella quindecim libras annui redditus competentes loco redditus supradicti, pro remedio animarum nostrarum et antecessorum nostrorum, de proprio redditu nostro comitatus Niuernensis prope Interannem bone fide assignabimus.

In cuius rei testimonium presentes litteras fecimus sigillorum nostrorum munimine roborari. Actum anno Domino MCC XX sexto, mense Ottobrorum.

See also the following document.

72

February 1228

Mathilda, countess of Nevers, reassures Bishop Henry of Auxerre that he and his successors shall have the chapel at Entrains when she dies. In the meantime, he grants it to her, excepting only parish rights.

---

1 Wigo, count of Forez (d. 1241), second husband of Mathilda, heiress of Nevers (d. ca 1257).

2 Hervé, count of Nevers (1199–1222), Mathilda's first husband.

3 Entrains, 65 km southwest of Auxerre.

4 Gui of St-Pol had married Agnes, Mathilda's daughter and heiress to Nevers. Both Gui and Agnes had just died when this document was issued.

MANUSCRIPT: Bishops' cartulary, fol. 54v.
EDITIONS: Lebeuf 2:48, no. 106, from the cartulary. Lebeuf 4:93, no. 157.

Item littera de collatione eiusdem capelle.

Ego Matildis comitissa Niuernensis,[1] omnibus notum facimus quod nos uolumus et approbamus ut uenerabilis pater et dominus H[enricus] Dei gratia episcopus Autissiodorensis[2] post decessum nostrum, uel episcopus Autissiodorensis qui pro tempore erit, habeat donacionem et collacionem capelle que est in domo nostra de Interanne,[3] cuius capelle donacionem et collacionem dominus H[enricus] episcopus Autissiodorensis nobis ad uitam meam concessit, saluo in ominibus iure ecclese parochialis de Interanne.

Quod ut ratum sit et firmum, presentes litteras fecimus sigilli nostri munimine roborari. Actum anno Domini MCC XX septimo, mense Februarii.

February of 1227 was the beginning of 1228 in 'new style'. See also the previous document.

73

August 1239

The cantor and chapter of Gien asset to the end of their quarrel with Bishop Bernard of Auxerre, reiterating the text of his charter. The bishop promises to pay for the support of the vicars in the church of St-Étienne there.

MANUSCRIPT: Bishops' cartulary, fols. 54v–55r.
EDITION: GC 12, instr. col. 159, no. 87; abbreviated, the bishop's document only.

Item littera de uicaria de Giemo.

Omnibus presentes litteras inspecturis, G cantor totumque capitulum Giemensis,[1] salutem in Domino. Nouerint uniuersi quod cum contencio uerteretur inter nos ex una parte et uenerabilem patrem B[ernardum] Dei gratia Autissiodorensis episcopum[2] ex altera super collacione uicariarum que sunt in ecclesia Beati Stephani de Giemo, tandem saniori usi consilio uolumus et concessimus quicquid idem uenerabilis pater B[ernardus] Dei gratia

1 Mathilda, countess of Nevers (d. ca 1257).
2 Henry, bishop of Auxerre (1220–35).
3 Entrains, 65 km southwest of Auxerre.

1 Gien, 76 km west-southwest of Auxerre.
2 Bernard of Sully, bishop of Auxerre (1235–45).

Autissiodorensis episcopus super predictis collacionibus de speciali gratia ordinaret. Tenor cuius ordinacionis continetur sub hac forma.

Omnibus presentes litteras inspecturis, B[ernardus] Dei gratia Autissiodorensis episcopus, salutem in Domino. Nouerint uniuersi quod cum contencio uerteretur inter nos ex una parte et dilectos filios cantorem et capitulum Giemensis ex altera super collacione uicariarum que sunt in ecclesia Beati Stephani de Giemo, tandem saniori usi consilio uoluerunt et concesserunt et promiserunt tenore quicquid super predictis uicariis a nobis fuisse ordinatum. Nos uero habito bonorum uirorum consilio de speciali gratia concessimus eisdem collacionem altarium Beate Marie et Beati Iohannis. Collacionem autem tam aliorum altarium quam uicariarum nobis et successoribus nostris retinentes, et etiam aliorum tam altarium quam uicariarum, si de nouo contingerit in eadem ecclesia constitui uel creari, prout ad nos de iure communi noscitur perinere. Dicti uero cantor et capitulum post decessum capellanorum duorum altarium supradictorum tenentur concorditer eligere infra quadraginta dies, et ante institutionem nobis et successoribus nostri presentare, alioquin a collacione dictorum altarium priuabuntur ea uice. In cuius rei testimonium presentes litteras sigilli nostri munimine fecimus roborari. Actum anno Domini MCC XXX nono.

Nos autem predictas litteras ratas et gratas habemus et quicquid in eis plenarie continetur. Quod ut ratum et stabile habeatur, presentes litteras sigilli nostri munimine fecimus roborari. Actum anno Domini MCC trecesimo nono, mense Augusto.

See also the following document.

74

April 1237

The archdeacon of Nevers and cantor of Auxerre attest to the end of a quarrel between the bishop of Auxerre and the knight Hugh of 'Nomato,' who claims that he has the right to name the vicar in the church of St-Étienne of Gien, which position his late mother had established, along with him and his brothers. Although it is settled that only the bishop names the vicar, it is agreed that he will name a certain person when the position becomes vacant.

MANUSCRIPT: Bishops' cartulary, fol. 55r–v.

Item littere de collacione uicariarum de Giemo.

Omnibus presentes litteras inspecturis, I. Niuernensis archidiaconus et R. cantor Autissiodorensis, salutem in Domino. Nouerint uniuersi quod cum controuersia uerteretur inter uenerabilem patrem episcopum Autissiodorensis[1] ex una parte et Hugonem de Nomato militem ex altera super eo quod idem miles dicebat quandem uicariam quam defuncta Elizabet domina de Nomato, Guillelmus, Hugo et Herueus ipsius filii, constituerant in ecclesia Beati Stephani de Giemo[2] ad donacionem suam pertinere, dicto episcopo contrarium aserente. Tandem coram nobis cognitum fuit et declaratum quod ius conferendi dictam uicariam ad dictum episcopum pertinebat. Dominus autem episcopus ad instanciam nostram et preces ipsius militis ex mera gratia cuidam persone predictam uicariam contulit tunc uacantem.

In cuius rei testimonium et memoriam, presentes litteras sigillorum nostrorum munimine fecimus roborari. Actum anno Domini MCC XXXVII, mense Aprili.

This document has not been previously printed. See also the previous document.

75

Coulanges-sur-Yonne, 31 May 1249

Countess Mathilda of Nevers attests to the end of a quarrel between Bishop Gui of Auxerre and her liegeman Geoffrey of 'Corbolano.' The latter had damaged the bishop's interests at his castle. The countess makes peace by establishing that everything may stay as it now is, but that Geoffrey shall not make further additions to the castle.

MANUSCRIPT: Bishops' cartulary, fol. 55v.

Item littera de Breteschia de Corbolano attestata.

Nos M[atildis] comitissa Niuernensis,[1] notum facimus uniuersis quod cum discordia uerteretur inter uenerabilem patrem et dominum nostrum Guidonem Dei gratia episcopum Autissiodorensis[2] ex una parte et Gaufridum de Corbolano[3] armigerum hominem nostrum ligium ex altera, super hoc quod idem episcopus dicebat dictum armigerum fecisse in domo sua de Corbolano quandam

1 Bernard of Sully, bishop of Auxerre (1235–45).

2 Gien, 76 km west-southwest of Auxerre.

1 Countess Mathilda of Nevers (d. ca 1257).

2 Gui of Mello, bishop of Auxerre (1247–70).

3 It is possible that this is Corvol, 45 km south-southwest of Auxerre.

Breteschia ligneam et quedam alia ad forterициam pertinencia in eius et episcopatus Autissiodorensis preiudicium et grauamen.[4] Tandem eodem episcopo et dicto armigero in nostra presencia constitutis, nos de assensu et uoluntate dictarum partium super discordia supradicta ordinauimus in hunc modum.

Scilicet quod ea que usque ad presentem diem in domo predicta facta sunt in statu in quo sunt remanebunt. Ita tamen quod ibidem aliquid ad fortericiam pertinens poterit de cetero superadi, sine accedu non posset nec hiis que ad primis ibidem fatam sunt aliquid ad fortericiam. Nos autem ad requisicionem predicti armigeri bona fide promisimus episcopo supradicto, quod si aliquid ad fortericiam pertinens de cetero in loco predicto fieret uel contingeret superadi, nos illud destinere tenemus. Hec autem omnia et singula supradicta rata et grata habuit coram nobis armiger supradictus.

In cuius rei memoriam et perpetuam firmitatem, nos ad peticionem dictarum partium sigillum nostrum direximus presentibus litteris apponendum. Actum apud Colungias super Yonam[5] ultima die Maii, anno Domini MCC quadragesimo nono.

Item alia littera consimilis.

This document has not been previously printed.

76

July 1248

William of Mello, lord of St-Bris, receives Baulche in fief from Bishop Gui of Auxerre. He and all his heirs will be the bishop's liegemen for all his other houses. Any of these heirs who hold Baulche and are lords of St-Bris will, if possible, first be liegemen of the count of Auxerre for St-Bris, and then liegemen of the bishop.

MANUSCRIPTS: Bishops' cartulary, fols. 55v–56r. Bibl. Auxerre, MS 153, fol. 402r; seventeenth-century copy by Dom Viole. Coll. Bourgogne 3, fol. 14r–v (abbreviated).

EDITION: GC 12, instr. col. 163, no. 94; abbreviated.

SUMMARY: Q 3:393, no. 763.

4 The cartulary reads 'grauamem.'

5 Coulanges-sur-Yonne, 30 km south of Auxerre.

Item littere de feodo de Belca.

Omnibus presentes litteras inspecturis, Guillelmus de Melloto dominus Sancti Prisci,[1] salutem in Domino. Notum facio uniuersis quod ego domum meam de Belca[2] cum omnibus pertinenciis eiusdem domus, excepto nemore quod habeo in brueria, recepi in feodum ligium et casamentum a reuerendo patre ac domino Guidone Dei gratia episcopo Autissiodorensis,[3] iurabilem et reddibilem dicto episcopo et successoribus ad paruam uim et ad magnam, et factus sum homo ligius post alios dominos meos quos modo habeo dicto episcopo, et heredes mei erunt homines ligii dicto episcopo et successoribus eius imperpetuum de dicta domo et pertinenciis, ita quod si ille de heredibus meis qui erit dominus Sancti Prisci tenuerit domum predictam de Belcha, post ligiacionem quam debebit comiti Autissiodorensis ratione feodi Sancti Prisci, erit homo ligius ante omnes homines dicto episcopo et successoribus eius imperpetuum, si de iure possit esse.

Si uero alius de heredibus meis quam ille qui erit dominus Sancti Prisci habuerit uel tenuerit dictam domum, ipse et heredes sui erunt homines ligii ante omnes dicto episcopo et successoribus eius, si de iure possit esse, et si ego uel heredes mei aliquid acquisiuimus uel acquiremus in futurum circa uel iuxta domum predictam quod non sit de feodo alterius, ego et heredes mei quos ad hoc obligo, illud tenebimus a dicto episcopo et successoribus eius in feodum cum aliis rebus que sunt de feodo supradicto. Et ad omnia predicta tenenda complenda et firmiter obseruanda, obligo me et heredes meos specialiter et expresse.

Et in testimonium predictorum et robur firmitatis, sigillum meum duxi presentibus apponendum. Actum anno Domini MCC XL ottauo, mense Iulio.

Fol. 56 has a long diagonal slice, mended, down the middle. The bishop was Lord William's brother. See also the following document, in which William's brother Droco confirms.

77

July 1248

Droco of Mello attests that his brother William, lord of St-Bris, has received his house at Baulche in fief from Bishop Gui of Auxerre.

---

1 William of Mello, lord of St-Bris, 10 km southeast of Auxerre.

2 Baulche, 4 km west of Auxerre.

3 Gui of Mello, bishop of Auxerre (1247–70).

MANUSCRIPTS: Bishops' cartulary, fol. 56r–v. Coll. Bourgogne 3, fol. 14v; abbreviated.

EDITION: GC 12, instr. cols. 163–4, no. 95.

Item alia littera consimilis.

Ego Droco de Melloto dominus Locharum et Meduane,[1] notum facio uniuersis quod in presencia mea constitutus, karissimus frater meus Guillelmus de Melloto dominus Sancti Prisci[2] recepit in feodum ligium et casamentum a reuerendo patre ac domino Guidone Dei gratia episcopo Autissiodorensis[3] domum suam de Belcha,[4] cum omnibus pertinenciis eiusdem domus excepto nemore quod habet in brueria, iurabilem et reddibilem eidem episcopo et successoribus eius imperpetuum ad paruam uim et ad magnam, et factus est homo ligius coram me dicto episcopo post alios dominos suos quos modo habet, et erunt similiter heredes sui homines ligii dicto episcopo et successoribus eius imperpetuum, ita quod si ille de heredibus dicti Guillelmi qui erit dominus Sancti Prisci tenuerit dictam domum post ligiacionem quam debet comiti Autissiodorensis ratione feodi Sancti Prisci erit homo ligius ante omnes dicto episcopo et successoribus eius, si de iure possit esse.

Si uero alius de heredibus dicti Guillelmi quam ille qui erit dominus Sancti Prisci tenuerit dictam domum, erit homo dicto episcopo et successoribus eius ligius ante omnes, si de iure possit esse. Promisit etiam idem Guillelmus coram me quod ipse uel heredes sui quos ad hoc obligauit specialiter et expresse contra predicta uel aliquod predictorum non uenient aliquatenus in futurum.

In cuius rei testimonium sigillum meum duxi presentibus apponendum. Datum anno Domini MCC XL ottauo, mense Iulio.

This repeats the arrangements spelled out in the previous document. See also the following document.

78

June 1258

Archbishop William of Sens attests that Droinus of Mello confirms the agreements over fiefs that his grandfather William, lord of St-Bris, and William's brother Droco made with the bishop of Auxerre.

---

1 Loches, in the valley of the Loire, and Mayenne, in Normandy.

2 St-Bris, 10 km southeast of Auxerre.

3 Gui of Mello, bishop of Auxerre (1247–70).

4 Baulche, 4 km west of Auxerre.

MANUSCRIPTS: Bishops' cartulary, fol. 56v. Bibl. Auxerre, MS 153, fol. 411r; seventeenth-century copy by Dom Viole. Coll. Bourgogne 3, fol. 14v; abbreviated.

EDITION: GC 12, instr. col. 169, no. 103; abbreviated.

Item littera testimonii sub sigilo archiepiscopi Senonensis.

Vniuersis presentes litteras inspecturis, Guillelmus Dei gratia Senonensis archiepiscopus,[1] salutem in Domino. Notum facimus quod in nostra presencia constitutus Droynus de Melloto[2] armiger, Spissie et Castri Canini[3] dominus, super sancta Dei euuangelia iurauit et per iuramentum suum promisit quod elemosinas, legata et feuda atque dona que nobiles uiri bone memorie G[uillelmus] de Melloto quondam dominus Sancti Prisci auus suus et Droco de Melloto quondam dominus Locharum[4] frater eiusdem Guillelmi contulerunt seu legauerunt quibuscunque latis uel personis soluet integre et plenarie,[5] prout uenerabilis frater Autissiodorensis episcopus,[6] patruus eiusdem Droini, ordinauerit uel quocumque modo duxerit statuendum et assignacionem quam de donis, legatis seu elemosinis et feodis supradictis facere duxerit super terram ipsius Droini predictus Autissiodorensis episcopus ratam habebit et gratam idem Droynus, nec contra ueniet per se uel per alium aliquatenus in futurum. Sed quantum ad hoc iuridicioni nostre et successorum nostrorum supponeus dictus Droinus ubicunque maneat uel existeat.

In cuius rei testimonium et munimen ad peticionem dicti Droini sigillum nostrum una cum sigillo ipsius Droini presentibus litteris duximus apponendum. Datum anno Domini MCC quinquagesimo ottauo, mense Iunio.

Droinus of Mello had presumably just inherited and was not yet a knight. See also the two preceding documents.

79

July 1248

William of Mello, lord of St-Bris, recognizes that he holds Baulche in fief from the bishop of Auxerre. In return the bishop gives him fifty pounds.

---

1 William, archbishop of Sens (1258–68).

2 He was mentioned as the son of Droco of Mello ten years earlier; see document 52.

3 Epoisse, 58 km southeast of Auxerre, and Château-Chinon, 86 km south-southeast of Auxerre.

4 Loches, in the valley of the Loire.

5 This is a reference to document 34.

6 Gui of Mello, bishop of Auxerre (1247–70).

MANUSCRIPT: Bishops' cartulary, fols. 56v–57r.

Item alia littera de eodem.

Omnibus presentes litterarus inspecturis G[uillelmus] de Melloto dominus Sancti Prisci[1] salutem in Domino. Nouerint uniuersi quod ego domum meam de Belcha[2] a reuerendo patre G[uidone] Dei gratia Autissidorensis episcopo[3] in feodum cepi, pro qua re michi dedit quingentas libras Turonenis episcopus supradictus, quas ab eo recepi in pecunia numerata.

In cuius rei testimonium sigillum meum presentibus est appensum. Actum anno Domini MCC XL ottauo, mense Iulio.

This document has not been previously printed. See also document 76, part of the same agreement.

80

April 1269

Droco of Mello, lord of St-Bris and Château-Chinon, attests that he is the liegeman of his uncle Gui, bishop of Auxerre. His heirs will be the liegemen of future bishops. The bishop gives him two hundred pounds worth of land. Droco also agrees that he is the bishop's liegeman for Baulche.

MANUSCRIPTS: Bishops' cartlary, fol. 57r. Bibl. Auxerre, MS 153, fol. 409r; seventeenth-century copy by Dom Viole; repeated on fol. 416r. Coll. Bourgogne 3, fol. 14v; abbreviated.

EDITION: GC 12, instr. cols. 172–3, no. 107.

Item littera de eodem feodo.

Ego Droco de Melloto miles dominus Sancti Prisci et Castri Canini,[1] notum facio uniuersis quod ego sum homo ligius et heredes mei similiter esse debebunt homines ligii reuerendi patris et karissimi patrui mei Guidonis de Melloto Dei gratia Autissiodorensis episcopi,[2] nomine Autissiodorensis ecclesie, et successorum suorum episcoporum Autissiodorensis qui pro tempore erunt, de

1 St-Bris, 10 km southeast of Auxerre.

2 Baulche, 4 km west of Auxerre.

3 Gui of Mello, bishop of Auxerre (1247–70). He was William's brother.

1 St-Bris, 10 km southeast of Auxerre, and Château-Chinon, 86 km south-southeast of Auxerre.

2 Gui of Mello, bishop of Auxerre (1247–70).

ducentis libratis terre ad Parisis redditualibus datis, assessis et assignatis michi ab eodem patruo meo, ratione successionis hereditarie deuenerunt, et quod eas recepi in feodum ligium ab eodem, et quod de ipsis feci eidem patruo meo nomine dicte ecclesie homagium manuale. Item notum facio et publice recognosco quod ego et heredes mei esse debebimus homines ligii predicti episcopi nomine dicte ecclesie et successorum suorum episcoporum Autissiodorensis, de toto eo quod ad nos deuenerit ultra predictas ducentas libratas terre ex residuo tocius hereditatis paterne, que ad ipsum episcopum in predicta terra de Belcha[3] ratione hereditarie successionis deuenit, et de hoc similiter facere tenebimur ligium homagium episcopis Autissiodorensis qui pro tempore erunt.

In cuius rei testimonium et munimen presentes litteras dicto domino episcopo tradidi sigilli nostri munimine roboratas. Datum anno Domini MCC sexagesimo nono, mense Aprili.

Lord Droco is the same as the Droinus of document 78; Droinus was presumably a diminutive. See also the following document.

81

April 1269

Droco of Mello, lord of St-Bris and Château-Chinon, received Baulche from the inheritance of his late grandfather William. He now affirms that Baulche is held in fief from the bishop of Auxerre. William was father of the bishop, Droco's uncle. Droco does liege homage.

MANUSCRIPTS: Bishops' cartulary, fol. 57r–v. Coll. Bourgogne 3, fol. 15r; abbreviated. BnF MS fr. 18692, pp. 130–1, from the cartulary; abbreviated. Arch. Yonne G 1592, fols. 71v–72r, from the preceding.

EDITION: GC 12, instr. 162, no. 106; abbreviated.

SUMMARY: Q 3:394, no. 771.

Item alia littera de eodem.

Ego Droco de Melloto miles dominus Sancti Prisci et Castri Canini,[1] notum facio uniuersis quod domus fortis de Belcha[2] prope Autissiodorensem que fuit nobilis uiri defuncti Guillelmi de Melloto quondam domini Sancti Prisci aui

3 Baulche, 4 km west of Auxerre.

1 St-Bris, 10 km southeast of Auxerre, and Château-Chinon, 86 km south-southeast of Auxerre.

2 Baulche, 4 km west of Auxerre.

mei cessit in partem et porcionem meam et ad me deuenit, per legitimam particionem et diuisionem factam inter me et heredes meos de hereditariis bonis nostris. Item notum facio et publice recognosco quod predicta domus est et mouet ac esse et mouere debet de ligio feodo episcopi Autissiodorensis quicunque sit nomine Autissiodorensis ecclesie et quod predictus karissimus auus meus receperat a tempore quo decessit tenebat nomine Autissiodorensis ecclesie predictam domum in feodum ligium a karissimo patruo meo et filio suo Guidone de Melloto Dei gratia episcopo Autissiodorensis[3] et quod de ipsa fecit eidem episcopo filio suo nomine Autissiodorensis ecclesie ligium homagium manuale. Item publice recognosco quod ego eandem domum recepi et teneo ab eodem patruo meo episcopo Autissiodorensis nomine Autissiodorensis ecclesie in feodum ligium, et de ea feci sibi nomine Autissiodorensis ecclesie homagium manuale, et quod ego sum et esse debeo homo dicti episcopi de dicta domo et heredes mei, qui dictam domum tenebunt post me. Similiter esse debent homines dicti episcopi de dicta domo, nomine Autissiodorensis ecclesie et successorum suorum episcoporum Autissiodorensium qui pro tempore erunt, et dictam domum ab eis recipere et tenere debent nomine dicte ecclesie et de ea eis facere ligium homagium manuale.

In cuius rei testimonium et munimen presentes litteras dicto episcopo tradidi, sigilli mei munimine roboratas. Datum anno Domini MCC LX nono, mense Aprili.

This document was given at the same time as both the preceding and following ones. Droco's grandfather William had doubtless died in 1261, when Bishop Gui, Droco's uncle, had been executor of his testament.[4]

82

April 1269

Droco of Mello, lord of St-Bris and Château-Chinon, attests that his heirs will do liege homage to the bishop of Auxerre for Baulche and the two hundred pounds worth of land that the bishop has given him. The bishop is his uncle.

MANUSCRIPT: Bishops' cartulary, fol. 57v.

EDITION: GC 12, instr. col. 173, no. 108.

---

3 Gui of Mello, bishop of Auxerre (1247–70).

4 *Le premier cartulaire de l'abbaye cistercienne de Pontigny (XIIe–XIIIe siecles)*, ed. Martine Garrigues, pp. 287–8, no. 257. Garrigues mistakenly calls Bishop Gui 'Guillaume de Brosse.'

Item alia littera de eodem.

Ego Droco de Melloto miles, dominus Sancti Prisci et Castri Canini,[1] notum facio uniuersis quod ego uolo consencio et concedo quod si domum forte de Belcha[2] prope Autissiodorum quam recepi et teneo in ligium feodum a reuerendo patre et karissimo patruo meo Guidone de Melloto Dei gratia Autissiodorensis episcopo[3] nomine Autissiodorensis ecclesie, et ducentas libratas terre ad Parisiensis reddituales quas idem karissimus patruus meus episcopus Autissiodorensis michi dedit et assignauit in ligium feodum et perpetuum hereditagium super bonis illis patrimonialibus, qui in dicta terra de Belcha ex patre patris sui ratione successionis deuenerint ad ipsum ac illud totum quod ad me uel heredes meos de predictis bonis patrimonialibus ultra dictas ducentas libratas terre deuenerit seu aliquid de predictis inter plures coheredes diuidi aut partiri contingeret in futurum, quotquot fuerint heredes tot homagia singuli singulariter pro rata sua in forma consimuli episcopis Autissiodorensis qui pro tempore fuerint facere teneantur.

In cuius rei testimonium et munimem presentes litteras dicto domino episcopo tradidi sigilli nostri munimine roboratas. Datum anno Domini MCC LX nono, mense Aprili.

This document was given at the same time as the preceding one.

Fol. 58r.

In scrinio signato per N inuenientur littere de fundacione parrochiorum de Karitate et plures alie.

83

26 February 1210

William of Seignelay, bishop of Auxerre, establishes three new parish churches at La Charité, where there had only been one. He does so with the consent of Geoffrey, prior of the house there.

1 St-Bris, 10 km southeast of Auxerre, and Château-Chinon, 86 km south-southeast of Auxerre.

2 Baulche, 4 km west of Auxerre.

3 Gui of Mello, bishop of Auxerre (1247–70).

MANUSCRIPTS: Bishops' cartulary, fol. 58r. Bibl. Auxerre, MS 153, fol. 295r; seventeenth-century copy by Dom Viole. BnF MS fr. 18692, p. 115, from the cartulary. Coll. Bourgogne 3, fol. 15r.

EDITIONS: GC 12, instr. col. 150, no. 70; abbreviated. PL 216:377–8, no. 209, with the documents of Innocent III.

Guillelmus Dei gratia Autissiodorensis episcopus,[1] omnibus presentes litteras inspecturis, in Domino salutem. Vniuersitatem uestram scire uolumus quod cum uilla de Karitate[2] ab antiquo non habuisset nisi unicam parrochialem ecclesiam, tanquam nouella plantacio que paucos habebat habitatores tandem crescente multitudine plebis in tantum quod unius non sufficiebat ad eam regendam, sollicitudo pastoris de assensu et uoluntate dilecti filii Gaufridi prioris et conuentus, ibidem constituimus tres parrochiales ecclesias, scilicet ecclesiam Beate Marie, ecclesiam Sancti Petri, et ecclesiam Sancti Iacobi, saluo iure monachorum, uidelicet ut id iuris habeant in singulis trium quod habebant in una, tam in presentacionibus personarum quam in aliis.

Quod ut ratum sit et firmum, presentem cartam fecimus sigillo nostro confirmatam. Actum anno gratie MCC nono, iiii kalendas Marcii.

The Cluniac monks of La Charité would have had authority over the parish church there. Because this document was given before Easter, it should be dated 1210 in 'new style.' This folio is missing its top outer corner.

84

Lateran, 19 September 1210

Pope Innocent III confirms the establishment of new parish churches at La Charité. He indicates that this is particularly important because of the danger of heresy there.

MANUSCRIPTS: Bishops' cartulary, fol. 58r. Bibl. Auxerre, MS 153, fol. 295r; seventeenth-century copy by Dom Viole. BnF MS fr. 18692, p. 115.

EDITION: PL 216:376–7, no. 211.

SUMMARY: August Potthast, *Regesta pontificum Romanorum*, 1:352, no. 4092.

1 William of Seignelay, bishop of Auxerre (1207–20).

2 La Charité, 86 km southwest of Auxerre.

Item littera papalis confirmatoria super hoc.

Innocentius episcopus seruus seruorum Dei,[1] uenerabili fratri Autissiodorensis episcopo,[2] salutem et apostolicam benedictionem. Solet annuere sedes apostolica piis uotis et honestis petencium precibus fauorem beneuolum impertiri. Sane sicut ex tua insinuacione recepimus cum in tribus capellis que sunt apud burgum de Karitate[3] unicus consueuerit presbiter ministrare ut multitudini populi eiusdem loci exhiberi possent commodius ecclesiastica sacramenta, maxime cum idem locus infectus dudum fuerit fermento heretice prauitatis, de tuo et prioris atque conuentus de Karitate consensu extitit constitutum ut in quacumque capellarum ipsarum sacerdos proprius ministraret, certis parrochianis earum cuilibet assignatis. Nos igitur tuis precibus inclinati constitutum ipsum, sicut pie ac prouide factum est, auctoritate apostolica confirmamus et presentis scripti patrocinio communimus.

Nulli ergo omnino hominum liceat hanc paginam nostre confirmacionis infringere uel ei ausu temerario contraire. Si quis autem hoc attemptare presumpserit, indignacionem omnipotentis Dei et beatorum Petri et Pauli apostolorum eius se nouerit incursurum.

Datum Latarani xiii kalendas Octobrorum, pontificatus nostri anno tercio decimo.

Heresy had appeared in La Charité during the 1190s, under Bishop William's predecessor.[4] See also the preceding document.

85

Lateran, 3 April 1219

Pope Honorius III writes the bishop of Auxerre about burghers of La Charité who are practising usury. They try to claim that they are not subject to the bishop by moving temporarily to parishes not under his jurisdiction.

MANUSCRIPT: Bishops' cartulary, fol. 58v.

---

1 Pope Innocent III (1198–1216).

2 William of Seignelay, bishop of Auxerre (1207–20).

3 La Charité, 86 km southwest of Auxerre.

4 *Gesta*, 2:147. See also Constance Brittain Bouchard, *Spirituality and Administration*, pp. 103–4.

Item littera papalis contra usuarios facientes burges iam in uillam regis.

Honorius episcopus seruus seruorum Dei,[1] uenerabili fratri Autissiodorensis episcopo,[2] salutem et apostolicam benedictionem. Ad audienciam nostram te significante peruenit quod quidam burgenses de Karitate,[3] licet in ea per totum fere annum uel pro maiori parte morentur et contrarius excerceant usuarium in tribus tamen festiuitatibus annualibus se ad uillas regis uel aliorum principium extra tuam dyocesam transferunt iura parrochialia excertentes ibidem ut sit se parrochianos alterius mentientes tuam iuridicionem eludant coram te iuri parere penitus contempnendo. Quia igitur fraus et dolus nemini debent puntamunii impertiri, ut usurarios supradictos si res ita se habet ad exhibendum tibi tanquam patri et pastori suo reuerenciam et obedientiam debitam recipiendo tua salubria monita et precepta iuridictione premissa per censuram ecclesiasticam, non obstante frustratorie appellacionis obiectu compellas ad exemplar felicis recordacionis Innocentii pape predecessoris nostri[4] liberam tibi auctoritate prenemiri concedimus facultatem.[5]

Nulli ergo omnino hominum liceat hanc paginam nostre concessionis infringere uel ei ausu temerario contraire. Si quis autem hoc attemptare presumpserit, indignacionem omnipotentis Dei et Beatorum Petri et Pauli apostolorum eius se nouerit incursurum. Datum Laterani iii non. Aprilis, pontificatus nostri anno tercio.

This document has not been previously printed or indeed noted. Pope Honorius III is known from other documents to have been at the Lateran at this time. Although which Pope Honorius is not explicitly stated, it cannot be Honorius IV because he died on 3 April of the third year of his rule, and it also cannot be Honorius II, because the only Pope Innocent who preceded him was Innocent I in the fourth century. In addition, the document would appear to be given close in time to the two preceding ones.

86

14 March 1274/November 1276

The abbot of St-Denis repeats a bull of Pope Gregory X, in which he is asked to mediate between the bishop of Auxerre and the prior of La Charité. The prior

1 Pope Honorius III (1216–27).

2 William of Seignelay, bishop of Auxerre (1207–20).

3 La Charité, 86 km southwest of Auxerre.

4 Pope Innocent III (1198–1216).

5 This is a reference to document 84.

had refused to recognize the interdict that the bishop had imposed, even after peace between them had supposedly been attained by the archbishop of Sens and the abbot of Cluny. The pope then asked the abbot of St-Denis to settle the case. The abbot now asks the prior of St-Laurent to force the prior of La Charité to come to Paris to have the case heard.

MANUSCRIPT: Bishops' cartulary, fols. 58v–59r.

Abbas Sancti Dyonisii in Francia Parisis diocesis,[1] iudex autem apostolica delegatus, dilecto sibi in Christo priori abbatie Beati Laurencii Autissiodorensis dyocesis,[2] salutem in Domino. Noueritis mandatum apostolicum ad nos directum in hec uerba.

Gregorius episcopus seruus seruorum Dei,[3] dilecto filio abbati monasterii Sancti Dyonisii in Francia Parisis dyocesis, salutem et apostolicam benedictionem. Qua nobis uenerabilis frater noster Autissiodorensis episcopus peticionem monstrauit quod cum ipse dudum parrochiales ecclesias et uillam de Caritate Autissiodorensis dyocesis[4] eidem episcopo lege dyocesana subiectas, ex iustis et rationabilis causis supposuisset ecclesiastico interdicto. Tandem inter eundem episcopum et priorem eiusdem loci de Caritate Cluniacensis ordinis super eo quod idem prior interdictum huius temere uiolarat, in eiusdem episcopi preiudictum et grauamen, ac aliis diuersis articulis, orta fuit materia questionis. Deinde super hiis a patribus in bone memorie P[etrum] archiepiscopum Senonensis et Yuonem abbatem Cluniacensis[5] tanquam in arbitratorum et amicabiles compositores sub certa forma extitit concorditur compromissum et licet archiepiscopus et abbas prefati equm. Super predictis arbitrum tulerunt inter partes.[6] Idem tamen prior illud obseruare indebite contradixit. Quare idem episcopus humiliter petebat a nobis ut eundem priorem ad obseruacionem ipsius arbitrii sicut est equm et ab utraque parte sponte receptum per penam in compromisso expressam compelli per discretum aliquem manderemus. Quocirca discretioni tue de utriusque partis procuratorum assensu per apostolica scripta mandamus quatinus partibus conuocatis eam parte audias eamque iudicio uel si de partium uoluntare predessent concordia terminare procures, faciens quod deceteris per censuram ecclesiasticam firmiter obseruari. Testes autem qui fuerunt nominati. Si se gracia odio uel timore subtraxerint censura

1 The abbot of St-Denis.
2 St-Laurent-l'Abbaye, 66 km southwest of Auxerre.
3 Pope Gregory X (1271–76).
4 La Charité, 86 km southwest of Auxerre.
5 Peter, archbishop of Sens (1268–74), and Ivo, abbot of Cluny (1256–75).
6 This is a reference to documents 87–8.

simuli appelacione cessante compellas ueritati testimonium perhibere. Datum Lugdunensis ii idus Marcii, pontificatus nostri anno tercio.

Huius igitur auctoritate mandati uobis precipiendo mandamus quatinus ad predictum priorem de Karitate personaliter accedentes ut ipsum coram nobis auctoritatem predictam Parisius ad diem crastinam ottabarum purificacionis Beate Marie uirginis. Si non fuerint feriata uel ad diem sequentem immediate non feriatam si dicta dies crastina fuerint feriata processurum in causa seu negotio predicto nobis commisso prout de iure fuerint procedendum et predicto reuerendo patri E[rardo] Dei gratia Autissiodorensis episcopo[7] uel eius proemus quod iustum fuerit responsurus.

Datum anno Domini MCC LXXVI, die sabbati post yemalis festum Beati Martini. Redditas litteras sigillo in signum mandati executi.

This document has not been previously printed or even noted. Pope Gregory X was indeed in Lyon on this date. The case seems to have dragged out for at least six years; see the following document.

Fol. 59r.

Item in eodem scrinio littera papalis contenta in litteras prescripta.

Item totus processus sub manu publice Bartholomei[1] de Cersine auctoritate apostolica notus.

87

Paris, November 1271

Erard, bishop of Auxerre, and Milo, prior of La Charité, recall that, before Bishop Gui died, he and Prior Milo had agreed that their quarrel be settled by the archbishop of Sens and the abbot of Cluny.

MANUSCRIPT: Bishops' cartulary, fol. 59r–v.

Item littera compromissi in P. archiepiscopum Senonensis.

Vniuersis presentes litteras inspecturis, E[rardus] miseracione diuina Autissiodorensis episcopus, et M[ilo] humilis prior de Caritate ordinis

7 Erard of Lézinnes, bishop of Auxerre (1270–8).

1 The cartulary reads 'Batholomei.'

Cluniacensis,[2] salutem in Domino. Notum facimus quod de omnibus contencionibus motis inter nos E[rardum] miseracione diuina Autissiodorensis episcopum nomine ecclesie nostre Autissiodorensis ex una parte et nos M[ilonem] priorem de Karitate nomine monasterii nostri ex altera, necnon de omnibus contentionibus inter reuerendum patrem bone memorie G[uidonem][3] Dei gratia quondam Autissiodorensis episcopum nomine ecclesie sue Autissiodorensis ex una parte et nos priorem de Karitate ex altera nomine monasterii nostri motas tempore quo decessit compromisimus alte et basse in reuerendum patrem P[etrum] Dei gratia archiepiscopum Senonensis[4] et religiosum uirum Yuonem abbatem Cluniacensis,[5] tanquam in arbitratores seu amicabiles comprortores et ordinatorum ipsorum stare, promisimus super predictis contencionibus omnibus motis uel que moueri possent inter nos usque ad datam presentium litterarum. Promittentes bona fide nos E[rardus] Autissiodorensis episcopus et nos M[ilo] prior de Caritate per stipulacionem unius alteri sub pena ducentarum marcharum argenti soluenda a parte non parente arbitrio, seu ordinacionem predictorum parti parenti, quod quicquid predicti duo infra instantem purificacionem Beate Marie uirginis de predictis contencionibus arbitrandis duxerint aut ordinauerint firmiter et inuiolabiliter obseruabimus infirmum, nec per nos uel per alium imposterum in contrarium ueniemus potestate dictorum arbitratorum post lapsum dicte purificacionis beate uirginis minime duratura. Si autem alterutram partem contra ordinacionem uel dictum prolatum infra dictum festum purificacionis beate uirginis in aliquo uenire contingeret, pena predicta ipso facto commissa contra partem non parentem ordinatum, seu arbitrio predictorum et soluenda parti parenti inthilous arbitrium seu dictum in sua firmitate manebit. Nos uero E[rardus] episcopus Autissiodorensis promittimus nos procuraturos quod capitulum nostrum Autissiodorensis per suas litteras hinc consentiet compromisso, et nos M[ilo] prior de Caritate similiter promittimus nos procuraturos quod conuentus noster de Caritate hiis omnibus per suas litteras prestabit assensum compromissum huior concedendo.

In cuius rei testimonium sigilla nostra presentibus litteris duximus apponenda. Datum Parisis, anno Domini MCC septuagesimo primo, die sabbati ante festum Sancti Andre apostoli.

Item litteras de eodem transcripta sub sigillo Erardi episcopi.

---

2 Erard, bishop of Auxerre (1270–8), and Milo, prior of La Charité (1262–73). La Charité is 86 km southwest of Auxerre.

3 Gui of Mello, bishop of Auxerre (1247–70).

4 Peter, archbishop of Sens (1268–74).

5 Ivo, abbot of Cluny (1256–75).

For this agreement, not previously printed, see also the preceding and following documents.

88

St-Sauveur-en-Puisaye, December 1271

Peter, archbishop of Sens, and Ivo, abbot of Cluny, settle the quarrel between Bishop Erard of Auxerre and Prior Milo of La Charité. The bishop had put La Charité under interdict after a young woman there was accused of heresy, and the monks now persuade him to lift it so that the dead may be buried. The archbishop and abbot rule that the prior must observe any interdict imposed by the bishop of Auxerre.

MANUSCRIPT: Bishops' cartulary, fols. 59v–60v. Bibl. Auxerre, MS 153, fols. 450r–451r; seventeenth-century copy by Dom Viole.
EDITION: GC 12, instr. cols. 173–4, no. 109.

Item prolacio arbitri commissi in archiepiscopum Senonensis.

Petrus miseracione diuina Senonensis archiepiscopus et frater Yuo eadem miseracione Cluniacensis ecclesie minister humilis,[1] uniuersis presentes litteras inspecturis, salutem in Domino. Noueritis quod cum super diuersis articulis inter uenerabilem fratrem et patrem E[rardum] Dei gratia Autissiodorensis episcopum nomine ecclesie sue Autissiodorensis ex parte una et religiosum uirum M[ilonem] priorem de Caritate ordinis Cluniacensis[2] nomine monasterii sui ex altera, materia questionis et discensionis suborta fuisset, lataque sententia interdicti de mandato et auctoritate predicti episcopi in uillam et ecclesias de Karitate, occasione cuiusdam muliercule suspecte de heresi, que a preposito de Karitate temporalem iurisdictionem exercente, loco prioris predicti in uilla de Caritate, pro suspicione heresis capta fuerat et detenta. Tandem in nos super predictis omnibus articulis sub certa forma a dictis partibus extitit compromissum, prout in litteris sigillis dictorum episcopi et prioris sigillatis, plenius continetur.

Nos autem die Iouis post festum natiuitatis Domini apud Sancti Saluatorem in Puiseya,[3] partibus in nostra presentia constitutis, tractatibus aliquibus habitis

1 Peter, archbishop of Sens (1268–74), and Ivo, abbot of Cluny (1256–75).
2 Erard, bishop of Auxerre (1270–8), and Milo, prior of La Charité (1262–73). La Charité is 86 km southwest of Auxerre.
3 St-Sauveur-en-Puisaye, 35 km southwest of Auxerre.

cum eisdem, pro bono pacis arbitrando pronunciamus, quod unus ex monachis de Caritate pro omnibus, qui ut interdictum ferrent in uilla de Karitate, et in uiolatione eiusdem interdicti culpabiles extiterunt, humiliter et deuote flexis genibus, ueniam fratri et patri domino E[rardo] Dei gratia Autissiodorensi episcopo supplicabit, ut interdictum latum in predicta uilla relaxet, et eidem episcopo tam pro interdicto quam pro uiolacione in nostra presentia emendabit, et episcopus teneatur sententiam per suas patentes litteras relaxare. Item quod de quolibet cimiterio ecclesiarum parrochialium de Karitate exhumabuntur uiginti corpora extra cimiterium existenda, quo usque una missa de defunctis pro ipsis fuerit celebrata, que incontinenti post exhumationem incipietur, et quod heredes uel successores huius defunctorum teneantur rectoribus ecclesiarum parrochialium exsoluere, quod in talibus fidelium deuotione in parrochiis illis extitit introductum, et quod si qui ultra uiginti in quolibet cimiterio durante interdicto sepulti fuerint, nisi heredes uel successores satisfecerint, rectoribus antedictis secundum piam consuetudinem supradictam, sicut et uiginti debeant exhumari, et quod prior compellat homines suos ad satisfaciendum rectoribus antedictis.

Si uero monachi aliquid receperunt a peregrinis et transeuntibus, quod habuissent rectores, uel habere debuissent, se per eos uel capellanos suos tradui fuissent ecclesiastice sepulture, illud prior de Caritate restitui faciet rectoribus antedictis. Si autem aliqui nominatim excommunicati in cimiteriis infra septa, siue clausuram prioratus de Karitate existentibus, sepulti fuerint, extrahentur ex eisdem, et ecclesiastica sepultura carebunt, nisi in ipsis uiuentibus signa penitencie apparuerint, et tunc absolutione ipsorum a iudicibus competentibus impetrata, tradentur ecclesiastice sepulture.

Quia uero monachi dicunt quod habent priuilegia a sede apostolica, quod durantibus interdictis possunt admittere in suis cimiteriis ad ius ecclesiastice sepulture omnes illos qui non sunt nominatim excommunicati uel interdicti, uel qui causam uel occasionem interdicto ferendo nullatenus prestiterant, parte episcopi contrarium asserente et maxime in hoc casu cum aliis quibusdam articulis hinc inde exhibitis coram nobis, quia cause cognitionis longiorem dederant, de uoluntatem partium secundum tenorem peregrinacionis facte nostre arbitrali fine reseruamus. Si uero aliquid uel aliquod premissorum partes dubium reputauerint uel dixerint, declarationem nostro arbitrio similiter reseruamus. Sane pro certo tenentes priorem et conuentum de Karitate nullum priuilegium habere, uel habere posse in eis, uel contra ea que sunt contra hereticos a sacris canonibus instituta, per ea tamen que arbitrando protulimus, priuilegiis que alias habent, seu in aliis casibus, non intendimus, nec uolumus in aliquo derogari.

In cuius rei testimonium presentes litteras sigillis nostris fecimus sigillari. Datum die et loco predictis, anno Domini MCC septugesimo primo.

This agreement was not long observed; see document 86.

89

7 September 1237

Bernard, bishop of Auxerre, recalls an earlier ruling by Bishops William of Auxerre and Hervé of Troyes that someone suspected of heresy cannot be provost of La Charité.

MANUSCRIPT: Bishops' cartulary, fol. 60v.

Item littera quod nullus suspectus de heresi non potest esse propositus de Karitate.

B[ernardus] Dei gratia Autissiodorensis episcopus,[1] presbitero Beate Marie de Karitate,[2] salutem. Cum in iure uocassemus colinum morandi eidem sub pena extremis inhibuimus ne esset prepositus de Karitate, eo quod auctoritate apostolica statutum esset a bone memorie Guillelmo Autissiodorensis et Herueo Trecensis[3] ne aliquis suspectus de heresi aut qui sane opinionis non esset preposituram apud Karitatem haberet, et cum idem colinus de heresi esset suspectus in pote filius heretici et qui hereticus fuerat secundum statuta predicta nec etiam secundum iura dictus colinus preposituram apud Karitatem non poterat exercere, a qua inhibicione dictus colinus a nostra audiencia ad Senonensis curiam appellauit nichilominus dictam preposituram excercens sicut coram nobis publice recognouit rerum cum officiale Senonensis eius appellacionem non admiserit uobis districte precipiendo mandamus quatinus ipsum tribus dicbus continuis prius notatum exercoretis et exercoritur mericiens.

Datum die hinc ante natiuitate Beate Marie, anno Domini MCC trecesimo septimo. B. litt. Sigill.

This document has not been previously printed. The earlier document to which this one refers does not survive.

1 Bernard, bishop of Auxerre (1235–45).

2 La Charité, 86 km southwest of Auxerre.

3 William of Seignelay, bishop of Auxerre (1207–20), and Hervé, bishop of Troyes (1207–23).

Fol. 60v.

In scrinio signato per O inuenientur littere de subiectione Sancti Germani et plures alie.

90

Sens, April 1215

Hervé, bishop of Troyes, along with the abbots of Ste-Colombe and Escharlis, settle the quarrel between Bishop William of Auxerre and Abbot William of St-Germain over episcopal visitation of the monastery. They rule in favour of the bishop.

MANUSCRIPTS: Bishops' cartulary, fols. 60v–61r. Coll. Bourgogne 3, fol. 15r–v.
EDITION: GC 12, instr. cols. 153–4, no. 77.
SUMMARY: Q 3:392, no. 752.

In nomine patris et filii et spiritus sancti amen. Herueus Trecensis episcopus,[1] H[elias] Sancte Columbe Senonensis et N. Eschalleiarum abbates[2] in causa que uertitur inter uenerabilem patrem Willelmum episcopum Autissiodorensis[3] ex una parte et Vuillelmum abbatem et conuentum monasterii Sancti Germani Autissiodorensis[4] ex altera, super uisitacione et correctione eiusdem monasterii, iudices a summo pontifice delegati, dictis episcopo et abbate personaliter et conuentu per procuratorem in nostra presencia constitutis, eodem episcopo petente predictos abbatem et conuentum compelli a nobis ad obediendum, et in uisitacione et correctione sepefatti monasterii, lite coram nobis super hoc contestata, eorumdem abbatis et conuentus procuratoribus dicentibus quod episcopus Autissiodorensis non habebat uisitacionem neque correctionem in illo monaserio, et quod hoc probarent per priuilegia et alia, pluribus diebus eis a nobis assignatis ad probationes suas faciendas sub quadruplici dilatione, ad quos omnino defecerunt, ipsis abbate et conuentu per contumaciam absentibus, de consilio bonorum uirorum per sententiam diffinitiuam iudicamus quod predicti abbas et conuentus Sancti Germani Autissiodorensis debent obedire episcopo Autissiodorensis in uisitacione et correctione monasterii eorumdem.

1 Hervé, bishop of Troyes (1207–23).
2 Helias, abbot of Ste-Colombe of Sens (1196–1217), and the abbot of Escharlis, whose name is not known.
3 William of Seignelay, bishop of Auxerre (1207–20).
4 William, abbot of St-Germain of Auxerre (1208–21).

Actum Senonis anno incarnacionis dominice MCC quatrodecimo, mense Aprili, die Iouis ante ramos palmarum.

Because this was given before Easter, the year is 1215 in 'new style.' Pope Innocent III confirmed this agreement; see document 94. See also the following document.

Fol. 61r.

Item alia littera consimilis.
Item eadem littera sub sigillo N. Sancti Mariani et A. Sancti Petri abbatum et excommunicacio a predictis abbatibus in dictam abbatiam Sancti Germani lata.
Item in eodem scrinio totus processus et simile late in dictam abbatiam.
Item littera de recognicione obediencie et subiectionis abbatis Sancti Germani.

91

April 1215

William, abbot of St-Germain, agrees that he is subject to the bishop of Auxerre.

MANUSCRIPTS: Bishops' cartulary, fol. 61r. Coll. Bourgogne 3, fol. 15v.
EDITION: GC 12, instr. col. 154, no. 77; printed as part of preceding document.

Nouerint uniuersi presentes litteras inspecturi quod ego Willelmus, Sancti Germani Autissiodorensis dictus abbas,[1] confiteor et protestor me esse subiectum uenerabili patri domino et episcopo meo Vuillelmo[2] et successoribus ipsius et ecclesie Autissiodorensis in omnibus et per omnia in quibus abbas subiectus est episcopo sue. Confiteor etiam et protestor quod quando ab eo in abbatem sui benedictus, eidem tanquam domino et episcopo meo obedienciam et professionem publice feci et sicut moris est ore promisi et manu subscribendo confirmaui, quod etiam alii predecessores mei predecessoribus ipsius fecerunt. Promisi etiam et promitto me eidem sicut domino et episcopo meo et successoribus ipsius obedienciam et subiectionem firmiter et fideliter seruaturum.

Although not explicitly dated, this document was doubtless given at the same time as the preceding one.

---

1 William, abbot of St-Germain of Auxerre (1208–21).
2 William of Seignelay, bishop of Auxerre (1207–20).

Fol. 61r.

Item alia littera consimilis.

92

1263

Abbot John of St-Germain asks the bishop of Auxerre to excuse him from his upcoming synod, which he will be unable to attend.

MANUSCRIPTS: Bishops' cartulary, fol. 61r. Coll. Bourgogne 3, fols. 15v–16r.
EDITION: GC 12, instr. cols. 169–70, no. 104.
SUMMARY: Q 3:393, no. 769.

Item alia littera quod debent interesse sinodo.

Reuerendo patri ac domino G[uidoni][1] Dei gratia Autissiodorensis episcopo, frater Iohannes humilis abbas Sancti Germani Autissiodorensis,[2] salutem et cum omni reuerencia et honore obedienciam tam debitam quam deuotam. Cum nos hac instanti die Martis post octabas penthecostes ad uestram sinodum non possumus personaliter interesse, diuersis et ineuitabilibus ecclesie nostre negotiis impediti, paternitatem uestam rogamus quatenus absenciam nostram habere dignemus excusatam. Datum anno Domini MCC sexagesimo tercio, die Lune ante dictum diem.

Fol. 61r.

Item alia littera consimilis.
Item alia papalis confirmatoria quod abbas Sancti Germani non debet inuestiri per abbatem Cluniacensis.

93

Besançon, 7 May 1148

Pope Eugenius III settles the quarrel between the bishop of Auxerre and the abbot of Cluny by forbidding the abbot of Cluny to invest new abbots of St-Germain of Auxerre, which would be to the bishop's detriment.

1 Gui of Mello, bishop of Auxerre (1247–70).
2 John, abbot of St-Germain of Auxerre (1243–77).

MANUSCRIPTS: Bishops' cartulary, fol. 61v. BnF MS fr. 18692, p. 113, from the cartulary.

EDITIONS: GC 12, instr. cols. 122–3, no. 32. RHGF 15:450, no. 48, from GC. PL 180:1348, no. 299, from GC.

SUMMARY: Philip Jaffe, *Regesta pontificum Romanorum*, new ed. by Wilhelm Wattenbach, 2:57, no. 9259 (6433).

Eugenius episcopus seruus seruorum Dei,[1] uenerabili fratri Hugoni Autissiodorensis episcopo,[2] salutem et apostolicam benedictionem. Postquam controuersia que inter te et dilectum filium nostrum P[etrum] Cluniacensis abbatem[3] super Sancti Germani monasterio agebatur in nostra fuit presencia terminata, et dominus idem filius noster abbatem qui fratribus inibi Domino seruientibus preest per baculum inuestiuit, in quo quia dignitas ecclesie tue obfuscari et supprimi uidebatur, inter uos de quo paterne caritatis debito condolemus est suborta contencio. Quia igitur paci et transquilitati ecclesiarum attenta sollicitudine prouidere compellimur presencium scriptorum auctoritate statuimus ne quod ab ipso factum est tibi uel ecclesie tue imposterum preiudicium faciat uel aliquod inferat detrimentum, et ne de cetero abbas Sancti Germani a Cluniacensis abbate inuestituram per baculum suscipiat prohibemus. Datum Bisuntii, nonis Madii.

The pope wrote to Peter the Venerable, abbot of Cluny, on the same topic.[4] The recent death of Abbot Gervais of St-Germain had started the disagreement. The year of this charter is determined by the pope's itinerary.

Curiously, the papal bulls preserved at the abbey of St-Germain – the monastery's cartulary begins with a run of forty-five papal privileges dating between the mid-twelfth and mid-thirteenth centuries – have no overlap with the contemporary papal charters concerning St-Germain that were preserved by the bishops. The monks copied into their cartulary bulls confirming their liberty, while the scribe of the bishops' cartulary copied bulls confirming their subjection. Indeed, one would never know from the monks' cartulary that they owed obedience to the bishop. It may in part have been in reaction to this bull for the bishop that the monks obtained a confirmation of all their rights and

1 Eugenius III, pope (1145–53).

2 Hugh of Mâcon, bishop of Auxerre (1136–51).

3 Peter the Venerable, abbot of Cluny (1122–56).

4 PL 180:1294–5, no. 239.

privileges from the same pope, whose bull, dated January 1152, was the first entry in their thirteenth-century cartulary.[5]

94

Lateran, 5 January 1216

Pope Innocent III, having been shown the earlier ruling of Pope Eugenius III, orders the monks of St-Germain of Auxerre to be subject to correction by their bishop.

MANUSCRIPTS: Bishops' cartulary, fol. 61v. Coll. Bourgogne 3, fol. 16r.
EDITIONS: Lebeuf 2:45–6, no. 96. Lebeuf 4:79–80, no. 131. PL 217:255, no. 26, from Lebeuf 4.
SUMMARIES: Q 3:417, no. 972. August Potthast, *Regesta pontificum Romanorum*, 1:443, no. 5045.

Item alia littera papalis.

Innocencius episcopus seruus seruorum Dei,[1] uenerabili fratri Autissiodorensis episcopo,[2] salutem et apostolicam benedictionem. Postulante quondam dilecto filio magistro H. procuratore tuo abbatem et conuentum Sancti Germani Autissiodorensis ab impedimento quod tibi super uisitacionis et correctionis officio inferebant apostolice sedis auctoritate compesci, procurator partis aduerse respondit monasterium illud Cluniacensi esse subiectum, pro quo dilectus filius tunc abbas se in nostra presencia exhibuit defensorem. Super quibus uenerabili fratri nostri Trecensi episcopo et coniudicibus suis sub certa forma causam duximus commitendam.[3] Tandem uero te[4] ac dilecto filio Cluniacensis abbate apud sedem apostolicam constitutis per quoddam scriptum felicis recordationis Eugenii pape coram nobis exhibitum,[5] abbatem Cluniacensis in predicto autem monasterio ad receptionem et correpcionem

5 Bibl. Auxerre, MS 161, fol. 8r–v. The manuscript is described in *Catalogue général des manuscrits des bibliothèques publiques de France*, 6:62–3. For the relations between St-Germain and the bishops, see also *Les gestes des abbés de Saint-Germain d'Auxerre*, ed. Noëlle Deflou-Leca and Yves Sassier.

1 Pope Innocent III (1198–1216).
2 William of Seignelay, bishop of Auxerre (1207–20).
3 This is a reference to document 90.
4 The Lebeuf and PL texts mistakenly read 'nepote' for 'uero te,' creating a suggestion of a non-existent family relationship.
5 This is a reference to document 93.

canonicam restitutum fuisse ad Autissiodorensis uero episcopum tam abbas quam monachorum correpcionem canonicam inter alia pertinere. Quia uero quid ad correctionem ordinis et quid ad correctionem canonicam spectaret, secundum diuersos et aduersos partium intellectus in dubium ducebatur, nos sic declarauimus uerba predicta ut interruptio silentii retencio propriorum, contemptus obedientie in hiis que sunt ordinis, se negligentia in diuinis et aliaque considerantur circa obseruancium regule monachalis ad correctionem ordinis. Accusatio uero criminalis seu etiam ciuilis impetitio, et alia que ordinarie iurisdictionis existunt, ad correctionem canonicam pertinere dicantur, ita quod uterque uisitet et corrigat secundum declarationem predictam que fuerunt corrigenda in monasterio memorato.

Nulli ergo omnino hominum liceat hanc paginam nostre declarationis infringere, aut ei ausu temerario contraire. Si quis autem hoc attemptare presumpserit, indignacionem omnipotentis Dei et beatorum Petri et Pauli apostolorum eius se nouerit incursurum. Datum Laterani nonis Ianuarii, pontificatus nostri anno octauo decimo.

95

Lateran, 25 April 1154

Pope Anastasius IV confirms the earlier agreement between the bishop of Auxerre and St-Germain. New abbots of St-Germain shall be elected with the consent of the abbot of Cluny, but the bishop shall be able to decide whether or not to bless them, and once assuming office they shall owe the bishop obedience.

MANUSCRIPTS: Bishops' cartulary, fol. 62r–v. Bibl. Auxerre, MS 153, fols. 138r–139r; seventeenth-century copy by Dom Viole. Coll. Bourgogne 3, fols. 16r–17r.

EDITIONS: *Bullarium sacri ordinis Cluniacensis*, p. 66. GC 12, instr. cols. 123–4, no. 33. Q 1:519–21, no. 361 (abbreviated), from GC. PL 188:1065–6, no. 69, from GC.

SUMMARY: Philip Jaffe, *Regesta pontificum Romanorum*, new ed. by Wilhelm Wattenbach, 2:98, no. 9875 (6799).

Item littera papalis confirmator.

Anastasius episcopus seruus seruorum Dei[1] uenerabili fratri Alano Autissiodorensis episcopo[2] eiusque successoribus canonice substituendis.

1 Pope Anastasius IV (1153–4).

2 Alain, bishop of Auxerre (1152–67).

In perpetuum.[3]

Que a predecessoribus nostris per iudicium uel concordiam acta esse noscuntur in sua uolumus stailitate persistere ut in posterum robur obtineant confirmacionis nostre munimine roborari. Eapropter, dilecte in Domino fili Halane episcope, tuis iustis peticionibus gratum acommodantes assensum concordiam quam predecessor noster sancte memorie papa Eugenius super controuersia que agitabatur de monasterio Beati Germani inter Hu[gonem] bone memorie predecessorem tuum[4] et dilectum filium nostrum Petrum Cluniacensis abbatem[5] et monachos Sancti Germani fecisse dignoscitur.[6] Nos eius uestigiis inherentes apostolice sedis auctoritate firmamus, precipientes ut in abbacia Sancti Germani sine Cluniacensis abbatis consilio abbas nullatenus eligatur, electum uero approbandi uel reprobandi canonice et si dignus fuerit in abbatem benedicendi tam tu quam successores tui habeatis liberam facultatem, benedictus autem obedienciam episcopo Autissiodorensis promittat. Depositio quoque ipsius si talis quod absit apparuerit iudiciario ordine facienda, et tam abbatis quam monachorum canonica correctio ad te nichilominus pertinebit. Crisma, oleum sanctum, consecraciones altarium uel basilicarum, ordinaciones monachorum uel clericorum qui ad sacros ordines fuerint promouendi, abbas et monachi Sancti Germani ab Autissiodorensis episcopo tanquam a diocesano accipiant donec gratiam apostolice sedis habuerint. Preterea memorati predecessoris nostri pape Eugenii statuta sequentes presentis scripti pagina confirmamus ne quod a prefato Cluniacensis abbate de inuestitura per baculum ipsi abbati Sancti Germani factum est tibi uel ecclesie tue imposterum preiudicium faciat uel aliquod inferat detrimentum et ne de cetero abbas Sancti Germani a Cluniacensis abbate inuestituram[7] per baculum suscipiat prohibemus. Si quis autem huius nostre confirmacionis paginam sciens contra eam temere uenire temptauerit, honoris et officii sui periculum patiat aut extrema ultione plectatur nisi presumptionem suam digna satisfactione correxerit.

Ego Anastasius catholice ecclesie episcopus.[8]

Ego BB presbiter cardinalis tituli Calixti.

Ego Guido presbiter cardinalis tituli Sancti Grisogoni.

Ego Vmbaldus presbiter cardinalis tituli Sancte Praxedis.

Ego Aubericus presbiter cardinalis tituli S. Anastasie.

---

3 This phrase is represented by a monogram, doubtless copied from the original.

4 Hugh of Mâcon, bishop of Auxerre (1136–51).

5 Peter the Venerable, abbot of Cluny (1122–56).

6 This is a reference to document 93.

7 The cartulary reads 'inuestitura.'

8 There are crosses and other marks before and after each name, each slightly different, suggesting copying from the original.

Ego Iulius presbiter cardinalis tituli S. Marcelli.
Ego Iordanus presbiter cardinalis tituli Sancte Susanne et Felicitatis.
Ego Bidardus presbiter cardinalis tituli S. Stephani de Monte Celio.
Ego Iohannes presbiter cardinalis Sancti Iohannis et Pauli tituli Pamachii.
Ego Iohannes presbiter cardinalis tituli S. Siluestri et Martini.
Ego Imarus Tusculanus episcopus.
Ego Hugo Hostiensis episcopus.
Ego Censius Portuensis episcopus.
Ego Gregorius diaconus cardinalis et electus Sabiniensis.
Ego Rodulfus diaconus cardinalis tituli Lucie in septa solis.
Ego Guido diaconus cardinalis Sancte Marie in Porticu.
Ego Iohannes diaconus cardinalis Sanctorum Sergii et Bachi.
Ego Otto diaconus Sancti Nicholai in carcere Tulliano.

Datum Laterani per manum Rolandi Romane ecclesie presbiteri cardinalis et cancellarii, vii kalendas Maii, indictione ii, incarnationis dominice anno MCLIIII, pontificatus uero Domini Anastasii pape anno i.

Although the monks of St-Germain had received a bull from Eugenius III to confirm their rights and possessions only after the bishop of Auxerre had received one confirming his authority over the monastery (document 93), the monks were quicker to have Anastasius IV issue such a charter. His bull, the second in their cartulary, repeated much of what Eugenius had confirmed to them and preceded the bull of this document by two months.[9]

96

Lateran, 30 December 1142

Pope Innocent II, at the request of Bishop Hugh of Auxerre, confirms that the abbey of St-Germain of Auxerre owes obedience to the bishop. He also orders that no secular person may judge clerics for crimes in the diocese.

MANUSCRIPTS: Bishops' cartulary, fols. 62v–63r. Bibl. Auxerre, MS 153, fol. 100r–v; seventeenth-century copy by Dom Viole.

EDITIONS: GC 12, instr. cols. 112–13, no. 20. Q 1:361–2, no. 218, from Viole and GC. PL 179:616–17, no. 548, from GC.

SUMMARY: Philip Jaffe, *Regesta pontificum Romanorum*, new ed. by Wilhelm Wattenbach, 1:904, no. 8262 (5873).

9 Bibl. Auxerre, MS 161, fols. 8v–94.

Item alia littera papalis confirmatoria.

Innocencius episcopus seruus seruorum Dei,[1] uenerabili fratri Hugoni Autissiodorensis episcopo[2] eiusque successoribus canonice substituendis.

In perpetuum.[3]

Ex iniuncto a Deo nobis apostolatus officio fratribus nostris tam uicinis quam longe positis paterna nos conuenit prouisione consulere et ecclesiis in quibus Domino militare noscuntur suam iusticiam conseruare, ut quemadmodum patres uocamur in nomine, ita nichilominus comprobemur in opere. Ea propter uenerabilis frater Hugo episcope tuis iustis precibus clementer annimus et benedictionem abbatis Sancti Germani et ipsius debitam obedienciam et reuerenciam in aliis quoque ecclesiis episcopatui Autissiodorensis pertinentibus ius episcopale tibi tuisque sucessoribus concedimus et apostolica auctoritate confirmamus, sicut ecclesia tua hactenus habuisse cognoscitur.

Prohibemus quoque ne aliqua secularis persona clericos in episcopatu tuo pro quolibet crimine iudicandi uel puniendi habeat potestatem. Si qua igitur ecclesiastica secularis persona hanc nostre constitutionis paginam sciens, contra eam uenire temere temptauerit, secundo tertioue commonita, si non satisfactione congrua emendauerit, potestatis honorisque sui dignitate careat, reamque se diuino iudicio existere de perpetrata iniquitate cognoscat, et a sacratissimo corpore examine districte ultioni subiaceatur. Cunctis autem eidem loco iusta seruantibus sit pax Domini nostri Ihesu Christi quatinus hic bone actionis fructum percipiant, et apud districtum iudicem premia eterne pacis inueniant. Amen.

Ego Innocencius catholice ecclesie episcopus.[4]

Ego Otto diaconus cardinalis Sancti Georgii ad Velum Aureum.[5]

Ego Petrus diaconus cardinalis Sancte Marie in Agro.

Ego Petrus diaconus cardinalis Sancte Marie in Porticu.

Ego Stephanus Prenestinus[6] episcopus.

Ego Thomas presbiter cardinalis tituli Vestine.

Ego Hubaldus presbiter cardinalis titulis sancte Praxedis.

Datum Laterani per manum Geraldi sancte Romane ecclesie presbiteri cardinalis ac bibliothecarii, iii kalendas Ianuarii, Dominice anno MCXLII, pontificatus uero domini Innocentii ii pape anno xiii.

---

1 Pope Innocent II (1130–43).

2 Hugh of Mâcon, bishop of Auxerre (1136–51).

3 This phrase is represented by a monogram, doubtless copied from the original.

4 The cartulary reproduces the pope's seal.

5 This and the following names are all preceded by a cross, each slightly different, presumably copied from the original.

6 The manuscript reads 'Penestinus.'

The obedience owed by the Cluniac abbey of St-Germain was always a disputed topic, as the preceding documents demonstrate.

97

20 January 1229

Gregory, minister of the friars minor (Franciscans) in France, attests that the friars are settling at St-Eusèbe of Auxerre but are ready to leave if requested. They are there with the consent of Bishop Henry, along with his dean and chapter.

MANUSCRIPT: Bishops' cartulary, fol. 63v.
EDITION: GC 12, instr. col. 158, no. 84.
SUMMARY: Q 3:392, no. 756.

Item littera de hospitacione fratrum minorum in loco ubi sunt et ad quid tenentur.

Vniuersis presentes litteras inspecturis, frater Gregorius seruus et minister fratrum minorum qui sunt in Francia, salutem et pacem. Notum uobis facio quod fratres minores apud ciuitatem Autissiodorensis commorantes, de licencia uenerabilis patris et domini H[enrici] eiusdem ciuitatis episcopi,[1] domini M. decani et totius capituli Sancti Stephani, hospitantur infra muros ciuitatis in parrochia Sancti Eusebii. Item quod quocumque placuerit domino episcopo siue domino decano siue capitulo quod fratres a dicto loco recedant, ipsi sine contradictione locum dimittent et exibunt. Omni autem tempore quo dicti fratres in dicto loco morabuntur, excommunicatos uel interdictos scienter non recipient ad diuina. Si uero cathedralis ecclesia aliquando cessauerit, et ipsi fratres similiter cessabunt, cum a domino episcopo siue decano siue capitulo ipsis fuerit demandatum. Actum anno Domini MCC XVIII, xiii kalendas mense Ianuario, in festiuitate Sanctorum Fabiani et Sebastiani.

The church of St-Eusèbe had been a house of canons regular before the arrival of the friars. January 1228 is 1229 in 'new style.'

98

1260

The abbot of Pontigny attests that Bishop Gui of Auxerre has granted his monastery the right to have an altar and oratory at their house of St-Bris.

1 Henry, bishop of Auxerre (1220–35).

MANUSCRIPTS: Bishops' cartulary, fol. 63v. Coll. Bourgogne 3, fol. 17r (abbreviated).

EDITIONS: Lebeuf 2:61, no. 132. Lebeuf 4:114–15, no. 199, dated 15 March.

Item littera de altari et oratorio Sancti Prisci.

Vniuersis presentes litteras uisuris, frater P[etrus] dictus abbas Pontiniacensis[1] totusque conuentus eiusdem loci, salutem in Domino. Noueritis quod reuerendus pater G[uido] Dei gratia Autissiodorensis episcopus[2] ex mera liberalitate sua uoluit et concessit quod nos in domo nostra Sancti Prisci[3] oratorium et altare quandam sibi placuerit habere possumus et ibi saluo iure ecclesiarum parrochialum Sancti Prisci diuina quandiu sibi placuerit celebrare. Et hoc omnibus tenore presencium intimamus.

Datum anno Domini MCC sexagesimo, die lune post letare Iherusalem.

Fol. 63v.

In scrinio signato per P inuenientur littere de Conada.

99

Auxerre, 1157

Bishop Alain of Auxerre and Count William III of Nevers reach an agreement over Cosne. The castle and castellany are to be held from the bishop, who has direct authority over crimes committed there and also shall exercise justice over merchants and markets.

MANUSCRIPTS: Bishops' cartulary, fols. 63v–64v. 1157. Arch. Yonne G 1675 includes a vidimus, taken from the original, done in 1345. Arch. Yonne G 1690 includes a vidimus done in 1424, from the 1345 vidimus. Bibl. Auxerre, MS 153, fols. 128r–129v; seventeenth-century copy by Dom Viole, from the vidimus. BnF fr. 18692, pp. 317–21, from the cartulary. Arch. Yonne G 1592, fols. 163r–v, from the preceding.

EDITIONS: GC 12, instr. cols. 124–5, no. 34. Q 2:75–7, no. 73, 1157, from the 1345 vidimus and from GC.

The material in brackets comes from the vidimus.

---

1 Peter, abbot of Pontigny (1260–1).

2 Gui of Mello, bishop of Auxerre (1247–70).

3 St-Bris, 10 km southeast of Auxerre.

[In nomine sancte et indiuidue trinitatis.] Ego Alanus Dei gratia Autissiodorensis episcopus, et ego Willermus comes Niuernensis.[1] Notum esse uolumus tam futuris quam presentibus quod Sancta Maria et Beatus Stephanus et episcopus Autissiodorensis dinoscuntur[2] habere et habuisse in pace apud Conadam[3] hec omnia que per capitula in presenti carta subscripta sunt. Quicquid in castro et in castellania Conade continetur, de casamento uel de dominio episcopi est, fossetum de firmitate Conade [et piscatura] episcopi est, et forisfactum de fosseto. Si fuerit empiramentum fosseti, comitis est [cum piscatura de fosseto castri].

De omnibus hominibus, ubicumque steterint, qui mercaturam faciunt apud Conadam, iusticia episcopi est, forum et theloneum episcopi est et quicquid de foro exit, et iusticia de omnibus hominibus qui uenerint infractura castri, et rapina et incendium episcopi est[4], quicumque clamorem fecerit, episcopi est. Quicumque stat in terra episcopi, si bouem habet, curuatam debet episcopo bis in anno, si bouem non habet, duos homines habebit pro[5] curuata[6] ubi prepositus episcopi mittet eos. Censum habet episcopus [solus] in dominio suo de terra sua tota intra castrum, et de foris per Ligerim[7] a riuo[8] Alueriae, usque ad terram Villechaiul,[9] ubicumque nauis ad uendendum aliquid portabit uenditure et consuetudines sunt episcopi de hoc quod uendiderit uel[10] aplicuerit.

Omnes homines qui stant a Villechaiul [usque] ad riuum Alueriae, quicumque rete miserint in Ligerim, submonebit prepositus episcopi ad piscandum, et panem et uinum habebunt, quod si facere noluerint, rectum inde facient per legem qua uiuunt. Boscus de Culdreyo,[11] Beate Marie et Sancti Stephani et episcopi est. Credenciam suam habet episcopus in omnibus qui uendunt panem et uinum et carnem, et quicquid est necessarium ad comedendum.

Si episcopus uenit in uillam, uel hospites ei superuenint, accipiet patellam, cacabum, scutellas, cyphos, culcitias, quissinos[12] et pannos ad iacendum, mel et cera que exit de bosco predicto, et pasnagium, et quercus, et fagus, et omnes

1 Bishop Alain of Auxerre (1152–67) and Count William III of Nevers (1149–61).
2 Here and below the vidimus spells the word 'dignoscuntur.'
3 Cosne, 65 km southwest of Auxerre.
4 The vidimus reads 'est episcopi.'
5 The cartulary reads 'in.'
6 The cartulary adds the word 'episcopi' here instead of a few words later in the sentence.
7 The river Loire.
8 For 'a riuo' the cartulary reads 'de lo ru.'
9 Villechaud, 4 km southwest of Cosne. The vidimius spells the place name 'Villecheau' throughout.
10 The cartulary erroneously substitutes 'ubi.'
11 The vidimus reads 'Culdreio.'
12 The vidimus reads 'cuissinos.'

arbores que fructum portant episcopi sunt, et iusticia tocius bosci episcopi est. Mariscalcus episcopi hospitabitur equos dominorum qui sunt post episcopum, et de unoquoque illorum habebit panem [et] uinum et carnem, apud Villamchaiul, que est in casamento, habebit episcopus curuatam de bouum.[13] In terra que utatur foresta monachorum habet episcopus curuatam bouum. Ad custodiendas messes [necesses vid] et prata que sunt in terra episcopi, prepositus episcopi ponet ibi cutodem, et si aliquid forisfactum fuerit, iusticiam habebit episcopus a Conada usque ad saxum de Geury [et] usque ad quadriuium Cistilliaco, et quantum terra episcopi durat [ultra fosseta], et boscum et planum.

Si bestia uel aliquid ibi[14] uenditur, uenditure sunt episcopi a duodecim nummis. Insupra duella Conade sunt episcopi[15] a planea de riuo usque ad Villamchaiul, et usque ad Villam Villani et usque ad[16] Ligerim. Iusticia totius castallanie Conade episcopi est. [In burgo Sancti Aniani, nec etiam in aliqua terra episcopi que sit extra municionem Conade, ego comes consuetudinem aliquam, nec iusticiam, nec censum, nec pedagium habeo. Infra municionem nec extra talliam uel questam licet michi facere, nisi in meis hominibus de corpore.]

Hec[17] que suprascripta sunt, ego W[illermus] Niuernensis comes sigillaueram, postea uero dominus meus A[lanus] Autissiodorensis episcopus et ego, que subscripta sunt concordauimus et huic cartule apposuimus, et eam tam meo quam suo sigillo signauimus. Nullus hominum episcopi qui maneat extra munitionem Conade consuetudinem uel iusticiam michi debet aliquam.

Si quis hominum meorum de Conada, uel de aliis castris, scilicet Castro Nouo, Mailliaco, Sancto Saluatore, Bitriaco, Vlmo[18] et eorum castellaniis que ab episcoo teneo, perrexerit ad uillam que sit episcopi, quandiu ibi manebit, episcopi erit, nec res ipsius saisire potero, cum autem redierit, meus erit. Si tamen ad Conadam rediens fiat feodatus seruiens episcopi, episcopi erit. Terram que de fundo est episcopi, non licet michi uel decimam aliquam acquirere, nisi per episcopum Autissiodoris, non licet michi inducere uel denuere aliquas consuetudines, nisi per episcopum de cuius feodo omnes eas (eas omnes cart) habeo. Quecumque habeo Autissiodori in foro, et in aliis consuetudinibus, et in

13 The cartulary reads 'bobum.'

14 The cartulary reads 'ubi.'

15 The vidimus adds 'sic.'

16 The preceding five words were omitted in the vidimus.

17 The vidimus does not include this or the following sentence.

18 The castles of Châteauneuf, 64 km south-southwest of Auxerre, Mailly-le-Château, 23 km south of Auxerre, St-Sauveur, 35 km southwest of Auxerre, Bétry, 20 km southeast of Auxerre, and Lormes, 60 km south-southeast of Auxerre. This is the earliest mention of the castle of Bétry, although the count had said in 1145 (document 1) that he held the other castles from the bishop; see Yves Sassier, *Recherches sur le pouvoir comtal en Auxerrois*, p. 65.

circuitu, preter clausuram murorum, de episcopi feodo est, preter illud modicum quod teneo a duce [Burgundie] ultra pontem. Liberi homines mei qui se transferunt ad aliquam uillarum episcopi, episcopi sunt.

[Hec que scripta sunt dominus meus Alanus Autissiodorensis episcopus et ego Willermus comes Niuernensis concordauimus et tam suo quam meo sigillo sigillauimus.] Huius rei testes sunt, R. archidiaconus, G. cantor, Stephanus cellararius, Ra. de Touci, Herueus prepositus, Olannus, hii ex parte episcopi.

Ex parte comitis magister Stephanus, magister Gaufridus, Gaudricus capellanus. Odo Grossus, Briennus de Cona, Raudus, Robertus, et alii quamplures ex utraque parte. [Actum Autissiodori, anno incarnacionis Domini millesimo centesimo quinquagesimo septimo.]

This document is the only one for which any medieval copies survive, other than the cartulary itself. It was done at the same time as document 101.

100

ca 1185

Hervé, lord of Gien, makes an agreement with the bishop of Auxerre that he shall not demand that the men of Cosne accompany his army unless they can return home the same day. He shall not exercise the wine ban at Cosne, except for his own wine for his personal use. He also yields to the bishop on their disputes over the fief of La Chapelle-St-André and the tithes of Entrains.

MANUSCRIPT: Bishops' cartulary, fol. 64v.

EDITIONS: Lebeuf 2, instr. p. 269, no. 317, dated ca 1210. Lebeuf 4:71, no. 108, dated ca 1210.

Item alia littera de Conada.

Ego Herueus Giemensis dominus,[1] notum fieri uolo tam futuris quam presentibus quod inter me et dominum meum Autissiodorensis episcopum[2] talis interuenit pactio, quod homines Conade[3] in exercitum ducere non debeo, nisi eadem die qua domum suam possunt reuerti. Bannum Conade facere non possum, nisi de uino me proprio quod ante festum Sancti Martini ad usus meos emptum sit, et in domo mea repositum. De rachatacione terre mee que de feodo ipsius est quam ipsi debeo, in beneplacito eius et in bona submonitione erit. De

1 Hervé III of Donzy, lord of Gien, 76 km west-southwest of Auxerre.

2 Hugh of Noyers, bishop of Auxerre (1183–1206).

3 Cosne, 65 km southwest of Auxerre.

feodo Capelle[4] de quo erat contencio in curia domini episcopi faciam iuris plenitudinem. De decima que est apud Interannum uillam[5] meam de qua canonici Beati Stephani Autissiodorensis se deuestitos esse conqueruntur, concessi quod si probatum fuerit temporibus patris uel aui mei eos prefatam decimam habuisse, eis illam restituam. Ad maiorem etiam pacis stabilitatem communi statutum est assensu quod si aliqua inter nos emerserit contencio, episcopus unum amicorum suorum eliget et ego unum, illi uero duo tertium, qui tres mediante iuramento bona fide litem terminabunt.

This document is undated, but certainly dates to the twelfth century, before Hervé IV of Donzy became count of Nevers in 1199, because he gave Gien to the king at that time in return for royal agreement to his marriage. In 1204, Bishop Hugh of Auxerre also granted his rights in Gien to the king, saying that it had been held from him as a liege fief.[6] The Hervé of the charter is most likely Hervé III, who died on the Third Crusade; he was forced to do homage to Bishop William of Auxerre for Gien in 1181.[7]

101

Auxerre, 1157

William III, count of Nevers, settles his quarrel with Bishop Alain of Auxerre over Cosne. He agrees that the bishop has primary right of justice there.

MANUSCRIPTS: Bishops' cartulary, fol. 64v. Coll. Bourgogne 3, fol. 17r–v.
EDITION: GC 12, instr. col. 125, no. 35.

Item alia littera de Conada.

Ego W[illelmus] Niuernensis comes[1] presentibus et futuris notifico extitisse discordiam inter me et dominum meum A[lanum] episcopum Autissiodorensis[2]

4 La Chapelle St-André, 48 km south-southwest of Auxerre. Count Gui of Nevers had given the bishop property there in 1173 (document 42). It is 17 km east of Donzy; its closeness was doubtless what had made Hervé raise claims.

5 Entrains, 65 km southwest of Auxerre.

6 GC 12, instr. cols. 146–7, no. 63.

7 *Gesta*, 2:123–5. For the lords of Donzy, see Constance Brittain Bouchard, *Sword, Miter, and Cloister*, pp. 327–9.

1 Count William III of Nevers (1149–61).

2 Alain, bishop of Auxerre (1152–67).

de banno et iusticia Conade[3] et burgo Sancti Aniani, unde talis facta est concordia. Bannum ex parte mea et episcopi clamababitur. Si clametur pro negotio episcopi uel me uel alterius infractura et emendacio erit episcopi, sed dampnum michi uel alteri restituetur per iustitiam episcopi. Iustitia omnium hominum manentium apud Conadam episcopi est. Quicumque clamorem fecerit pro qualicumque forisfacto episcopo uel preposito ipsius faciet etiam de illo forisfacto quod fiet in domo uel dongione meo ab hominibus meis uel alterius. Cognitum insuper fuit quod in burgo Sancti Aniani nec etiam in aliqua terra episcopi que sit extra munitionem Conade consuetudinem aliquam, nec iustitiam habeo infra munitionem nec extra talliam uel questum licet michi facere nisi in meis hominibus de corpore. Hominibus de Conada tenemur ego et episcopus credita nobis ab eis infra xl dies reddere.

Huius rei testes sunt magister Stephanus, Stephanus cellarius, magister Gaufridus, Odo Grossus, Briennis de Cona, Robertus prepositus. Actum Autissiodori anno ab incarnacione Domini MC LVII.

This document was drawn up at the same time as document 99.

Fol. 64v.

Item totus processus de litte quondam habita inter episcopum Autissiodorensis et comitem Niuernensis super Conada.
Item quadam cedula non sigillata super constiutione cantorie et lectorie de Conada.
Item tres littere de Codreto et de Liernois.

102

1212

Hugh, archdeacon of Auxerre, attests that the bishop has established prebends at St-Laurent of Cosne and given that church the church of 'Nusiacum.' The latter church shall be free of the archdeacon's procurations.

MANUSCRIPTS: Bishops' cartulary, fols. 64v–65r. Bibl. Auxerre, MS 153, fol. 298v; seventeenth-century copy by Dom Viole.
EDITION: GC 12, instr. col. 151, no. 73.

3 Cosne, 65 km southwest of Auxerre.

Item littera quod ecclesiam de Nuisiaco non debet procurationem archidiacono.

Hugo Autissiodorensis archidiaconus, omnibus presentes litteras inspecturis in Domino salutem. Nouerint uniuersi quod cum uenerabilis pater et dominus meus W[illelmus] Autissiodorensis episcopus[1] in ecclesia Beati Laurencii de Conada[2] instituisset prebendas, dedit et concssit de assensu et uoluntate nostra ecclesie Sancti Laurentii supradicte imperpetuum ecclesiam de Nusiaco,[3] iustituens ut quicumque fuerit prebendam unam de cetero absque residencia habet annexam archidiacono in ecclesia memorata. Ad peticionem quoque prefati domini mei episcopi concessi ut ecclesia de Nusiaco deinceps imperpetuum sit libera a procuracione archidiaconi.

In cuius rei memoriam, presentes litteras feci annotari et sigilli mei munimine roborari. Actum anno Domini MCC XII.

This charter confirms an episcopal charter given at the same time, by which Bishop William established canons at St-Laurent of Cosne with the consent of the chapter.[4]

Fol. 65v.

In scrinio signato per Q inuenientur simile de capella de Betleem.

103

August/September/October 1211

Manasses, bishop of Orléans, and Humbaud, a canon of Auxerre, attest to the settlement of the dispute over the church of Bethlehem at Clamecy, between the bishops of Auxerre and Autun. By papal authority, the quarrel was settled by canons of Bourges. Separate attestations are made by the arbiters and by both the bishops and the cathedral chapters of Auxerre and Autun.

MANUSCRIPT: Bishops' cartulary, fols. 65r–66v.

EDITION: GC 4, instr. col. 95, no. 63 (Bishop Walter's confirmation only, the final part of this entry).

1 William of Seignelay, bishop of Auxerre (1207–20).

2 Cosne, 65 km southwest of Auxerre.

3 This place is not identified. It is spelled differently in the rubric and the charter itself.

4 Lebeuf 4:73, no. 115.

Manasses Dei gratia Aurelianenis episcopus[1] et Humbaudus Autissiodorensis canonicus, omnibus presentes litteras inspecturis, in Domino salutem. Nouerint uniuersi presentes pariter et futuri quod cum inter uenerabiles patres Galterum Eduensis et Willelmum Autissiodorensis episcopos[2] super capella et domo de Betleem et burgo de Bethleem apud Clameciacum[3] cui iure diocesiano suboentur, coram uenerabilis uiris cantore, archipresbitero et Magistro Bonoamico canonicis Bituricensis,[4] auctoritate apostolica questio uerteretur. Tandem de assensu capitulorum suorum sub pena centum marcarum compromisunt in nos et uenerabilem uirum Magistrum Hugonem Bituricensis archidiaconum nostre forni qui in autenticis eorum decani et capitulorum suorum litteris inde constitutis et nobis traditis expressius continetur quorum seriem de uerborum presenti pagine duxere annotare.

Littere ex parte episcopi Eduensis.

Galterus Dei gratia Eduensis episcopus, omnibus presentes litteras inspecturis, in Domino salutem. Nouerint uniuersi quod cum inter nos ex una parte et uenerabilem patrem W[illelmum] Autissiodorensis episcopum ex altera super capella de Bethleem apud Clameciacum et iure parrochiali eiusque burgi coram cantore, archipresbitero et Magistro Bonoamico canonicis Bituricensis, auctoritate apostolica questio uerteretur. Tandem mediantibus uiris bonis et ad pacem interponentibus partes suas in uenerabilem Manassem Aurelianensis episcopum, Magistrum Hugonem Bituricensis archidiaconum et Humbaudum Autissiodorensis canonicum super illa controuersia sub pena centum marcharum Parisi hinc inde compromisimus uoluntate sub hac forma, quod arbitri ipsi de plano ius uterusque partis inquirent, et nos inconcusse seruabimus quicquid ipsi uel episcopus cum altero coarbitrorum suorum duxerit arbitrandum. Et condictum est quod propter tercii absenciam non impedietur quin episcopus cum coarbitro suo qui prius fuerit procedat. Super pena autem centum marcharum repetenda si centus in defftum plene supposuimus nos iuridicioni episcopi supradicti et ut manis robur obtineat compromissum istud tam per nostras quam per capituli nostri litteras duximus roborare. Durabit autem compromissum istud usque ad festum omnium sanctorum nisi de communi assensu partium fuerit prorogatum et ex tunc si non esset tam per arbitros terminata. Dominus Autissiodorensis episcopus ad iudices suos superius nominatos haberet recursum et esset negocium,

1 Manasses, bishop of Orléans (1207–21).

2 Bishops Walter of Autun (1189–1223) and William of Auxerre (1207–20). Bishop William was the brother of Bishop Manasses.

3 Clamecy, 37 km south of Auxerre.

4 The city of Bourges. Its diocese is west of that of Auxerre.

quo ad litteras apostolicas quorum auctoritate conueniebamus et quo ad omnia tam quo ad nos quam quo ad ipsum in eo statu in quo erat tempore compromissi, ita quod non posset huius compromissi pretextu exceptio aliqua ex parte nostra contra ipsum uel litteras predictas opponi. Actum mense Augusto, anno Domino M duecentesimo undecimo.

Littere capituli Eduensi.

Hugo decanus et uniuersum Eduensis ecclesie capitulum, omnibus presentes litteras inspecturis, in Domino salutem. Nouerint uniuersi quod cum inter uenerabiles patres dominum nostorum Galterum Eduensis ex una parte et Vuillelmum Autissiodorensis ex altera episcopos super capella de Betleem apud Clameciacum et iure parrochiali eiusdem burgi coram cantore archipresbitero et Magistro Bonoamico canonico Bituricensis auctoritate apostolica questio uerteretur. Tandem mediantibus uiris bonis et ad pacem interponentibus partes suas in uenerabilem patrem Manassem Aurelianensis episcopum, magistrum Hugonem Bituricensis archidiaconum et Humbaudum[5] Autissiodorensis canonicum super illa controuersia sub pena centum marchum Parisi uoluntate compromiserunt hinc inde sub tali forma, quod arbitri ipsi de plano ius uterusque partis inquirent et pars uterusque inconcusse seruabit quod arbitri ipsi uel episcopus cum altero coarbitrorum suorum duxit arbitrandum. Et condittum est quod propter tercii absentiam non impedietur quin episcopus cum coarbitro suo qui fuerit presens procedat. Super pena autem centum marcarum argenti repetenda si episcopus noster esset in defftum supposuit idem episcopus plene iuridicioni dicti Aurelianensis episcopi coherendus et ut manis robur obtineat compromissum, dominus noster episcopus illud duxit per suas ac nostras litteras roborare. Durabit autem compromissimum istud usque ad festum omnium sanctorum nisi de communi consensu partium fuerit ulterius prorogatum et ex tunc si non esset causa per arbitros teminata. Dominus Autissiodorensis ad iudices suos superius nominatos haberet recursum et esset negotium, quo ad litteras apostolicas quorum auctoritate conuenitur dominus noster episcopus et quo ad omnia tam quo ad predictum dominum nostrum, quam quo ad dominum Autissiodorensem in eo statu in quo erat tempore compromissi, ita quod non poterit huius compromissi pretextu exceptio aliqua contra dominum Autissiodorensem uel litteras suas predictas ab aduersa per tempore.

Nos itaque ea que ad pacem sunt cupientes huic compromisso assensum prebentes illud sub presentis pagine et sigilli nostri testimonium duximus roborare. Ratum et inconcussum in perpetuum hanc quicquid ex eo fuerit ordinatum. Actum mense Septembri, anno incarnacionis Dominice M CC XI.

5 The cartulary reads 'Humbaud.'

Littere ex parte Autissiodorensis episcopi.

Willelmus Dei gratia Autissiodorensis episcopus, omnibus presentes litteras inspecturis, in Domino salutem. Nouerint uniuersi quod cum inter nos ex una parte et uenerabilem patrem Galterium Eduensis episcopum ex altera super capella de Bethleem apud Clameciacum et iure parrochiali eiusdem burgi coram cantore, archipresbitero et Magistro Bonoamico canonico Bituricensis auctoritate apostolica questio uerteretur, tandem mediantibus uiris bonis et ad pacem interponentibus partes suas Manassem Aurelianensis episcopum, Magistrum Hugonem Bituricensis archidiaconum et Humbaudum Autissiodorensis canonicum, super illa controuersia sub pena centum marcarum Parisi hinc inde compromisimus uoluntate sub hac forma, quod arbitri ipsi de plano ius uterusque partis inquirent et uolicatus seruabimus quicquid ipsi uel episcopus cum altero coarbitrorum suorum duxerit arbitrandum. Et condittum est quod propter tercii absentiam non inpedietur quin episcopus cum coarbitror qui presens fuerit procedat. Super pena centum marcarum repetenda si centus in defftum plene supposuimus nos iuridicioni episcopi superdicti et ut manis robur obtineat compromissum illud tam per nostris quam per capituli nostri litteras duximus roborare. Durabit autem compromissum istud usque ad festum omnium sanctorum nisi de communi consensu partium fuerit prorogatum et ex tunc si non esset tam per arbitros terminata nos ad iudices nostros superius nominatos haberemus recursum et esset negotium, quo ad litteras apostolicas quorum auctoritate conueniebamus iamdictum Eduensis et quo ad omnia tam quo ad nos quoniam quo ad ipsum in eo statu in quo erat tempore comprimissi, ita quo non posset huius compromissi pretextu exceptio aliqua ex parte ipsius contra nos aut litteras nostras opponi. Actum mense Augusto, anno Domini M CC XI.

Littere capituli Autissiodorensis.

Regnaus[6] et uniuersum Autissiodorensis ecclesie capitulum, omnibus presentes litteras inspecturis, in Domino salutem. Nouerint uniuersi quod cum inter uenerabilem patres dominum nostrum Willelmum Autissiodorensis ex una parte et Galterum Eduensis episcopos ex altera super capella de Bethleem apud Clameciacum et iure parrochiali eiusdem burgi coram cantore, archipresbitero et Magistro Bonoamico canonico Bituricensis auctoritate apostolica questio uerteretur. Tandem mediantibus uiris bonis et ad pacem interponentibus, partes suas in uenerabilem patrem Manassem Aurelianensis episcopum et Magistrum Hugonem Bituricensis archidiaconum et Humbaudum Autissiodorensis canonicum super illa controuersia sub pena centum marcharum Parisi uoluntate compromisserunt hinc inde sub tali forma, quod arbitri ipsi de plano ius

6 He was mostly likely the dean of the chapter.

uterusque partis inquirent et pars uterusque inconcusse seruabit quicquid arbitri ipsi uel episcopus cum altero coarbitrorum suorum duxerit arbitrandum. Et condictum est quod propter tercii absenciam non impedietur quin episcopus cum coarbitro suo qui fuerit presens procedat. Super pena autem centum marcarum argenti repetenda si episcopus noster esset in defftum supposuit Eduensis idem episcopus plene iuridicioni dicti episcopi coherendus et ut manis robur obtineat compromissum dominus noster episcopus illud duxerit per suas ac nostras litteras roborare. Durabit autem compromissum usque ad festum omnium sanctorum nisi de communi consensu partium fuerit prorogatum et ex tunc si non esset causa per arbitros terminata. Dominus Autissiodorensis ad iudices suos superius nominatos haberet recursum et esset negotium quo ad litteras apostolicas quorum auctoritate conuenitur dictus Eduensis et ad omnia tam quo ad dominum predictum Eduensis quam quo ad dominum Autissiodorensis in eo statu in quo erat tempore compromissi, ita quod non poterit huius compromissi pretextu excepcio aliquam contra dominum Eduensis uel litteras predictas ab aduersa parte opponi. Nos itaque ea que ad pacem sunt cupientas huic compromisso assensum prebentes illud super presentis pagine et sigilli nostri testimonium duximus roborare. Ratum et inconcussam in perpetuum hanc quitquid ex eo fuerit ordinatum. Actum mense Septembri, anno incarnacionis Domini M CC XI.

Assignatis itaque nobis litteris supradictis nos duo arbitri, non obstante tercii scilicet archidiacono Bituricensis absente, secundum quod condictum fuerat compromisso qui tamen litteraliter excusauit in arbitrio, processimus et per testes idoneos hinc inde productos ius uterusque partis diligentius inquirentes omnibusque uti et ea sollemnitate peractis que decint cum sola esset diffinitiam preferenda Eduam accessimus et ibi presentibus partibus formam de prudencium et iuris peritorum siunam permitiamus diffiniter et finaliter decernimus capellam et domum et burgum de Bethleem apud Clameciacum Autissiodorensis episcopo ut pote dyocesano loci altius pleno iure subesse et episcopum Eduensum nichil iuris penitus habere ibidem. Vnde ei perpetuum silencium imposimus super premissis. Ipse uero Eduensis episcopus prolata siuna statuii se traxit in partem et habito cum canonicis suis quorum magna pars presens erat consilio, reuersus publice protestatus est quod sentenciam illam approbabat et quod ei nullatenus obuiaret et tam subter dicte domus quam hominibus burgi de Bethleem per litteras suas patentes denunciauit id ipsum quarum tenor hic erat.

Galterus Dei gratia Eduensis episcopus, dilectis in Christo fratribus de Bethleem et omnibus in burgo de Bethleem apud Clameciacum manentibus, salutem in Domino. Noueritis quod per sentenciam reuerendi patris Manasse Aurelianensis episcopi et dilecti nostri Humbaudi Autissiodorensis canonici in quos compromiseramus super capella et iuridicione burgi de Bethleem, diffinitum est et declaratum quod capella, domus et burgus quoad ecclesiasticam iuridicionem pleno iure spectant ad episcopum Autissiodorensis, et nos eidem sententie parentes, id uobis notificamus et presenti insinuatione a cetero denuciamus. Datum anno gratie MCC XI, mense Ottobris, iiii kalendas Nouembris.

Nos igitur arbitri ne ea que per nos et a nobis rite ac tam sollempniter acta sunt procedente ipse possit per obliuione deleri acta ipsa in scriptum redegiri hoc presenti pagine annotata sigillorum nostrorum munimine duximus roborare. Actum anno Domini MCC XI.

Count William II of Nevers had established a Maison-Dieu at Clamecy, which William IV gave to the church of Bethlehem when he died there in 1168. With the fall of the Kingdom of Jerusalem in 1187, the Latin bishop of Bethlehem was invited to come settle along the Yonne, which he did, creating a continuing irritation for the rest of the Middle Ages for the bishop of Auxerre, who thus had another self-proclaimed independent diocese within his own diocese.[7] It did not help that Clamecy was on the diocesan border with the bishopric of Autun.

Fol. 66v.

Item littera papalis confirmatorum.

Item totus processus de Bethleem.

Item littera comitis Ioigniaci de feodo quod tenet ab episcopo Autissiodorensis sub castellum de Mons, duas uillas scilicet Rollen et Marsengi.

Item in scrinio signato per S inuenientur littere de conquestibus domus Parisis.

Item littere de ordinibus factis a Guillelmo de Gressibus Autissiodorensis episcopo inuenientur in scrinio[1] signato per T.

7 GC 12, instr. cols. 371–4, nos. 1–2.

1 The cartulary reads 'scrino.'

THE CATHEDRAL CHAPTER'S CARTULARY

1

Auxerre, 30 April 1166

The cathedral chapter of Auxerre reaches an agreement with Bishop Alain, before the abbots of Reigny and Les Roches and the prior of St-Eusèbe, that the office of provost will be attached to the chapter. The bishop will make the provostry a gift for his soul when the current provost dies or otherwise leaves office.

MANUSCRIPTS: Chapter cartulary, fol. 1r (closing only). Bibl. Auxerre, MS 153, fol. 146r–v; seventeenth-century copy by Dom Viole.

EDITIONS: Lebeuf 2, instr. p. 23, no. 45. Lebeuf 4:48, no. 59, from Lebeuf 2.

[In nomine Domini nostri Iesu Christi. Notum sit presentibus et futuris quod ego Alanus, Dei gratia Autissiodorensis episcopus,[1] conuocatis personis, scilicet Petro archidiacono, Guillelmo decano, Radulpho thesaurario, Stephano cantore, et ceteris canonicis Autissiodorensis ecclesie ipsius utilitati et paci cupiens in posterum prouidere. Dedi et concessi prepositurам cum omni iure suo totius capituli communitati post decessum Guidonis prepositi siue morte, siue habitus mutatione, siue dignitatis mutatione, ut post decessum meum singulis annis anniuersarium meum faciant, hoc quoque canonici laudauerunt, et tam persone quam alii qui adfuerant, se bone fide seruaturos, et ulterius prepositum non electuros iurauerunt. Accraantaui[2] etiam in capitulo canonicis et in uerbo ueritatis statui quod a personis et canonicis exteris substituendis, idem

1 Alain, bishop of Auxerre (1152–67).

2 This curious word appears both in Viole's copy of the charter and in Lebeuf's edition. It was presumably the spelling of the cartulary.

iuramentum fieri facerent, quod qui facere noluerit, tandiu beneficio prebenda careat, donec huius nostre institutionis formam, sicut alii iurauerunt se obseruaturum iuret. Vt autem hec nostra donatio et institutio firmior in posterum habeatur, huius rei donum per impositionem libri super altare B. Stephani, presentibus Ascelino abbate Regniacensi, et Ioanne abbate Rupium, et Gaufrido priore S. Eusebii, et tam personis quam canonicis S. Stephani feci, ac ipsis presentibus omnes illos qui hoc iuramentum aliquo modo infregerint, et huic institutioni contraire tempauerint, ego et predicti abbates, et alii sacerdotes ecclesie, uinculo anathe]matis innodauimus. Actum est sollempniter in capitulo Autissiodorensis. Anno Domini MCLX sexto, pridie kalendas Maii. Presentibus Ascelino abbate Rigniacensis, Iohanne abbate Rupium, Gaufrido priore Sancti Eusebii, et de canonicis ecclesie Beati Stephani presbitero, archidiacono, Guillelmo decano, Rudulpho thesaurario, Stephano cantore, Roberto lectore, Regnaldo camerario, Germano succentore, et multis aliis.[3]

Because nothing but the dating formula and witnesses survives from this charter (the fragment picks up in the middle of a word), it is impossible to say, on the basis of the cartulary alone, what agreement it recorded. However, in the first half of the eighteenth century Jean Lebeuf printed a document whose ending exactly corresponds, saying that it was from the cathedral cartulary, so he must have seen the cartulary before it became fragmented. I have here given his text in brackets, although I have not followed him in restoring the classical -ae- diphthong. His text was repeated in the nineteenth-century re-edition of his work.

2

1219

Bishop William of Auxerre attests to an agreement between the cathedral chapter and the noble Lord Droco of Mello. He had erected gallows at St-Maurice Thizouaille, next to the chapter's villa of Egleny, which the chapter found disturbing, but he promises not to do so again.

MANUSCRIPT: Chapter cartulary, fol. 1r.
EDITION: Q 3:96, no. 216.

3 The abbots are Ascelin of Reigny (1162–75) and John of Les Roches (1152–67), both nearby Cistercian houses. Geoffrey was prior of St-Eusèbe of Auxerre, a house of Augustinian canons. The principal officers of the cathedral of Auxerre also signed.

[G]uillelmus Dei gratia Autissiodorensis episcopus,[1] omnibus presentes litteras inspecturis, in Domino salutem. Notum fieri uolumus quod cum dilecti filii capitulum Autissiodorensis querelas mouissent nobili uiro Droconi de Melloto super eo quod idem nobilis in terra capituli fulcas erigi fecerat. Videlicet in quondam monticulo qui est inter Sanctum Mauricium Tyroaille uillam suam et Egliniacum uillam capituli,[2] tandem nobis mediantibus, et per dictum nostrum tunc se partes supposuntur. Hinc inde id ordinantibus sepefactus nobilis fulcas utpote in preiudicium capituli fecit auferri, et concessit ut fulcas ibi de cetero nec ipse leuabit nec leuari permitet a suis. In cuius rei memoriam presentes litteras notari fecimus, et sigilli nostri inpressione muniri. Actum anno domini MCC nono decimo.

The chapter of Auxerre received extensive revenues from the inhabitants of Egleny, a practice that the king confirmed in 1211.[3] Droco of Mello had been royal constable.

3

August 1215

Bishop William of Auxerre grants Dean William and the rest of the cathedral chapter patronage over twelve churches, including tithes and justice rights.

MANUSCRIPT: Chapter cartulary, fol. 1r.
EDITIONS: Lebeuf 2:43, no. 91. Lebeuf 4:79, no. 129, from Lebeuf 2.

[G]uillemus Dei gratia Autissiodorensis episcopus,[1] dilectis filiis Guillelmo decano totique capitulo Autissiodoro, in Domino salutem. Cum a nobis petitur quod ratio exigit, aut equitas persuadet facilem uolumus et debemus prebere consensum. Eapropter dilecti in Domino filii, postulationibus uestris iustis beniguolum impartientes fauorem uobis uestrisque successoribus in futurum ecclesias in quibus ius patronatus hactenus habuistis, uidelicet de Bacernna, de Oissiaco, de Acolaio, de Creueno, de Coruun, de Monestrillo, de Chimiliaco,

1 William of Seignelay, bishop of Auxerre (1207–20).
2 St-Maurice Thizouaille, 16 km west-northwest of Auxerre, and Egleny, 3 km southeast of St-Maurice.
3 *Recueil des actes de Philippe Auguste, roi de France*, 3:290–1, no. 1189.

1 William of Seignelay, bishop of Auxerre (1207–20).

de Gurgiaco, de Puluereno, de Lindriaco, de Palliaco, de Bellouidere,[2] cum omni iure decimarum, iusticiarum hominum, siue prouentuum quocumque, quod in eisdem ecclesiis siue uillis usque nunc noscuntur habuisse. Auctoritate presentium confirmamus. Actum anno Domini MCC quinto decimo.

Jean Lebeuf's edition gives the last two sentences as, 'Auctoritate presentium confirmamus, et sigilli nostri patrocinio communimus. Actum anno Domini MCC quinto decimo, mense Augusto.' It is possible that his source was a different copy than the cartulary. He also spelled some of the place names slightly differently.

4

Troyes, December 1230

Theobold IV, count of Champagne and Brie, agrees to the sale to the cathedral chapter of the couple John of Montigny and his wife Maria, with their family. The knight Gui of Chamblin, who held in fief from the count, had sold them.

MANUSCRIPT: Chapter cartulary, fol. 1r.

EDITIONS: Lebeuf 2:50, no. 111 (abbreviated). Lebeuf 4:95, no. 162 (abbreviated), from Lebeuf 2.

SUMMARY: H. d'Arbois de Jubainville, *Histoire des ducs et des comtes de Champagne*, 5:295, no. 2079.

[E]go Theobaldus Campanie et Brie comes palatinus.[1] Notum facio omnibus presentibus et futuris quo ego laudo imperpetuum capitulo ecclesie Beati Stephani Autissiodorensis Iohannem de Montiniaco[2] et Mariam uxorem eiusdem, et eorum familiam, qui de feodo meo erant. Quos dilectus et fidelis meus

2 Bazarnes, 16 km south-southeast of Auxerre; Oisy, 37 km south-southwest of Auxerre; Accolay, 18 km southeast of Auxerre; Cravant, 16 km southeast of Auxerre; Moneteau, 5 km north of Auxerre; Chemilly, 11 km north of Auxerre; Gurgy, 8 km north of Auxerre; Lindry, 11 km west of Auxerre; Poilly, 16 km northwest of Auxerre; and Beauvoir, 15 km west of Auxerre. Beauvoir is just a short distance from the villa of Egleny that the chapter had long had. The other places are unidentified.

1 Count Theobold IV of Champagne (1225–53).

2 A number of places are named Montigny. The most likely in this context may be Montigny-la-Resle, 11 km northeast of Auxerre. This was the identification made by Lebeuf. The other possibility is the Montigny 5 km north-northeast of Chamblin. The chapter might have been more likely to buy a couple who lived close to Auxerre.

Guido miles de Chambelen[3] uendidit ecclesie supradicte. Quod ratum et firmum permaneat, presentem cartam sigilli mei munimine roboraui. Actum Trecensi anno Domini MCCXXX, mense Decembri.

This is the first complete edition of this charter.

5

1210

Count Peter of Auxerre and Tonnerre reaches an agreement with the cathedral chapter, that he shall neither claim nor receive the chapter's men into his lordship, and that the chapter shall do similarly with his men at Bétry and Mailly. Six specified men at Bétry, however, may return to the chapter's lands and lordship if they wish to do so. Peter asks the archbishop of Sens and the bishops of Auxerre and Langres to excommunicate him if he goes against this agreement and promises to have King Philip confirm it.

MANUSCRIPT: Chapter cartulary, fol. 1r–v.
SUMMARY: Léopold Delisle, *Catalogue des actes de Philippe-Auguste*, p. 291, no. 1267.

[E]go Petrus comes Autissiodorensis et Tornodensis.[1] Notum facio uniuersis presentibus et futuris quod de querelis et contentionibus quas capitulum Autissiodorensis habebat contra me ita pacificatus est inter me et ipsos, quod ego concessi eis et adhuc concedo bona fide, et iuramento prefacto firmaui, quod non ego non heredes mei de cetero hominem uel hospitem ad Autissiodorensem ecclesiam quoquo modo pertinentem uel qui quandoque pertinuerit in terram nostram recipiemus nec retinebimus nec recipi sustinebimus. Ne canonici homines nostros de Mailliaco, uel Betriaco,[2] retinebunt eodem modo. Homines autem eorum qui sunt apud Betriacum, uidelicet isti, Bernardus de Vallemarci,[3] et Theobaldus frater eius, Galterus Limaroris, Abbas auunculus eius, Bergundio, Hugonellus Planteronce, si ad terram ipsius capituli reuerti

3 Chamblin is a hamlet located 41 km northeast of Auxerre, near Ervy-le-Châtel, in the diocese of Troyes.

1 Peter of Courtenay (d. 1219) had become count of Nevers, Auxerre, and Tonnerre in 1184 by marrying the heiress. When his own daughter married in 1199 she took the county of Nevers to her husband, but Peter retained title to the other two.

2 Mailly-le-Château, 23 km south of Auxerre, and Bétry, 20 km southeast of Auxerre.

3 Val-de-Mercy, 14 km south of Auxerre.

uoluntur nobis placebit, et si quandoque reuersi fuerunt, nos eos non potimus retinere sicut nec alios. Preterea prepositi et seruientes nostri necnon et balliui nostri omnes qui se intermitent de Autissiodoro, de Mailliaco, et Betriaco quotiens mutabuntur iurabunt quod nichil capient uel capi facient de rebus ecclesie Autissiodorensis donec prius decano et capitulo monstratum fuerint, et ipsi de iure faciendo in capitulo defecerint. Si forte euenerit quod querela inter me et uestros oriatur super predictis, sine duello secundum testimonium duorum uel trium bonorum hominum cognoscetur et emendabitur. Quod si contra hec que predicta sunt me uel heredes meos in aliquo uenire uel attemptare contigerit, ego uenerabiles patres et dominos archiepiscopum Senonensem et Autisiodorensem et Lingonensem episcopos[4] rogaui, ut terram meam tandiu tenentur suppositam interdictionem et me excommunicatum donec esset competenter satisfeceri. Promisi etiam dicto capitulo et concessi bona fide quod ad hoc laborabo ut dominus meus Phillipus rex Francorum et Ludouicus filius eius[5] litteras suas eis tradant quod istas conuentiones teneri facient et firmiter obseruari. Ad cuius itaque rei confirmationem presentem cartulam sigilli mei munimine precepi roborari. Actum anno Domini MCC decimo.

This document has not been previously printed. King Philip confirmed this agreement, as the count promised he would; see document 7 below.

6

Auxerre, 1193

Count Peter of Nevers has, at the request of the king, obtained the agreement of the bishop and chapter of Auxerre that their men will assist him in completing the walls around the city of Auxerre, by building them along the waterfront. The bishop and chapter specify that they allow this out of free will, not because they are required to do so, and no later counts of Nevers shall demand such assistance.

MANUSCRIPTS: Chapter cartulary, fol. 1v. BnF MS lat. 17048, p. 102, from the cartulary.

EDITIONS: Lebeuf 2:33–4, no. 70. Lebeuf 4:60–1, no. 85, from Lebeuf 2. Q 2:449, no. 443, from Lebeuf.

---

4 Archbishop Peter of Sens (1200–23), Bishop William of Auxerre (1207–20), and Bishop William of Langres (1208–19).

5 King Philip II ('Augustus') (1180–1223) and his son and heir Louis VIII, future king (1223–6).

[E]go Petrus comes Niuernensis[1] notum uolo esse uniuersis ad quos litteras iste peruenerint quod dominus Autissiodorensis episcopus[2] et canonici Beati Stephani ceterique prelati ecclesiarum Autissiodorensis ad instantissimas preces domini regis Francorum[3] et meas de mera liberalitate sua uoluntur quod homines eorum iuuarent me ad faciendos muros, ex parte aque prefate ciuitatis, cum certissimum sit quod nec ipsi nec homines eorum aliquid ponere debeant ad faciendam quamlibet munitionem ipsius ciuitatis. Ne igitur ego uel successores mei comites Niuernenses hac occasione aliquid ab eis ad simile opus exigere debeamus, presenti pagina certifico, et ne in consuetudinem trahatur, modis omnibus fieri prohibeo. Promisi etiam eis quod litteras apertas domini regis eis habere facerem, antequam collecta super hoc facta de hominibus suis levaretur. Iniquum enim esset si beneficium quod de gratia et mera liberalitate mihi aliquando factum est, in preiudicium ecclesiarum in posterum redundaret.

Actum Autissiodori anno dominice incarnationis M ducentesimo[4] nonagesimo tercio.

Walls around the entire city of Auxerre had first been constructed during the middle decades of the twelfth century. Peter was here finishing the final section along the river.[5]

7

1211

King Philip II confirms the agreement reached between Count Peter of Auxerre and the cathedral chapter, that neither shall seize nor receive the other's men. Six specified men may however leave the count's lands at Bétry and return to the chapter's lordship if they wish.

MANUSCRIPT: Chapter cartulary, fols. 1v–2r.

EDITIONS: Lebeuf 4:70, no. 107. *Recueil des actes de Philippe Auguste*, 3:270–1, no. 1175.

SUMMARY: Léopold Delisle, *Catalogue des actes de Philippe-Auguste*, p. 291, no. 1268, dated March 1211.

---

1 Peter of Courtenay (d. 1219), count of Nevers through his marriage with the heiress in 1184.

2 Hugh of Noyers, bishop of Auxerre (1184–1206).

3 Philip II ('Augustus'), king of France (1180–1223).

4 This word should read 'centesimo.' Peter was count of Nevers in 1193, not 1293. This is the kind of slip that it would be easy for a thirteenth-century scribe to make.

5 See also Constance Brittain Bouchard, *Spirituality and Administration*, p. 116.

[I]n nomine sancte et indiuidiue trinitatis Phillipus Dei gratia Francorum rex.[1] Nouerint uniuersi presentes pariter et futuri quod sicut ex autentico dilecti consanguinei nostri Petri comitis Autissiodorensis[2] perpendimus super querelis et contentionibus quas capitulum Autissiodorensem habebat contra eundem comitem Petrum, ita pacificatum est inter ipsum et eos, quod dictus comes concessit eis et adhuc concedit bona fide et iuramento interposito firmauit, quod nec ipse nec heredes eius de cetero hominem uel hospitem ad Autissiodorensem ecclesiam quoquo modo pertinentem uel qui quandoque pertinuerit, in terram suam recipiet uel retinebit, uel recipi sustinebit. Nec canonici Autissiodorenses retinebunt homines eius de Malliaco uel de Betriaco[3] eodem modo. Homines autem eorum qui sunt apud Betriacum uidelicet isti, Bernardus de Vallemarci,[4] Theobaldus frater eius, Galterus Limateros, Abbas auunculus eius, Bergondio, Hugonellus Planteronce, si ad terram capituli reuerti uoluerint predicto comiti placebit, et si quandoque reuersi fuerint idem comes non poterit eos retinere sicut nec alios. Preterea ipsi et seruientes comitis necnon et omnes balliui eius qui se intromitent de Autissiodoro, de Malliaco et Betriaco, quotiens mutabuntur iurabunt quod nichil capient uel capi facient de rebus ecclesie Autissiodorensis, donec prius decano et capitulo Autissiodorensi monstratum fuerit et ipsi de iure faciendo in capitulo defecerint. Si uero inter comitem et ipsos super predictis orta fuerit querela, sine duello per testimonium duorum uel trium bonorum hominum cognoscetur et emendabitur. Quod si contra predictam comes uel heredes suos contraire uel in aliquo contigerit attemptare, idem comes amicos et fideles nostros archiepiscopum Senonensis, Lingonensis et Autissiodorensis episcopos rogauit ut terram eius tamdiu teneant interdicto suppositam, et ipsum comitem excommunicatum donec fuerit competenter emendatum. Promisit etiam dicto capitulo et concessit quod bona fide ad hoc laboraret quod nos conuentiones istas confirmaremus, et si dictus comes conuentiones istas non teneret, nos ad uniuersas res suas quas de nobis tenet assignaremus, quousque dicto capitulo super hoc esset satisfactum. Quod ut perpetuum robur obtineat, sigilli nostri auctoritate et regii nominis karactere inferius annotato, ad petitionem dicti comitis presentem paginam quantum ad nos pertinet confirmamus.

Actum anno Domini MCC decimo, regni nostri anno XXX secundo.

---

1 King Philip II ('Augustus') (1180–1223).

2 Peter of Courtenay (d. 1219) had become couint of Nevers, Auxerre, and Tonnerre in 1184 by marrying the heiress. His own daughter took the title of Nevers to her husband when she married in 1199, but Peter retained the county of Auxerre.

3 Mailly-le-Château, 23 km south of Auxerre, and Bétry, 20 km southeast of Auxerre.

4 Val-de-Mercy, 14 km south of Auxerre.

Here King Philip confirms the agreement spelled out in document 5, above. Because the new year was assumed to start at Easter, the first months of 1211, the thirty-second year of Philip's reign, would have been considered the end of the year 1210.

8

1209

Count Peter of Auxerre confirms that Alexander Fuignez has given a house in Auxerre to Walter of 'Meso.'

MANUSCRIPT: Chapter cartulary, fol. 2r.
EDITIONS: Lebeuf 2:37, no. 79. Lebeuf 4:69, no. 104, from Lebeuf 2.

[E]go Petrus comes Autissiodorensis[1] notum facio uniuersis quod laudo et condedo donationem quam Alexander Fuignez fecit Galtero de Meso[2] de domo sua que sita est ante monasterium Beati Renoberti apud Autissiodorum. Et ut hoc ratum habeatur imposterum et imotum, presentem paginam sigilli mei munimine roborari precepi. Actum anno Domini MCC nono.

Although this charter does not indicate that Walter of 'Meso' was a member of the cathedral chapter, the inclusion of this charter in the cartulary suggests that he was. The tiny monastery of St-Regnobert in Auxerre was located within the walls of the cathedral *cité*; this is the earliest mention of its existence.

9

1218

Droco of Mello renounces the market he had established at St-Maurice Thizouaille, at the request of the king, who had been approached by the cathedral chapter of Auxerre.

MANUSCRIPT: Chapter cartulary, fol. 2r.

1 Peter of Courtenay (d. 1219) had become count of Nevers, Auxerre, and Tonnerre by marriage to the heiress to these counties in 1184. After his own daughter married in 1199 and brought the title of count of Nevers to her own husband, he retained the title of count of Auxerre.

2 This place is not identified. It is possible that it is a nickname rather than a place.

[E]go Droco de Melloto notum facio omnibus presentes litteras inspecturis, quod cum ego de nouo fecissem mercatum apud Sanctum Mauricium Tiroaille uillam meam,[1] dominus meus rex[2] ad conquestionem decani et capituli Autissiodorensis iudicebit quod ibi non debet esse mercatum, et ego iudicium illud bonum et legitimum reputo. In cuius rei memoriam presentem cartam sigillo meo feci muniri. Actum anno Domini MCC octauo decimo.

Droco of Mello had repeated quarrels with the chapter concerning his villa of St-Maurice Thizouaille, located only a short distance from the chapter's villa of Egleny; see document 2, above. The chapter had complained to the king because Droco was royal constable. This document has not been previously printed.

10

Mailly, 1191

Agnes, countess of Nevers, attests that her mother Mathilda, countess of Tonnerre, had thought to establish an anniversary for her late husband Gui, Agnes's father, by giving the cathedral chapter half a house that she bought from Hugh of Bar; the other half she gave to St-Germain and St-Marien. After the house burned, however, she decided to give the entire property to the chapter.

MANUSCRIPTS: Chapter cartulary, fol. 2v. BnF MS lat. 17048, pp. 93, 120–1, from the cartulary.

EDITIONS: Lebeuf 2:33, no. 68. Lebeuf 4:60, no. 83, from Lebeuf 2. Q 2:435–6, no. 431.

[I]n nomine sancte et indiuidue trinitatis. Ego Agnes comitissa Niuernensis notum fieri uolo tam futuris quam presentibus quod cum karissima mater mea Mathildis comitissa Tornodensis medietatem domus quam emit ab Hugone de Barris pro remedio anime sue et pro faciendo anniuersario Guidonis comitis bone memorie patris mei et suo,[1] ecclesie et canonicis Beati Stephani dedisset,

---

1 St-Maurice Thizouaille, 16 km west-northwest of Auxerre.

2 King Philip II ('Augustus') (1180–1223).

---

1 Countess Agnes of Nevers, who married Peter of Courtenay, was daughter and heiress of Countess Mathilda (d. ca 1210) and of Count Gui of Nevers (1168–76).

et aliam medietatem ecclesiis Sancti Germani et Sancti Mariani,[2] saniori postmodum usa consilio, quod pro faciendis duobus anniuersariis parum uidebatur donasse ecclesie Beati Stephani, presertim cum domus illa communi incendio combusta fuisset, nec sine sumptuoso labore posset refici, totam illam domum cum cellario concessit, laudantibus fratribus prenominatarum ecclesiarum, et partes suas omnino quitantibus, ita quod medietas redditus qui proueniet de quinque operatoriis et cellario ipsius domus, in anniuersario Guidonis comitis patris mei, alia medietas in anniuersario prefate matris mee diuidetur canonicis qui seruicio intererunt, et ceteris clericis prout mos est in illa ecclesia diuidere.

Vt autem hoc pie deuotionis donum stabile foret et ratum, P[etrus] karissimus uir meus antequam Iherosolimam iret[3] et ego laudauimus et sigillis nostris confirmauimus. Insuper ut redditus perpetui manerent, et augeri potius possent quam minui, omnes illos qui quinque operatoria et cellarium sepedicte domus conduxintur ab exercitu et cheualchia et excubatione, scilicet a custodia uille de nocte, que uulgo cerchia dicitur, quitauimus et frangiuimus, et eos ab his tribus seruitiis immunes et quietos perempniter fore concessimus. Hanc uero ultime donationis mutationem et tocius domus sicut supradictum est ecclesie Beati Stephani a matre mea factam donationem, cum pretaxata hospitum franchia et libertate, ego Agnes comitissa Niuernensis iterum laudo et presenti pagina sigillo meo roborata confirmo. Debet autem sepenominata domus xii denarios de censu. Prioris donationis et confirmationis testes sunt Droco de Melloto, Lethericus Baledart, Milo Bornus, Petrus Choselli,[4] Petrus de Corcon, Regnaudus clericus comitisse Tornodensis, Gaufridus capellanus P[etri] comitis, et plures alii. Huius autem secunde confirmationis testes sunt, eadem mater mea, idem Petrus de Corcon, item Milo Bornus, magister Zacharias notarius meus. Datum apud castrum Malliacum,[5] anno Domini MC nonagesimo primo.[6]

Agnes was the first of a series of countesses who inherited the counties of Auxerre, Nevers, and Tonnerre during the course of the thirteenth century.

2 St-Germain was the major Benedictine monastery in Auxerre. St-Marien, located across the river from the cathedral, was a house of Premonstratensian canons.

3 Peter, count of Nevers, died on Crusade in 1219.

4 Choiseul, 30 km northeast of Langres.

5 Mailly-le-Château, 23 km south of Auxerre.

6 Both the Lebeuf and Quantin editions add, 'Regnante Philippo rege Francorum, Hugone uero episcopo, presidente sedi ecclesie Autissiodorensis.' This phrase is not in the cartulary but was added by Gaignières in 1680 when he copied the charter from the cartulary into MS lat. 17048.

11

1208–21

William, abbot of St-Germain of Auxerre, attests to an agreement between the cathedral chapter and Renaud Berard over a house at Mailly. He will pay the chapter seven solidi a year.

MANUSCRIPT: Chapter cartulary, fol. 2v.

[V]uillelmus Sancti Germani Autissiodorensis dictus abbas.[1] Omnibus ad quos presentes litteras peruenerint in Domino salutem. Nouerint uniuersi presentes pariter et futuri quod ad petitionem Regnaudi Berardi litteras presentes confecimus de conuentionibus quas habet ad capitulum Autissiodorensem super domo eiusdem capituli in castro Malliaci,[2] iuxta mercatum sita, quam magister Thomas tenuit a capitulo sepedicto. Siquidem ipse tenetur eidem capitulo per iuramentum suum de domo illa in censiua soluere Autissiodori in ipso capitulo annuatim in octauis natiuitate Domini septem solidos cursalis monete, et quinque preter ipsum successionem ...

The charter breaks off in the middle, at the end of the fragment. Without a dating formula, it is impossible to date the document more closely than to the abbacy of William.

1 William, abbot of St-Germain of Auxerre (1208–21).

2 Mailly-le-Château, 23 km south of Auxerre.

THE CARTULARY OF ST-JULIEN

1

631

Bishop Palladius of Auxerre establishes a convent in the suburb of Auxerre, associated with three basilicas, dedicated to Saint Mary, Saint Andrew, and Saint Julien, and establishes nuns there. He does so with the consent of King Dagobert. He also settles on the nuns property that had belonged to the cathedral. The nuns shall arrange for three masses a day and shall feed the poor daily, for the bishop's soul and that of the king.

MANUSCRIPTS: St-Julien cartulary, fol. 1r. Bibl. Auxerre, MS 152, pp. 641–4; seventeenth-century copy by Dom Viole.

EDITIONS: Jean Mabillon, *De re diplomatica*, pp. 465–6, no. 6.6, dated 634; somewhat abbreviated. Pardessus, J.M., *Diplomata chartae epistolae leges ad res Gallo-Francicas spectantia*, 2:36–7, no. 273; from Mabillon, dated 635. Q 1:7–9, no. 4, from the cartulary and Mabillon.

SUMMARY: M. de Brequigny, *Table chronologique des diplômes, chartes, titres et actes imprimés*, 1:50, dated 634.

Anno viii regni domni Dagoberti piissimi regis,[1] indictione vii, in nomine Dei omnipotentis patris et filii et spiritus sancti, Palladius quamuis peccator et fragilis, sancte Autissiodorensis ecclesie episcopus,[2] omnibus Dei fidelibus et in Christiana ueritate perseuerantibus, pax perpetua et salus eterna in Domino Ihesu Christo redemptore nostro. Magnum et mirabile donum Dei est cum de temporalibus et transitoriis atque caducis rebus premia acquiruntur in celis sine

---

1 Dagobert became king of Austrasia in 623, then king of all the Franks between 629 and 639.

2 Bishop Palladius of Auxerre (623–59).

fine mansura.[3] Vnde ego spem magnam et fiduciam habens in Domino cogitaui ut aliquod memoriale Deo deuouere et ad perfectum deducere non tardarem. Propterea cognoscat omnis sancta Dei ecclesia et omnes eius ministri tam sacerdotes et confessores quam et laici ordinis utriusque sexus, meis laboribus propriis et impensionibus pro uita eterna promerenda et Christiana religione amplificanda, in cellam siue cenobium in suburbano Autissiodorensi construxisse in basilicis tribus, id est domne Marie perpetue uirginis et matris Domini, et domni Andree apostoli, et Sancti Iuliani martyris cum oratoriiis sancti Ferreoli et Sancti Martini, annuente et consolante domno nostro Dagoberto piissimo rege.

Ordinaui et statui, qualiter ibi sanctimoniales puelle et uidue Domino deseruire sinceriter debeant, deputans quasdam res ex ipsa ecclesia episcopatus Sancti Stephani, que mihi indigno a Deo commissus est, et addens insuper tres agros nobilissimos, quos mihi prefatus domnus Dagobertus sua largicione concessit, id est Mitiganna in territorio Senonico cum omnibus appendiciis suis, et in territorio Autissiodorensi Vincella super Ycannam fluuium.[4] Similiter in eodem pago Truciacum,[5] cum omnibus iure ad se pertinentibus. De rebus autem ecclesie mee ordinaui, ut ibi deseruire debeant, in pago Autissiodorensi uillam que dicitus Vallis, et Clamiciacum super Ycannam fluuium, et Flaciacum[6] quam dominus Desiderius papa[7] de Godino et eius heredibus per pecuniam uisus est recepisse. Et in pago Aualense coloniam Audunacum,[8] et in territorio Senonico Campobassum, in pago quoque Trecasino agellum nuncupantem[9] Ruliacum, et in territorio Tornodorensi Criaus.[10] Item in pago Betorico terciam partem agri quod uocatur Sissima,[11] ad luminaria concinenda, reliquas duas ad lumen ecclesie senioris Sancti Stephani reseruatas. Ad hoc autem procurandum et instinsecus diuina religione stabiliendum, res quasdam militares et seruitutes ecclesie mee exercendo, Andegiscium uenerabilem diaconum constituimus

Ad hec addentes, ut singulis diebus in basilicis tribus singulas missas absque reliquo officio sacrarum horarum et diurnali missa cum oblationibus et oratio-

---

3 Luke 16:9.

4 Migennes, in the Senonais, 21 km north-northwest of Auxerre; and Vincelles in the Auxerrois, on the Yonne, 12 km south-southeast of Auxerre.

5 Trucy, 21 km south-southeast of Auxerre.

6 Vaux, 5 km south of Auxerre; Clamecy, 37 km south of Auxerre; and Flacy, 49 km north of Auxerre.

7 Bishop Desiderius of Auxerre (605–23), Palladius's predecessor.

8 Annay-la-Côte, 39 km southeast of Auxerre, in the region of Avallon, which is 42 km south-southeast of Auxerre. The following two places, in the regions of Sens and Troyes, have not been identified.

9 The cartulary reads 'nuncupante.'

10 Cry, 25 km southeast of Tonnerre.

11 The region is Bourges, but the field is not identified.

nibus celebrare non desinant, et xii pauperos cotidie pascant. Quinta uero feria omnibus ebdomadibus cum letaniis et crucibus omnis illa congregatio ad basilicam seniorem Sancti Stephani infra muros uenire non desinat, et ibidem missas celebrent, et triginta pauperos pascant. In cena uero Domini lx pascant et uestiant. In primis pro domino nostro piissimo rege Dagoberto et eius nobilissima stirpe tam preterita quam futura et omnibus Christianis regibus, et pro me pecatore et omnibus antecessoribus et successoribus meis qui in hac sancta sede sederunt uel sedem habebunt, et pro omni populo sancto Dei.

Si quis uero quod futurum esse non credo, nisi Deus fieri permittat, qui hanc religionem et elemosinam a mea paruitate institutam destruere presumpserit, aut de potestate huius ecclesie pontificis abstrahere uel minuere de hiis que supra diximus, uel que Deus ibi augere uoluerit, dyabolica plenus nequitia auferre temptauerit, queque ille sublimis uel mediocris persona exstiterit, conuocamus contra eum celum et terram, omnes angelos et archangelos, prophetas et patriarchas, et apostolos et martyrium Sancti Stephani et Sancti Iuliani, cum omnibus martyribus, confessoribus et uirginibus et omnibus sanctis Dei, quatinus in primis iram omnipotentis Dei incurrat, et a liminibus sanctorum alienus exsistat, et inferni cum uorago excruciet, et cum Dathan et Abyron, et cum Ananya et Saphyra et Simone Mago sententiam iudicii eterni incurrat, nisi condignam emendationem fecerit, tollatur ne uideat gloriam Dei, neque remittatur illi in presenti seculo, neque in futuro.

Palladius quamuis peccator et fragilis episcopus subscripsit.

I have dated this document to 631, the eighth year of Dagobert's rule as king of Austrasia. If however his regnal years are to be counted from the beginning of his rule as king of all the Franks, then the date is 637. Either date will do for Bishop Palladius. The indiction, however, would suggest 634, which is why that date is traditionally assigned. The establishment of this nunnery, the first in the region, is also mentioned in the ninth-century *Gesta* of the bishops of Auxerre. Before Bishop Palladius, it had been a male house.[12]

Although most Merovingian-era documents have been called forgeries at one time or another, this document gives every sign of authenticity. For example, the title of *papa* for Bishop Desiderius is an indication of a real seventh-century document, for a later forger would not have used the term for anyone but the pope. In addition, the cartulary scribe seems to have had trouble with the normal Merovingian -em abbreviation, rendered as a superscript -e, for there is a *nuncupante* that should be *nuncupantem.*

12 *Gesta,*1:105, 113.

2

814–40

Emperor Louis the Pious, at the request of Count Hugh, confirms the immunity of the nunnery of St-Julien, as his father and preceding kings of the Franks had granted. Louis had granted the nunnery to Hugh.

MANUSCRIPTS: St-Julien cartulary, fol. 1r–v. Bibl. Auxerre, MS 152, pp. 647–8; seventeenth-century copy by Dom Viole. Arch. Yonne H 1668, fol. 1r.

EDITION: Q 1:30–1, no. 15, dated 'ninth century.'

SUMMARY: J.F. Böhmer, *Regesta imperii*, new ed. by Engelbert Mühlbacher, vol. 1, p. 298, no. 744 (719), dated 821.[1]

In nomine Domini Dei et saluatoris nostri Ihesu Christi, Ludouicus diuina ordinante prouidencia imperator augustus.[2] Si erga loca diuinis cultibus mancipata, propter amorem Dei eiusque in eisdem locis si famulantes beneficia opportuna largimur premium, nobis apud Dominum eterne remunerationis rependi non diffidimus. Idcirco notum esse uolumus omnibus fidelibus sancte Dei ecclesie et nostris presentibus scilicet et futuris, quia adiens serenitatem culminis nostri uir illuster Hugo comes[3] nobis detulit preceptum immunitatis domini genitoris nostri Karoli imperatoris,[4] in quo continebatur insertum qualiter monasterium quo dicitur Sancti Iuliani puellarum, quod est situm non procul ab urbe Autissiodorense constructum in honore Sancte Marie semper uirginis, quod ipse largitionis nostre munere in beneficium habere uidetur, non solum idem domus et genitor noster sed antecessores eius, reges uidelicet Francorum, concessissent eidem monasterio ut nulli episcopi uel archidiaconi loci illius nisi orationem aut predicationem lucrando, nec ullus quilibet iudex publicus uel quislibet ex iudiciaria potestate accinctus, ne ut res uel rebus ipsius monasterii nullum debuisset habere introitum, petens ut similia ob anime nostre remedium predicto contulissemus monasterio.

Cuius petitioni libenter aurem accommodare placuit et hanc nostre auctoritatis preceptionem fieri iussimus per quam precipimus atque iubemus, ut sicut superius insertum est absque ullum introitum episcopi aut archidiaconi, nisi orationem aut predicationem faciendam, sed quod nullus iudex publicus uel quilibet ex iudiciaria potestate in ecclesia aut loca uel agros seu reliquas

---

1 This date is chosen because of the assumption that the Hugh is Hugh of Tours, who would have just become allied with the imperial family in 821.

2 Louis the Pious, emperor (814–40).

3 Hugh 'the Abbot,' of the Welf family. See Constance Brittain Bouchard, *'Those of My Blood,'* p. 18.

4 Charlemagne, king of the Franks (768–814).

possessiones predicti monasterii, quas moderno tempore iuste et legaliter in quibuslibet pagis et territoriis infra ditionem imperii nostri, iuste et legaliter possidet, uel ea que deinceps in iure ipsius monasterii uoluerit diuina pietas augeri, ad causas iudiciario more audiendas aut freda exigenda, aut mansiones uel paratas faciendas, aut fideiussores tollendos, aut homines ipsius monasterii distringendos, nec ullas redibitiones aut illicitas occasiones requirendas ullo unquam tempore ingredi audeat, uel ea que supra memorata sunt penitus exigere presumat, sed liceat rectoribus predicti monasterii sub immunitatis nostre defensione cum rebus et mancipiis ad idem monasterium iure pertinentibus quiete uiuere ac residere. Et quicumque ex inde fiscus noster sperare poterat nullatenus exactetur, nec requiratur qualiter sanctimoniales in eodem monasterio degentes pro nobis actum pro stabilitate imperii nostri, Domini misericordiam exorare delectet. Et ut hec auctoritas firmior habeatur, manu propria subter firmauimus et anuli nostri impressione signari iussimus.

This document is dated by the regnal years of Louis the Pious. It was most likely given late in his reign, when he was married to Judith, his second wife, for Count Hugh 'the Abbot' was her nephew. A less likely identification of the Count Hugh of this charter is Hugh of Tours (d. 837), father of the wife of Lothair I,[5] because a Count Hugh was still lay abbot of the house under Charles the Bald.

It is striking that Louis had no problem making one of his male allies the abbot of a nunnery. It is also striking that Louis's confirmation of immunities for St-Julien follows the seventh-century pattern – used both by Merovingian kings and by Pope Gregory the Great – of kings and bishops voluntarily restricting their access to a monastery and to its revenues. In general, Carolingian 'protection' of monasteries could better be termed 'control.'[6] Although Louis refers to what his father had granted, there is no evidence that a charter of Charlemagne for the nuns ever existed; see the following document.

3

840–75

A privilege of Charles the Bald for St-Julien, issued at the request of Hugh, the lay abbot. He refers to the earlier charters of Bishop Palladius and Louis the Pious.

---

5 This identification is made by Philippe Depreux, *Prosopographie de l'entourage de Louis le Pieux*, pp. 262–3, no. 164.

6 Barbara H. Rosenwein, *Negotiating Space*, pp. 42–97.

MANUSCRIPTS: St-Julien cartulary, fols. 1v–2r. Bibl. Auxerre, MS 152, pp. 649–50; seventeenth-century copy by Dom Viole. Arch Yonne, H 1668, fol. 1r–v.

EDITIONS: Q 1:51–3, no. 26. *Recueil des actes de Charles II le Chauve*, 2:377–80, from the cartulary; dated ca 850–5.

In nomine sancte et individue trinitatis, Karolus Dei gratia rex.[1] Si liberalitatis nostre munere locis Deo dicatis quiddam conferimus beneficii, necessitates ecclesiasticas nostro releuamus iuuamine atque regali tuemur munimine, id nobis et ad mortalem uitam temporaliter transiendam et ad eternam feliciter obtinendam profuturum liquido credimus. Itaque notum sit omnibus fidelibus sancte Dei ecclesie et nostris, presentibus scilicet atque futuris, quia satis dilectus et carissimus nobis Hugo,[2] abbas monasterii Sancte Marie genitricis Christi Sanctique Iuliani martyris Autissiodorensis ecclesie, ad nostram se conferens sublimitatem, obtulit obtutibus nostris quasdam priuilegiorum conscriptiones in quibus continebatur insertum qualiter quasdam res eidem monasterio uirginibusque ibidem Deo sub canonica auctoritate degentibus apostolice sedis antistes uenerandus Gregorius sua auctoritate confirmasset, idipsum a Beato Palladio prefate ciuitatis episcopo obtinente, insuper etiam ostendens auctoritates piissimi imperatoris augusti Ludouici,[3] in quibus continebatur quod non solum idem imperator excellentissimus, uerum etiam predecessores eius, imperatores uidelicet et reges Francorum, iam dictis Deo sacratis ad perpetualiter possidendum et ad supplementum uictus et uestitus preceptis et auctoritatibus annotassent. Sed pro rei infirmitate postulauit nobis prefatus abbas ut, paternum seu antecessorum nostrorum regum morem sequentes, hoc preceptum nostre auctoritatis fieri de uniuersis rebus iuste et legaliter ipsi monasterio competentibus, uidelicet de areis tribus in ciuitate sitis et de pratis et terris super fluvium Belche[4] et de rebus circa monasterium constitutis, scilicet de uilla que uocatur Vallis[5] cum cella Sancti Lupi et alteram iuxta eam que uocatur Poziacus, in Nantilla[6] quoque uilla mansum parceringum unum, et in Bercuaco uilla,[7] et

1 King Charles the Bald of the West Franks (840–77).

2 Hugh, called 'the Abbot,' of the Welf family, uncle of Rudolph I of Burgundy. See Constance Brittain Bouchard, *'Those of My Blood,'* p. 18.

3 These are references to documents 1 and 2. The confirmation of Pope Gregory is otherwise unknown. It most likely refers to Pope Gregory I the Great (590–604). According to the *Gesta* of the bishops of Auxerre, composed not long after this charter, Gregory the Great had written to Bishop Desiderius; *Gesta*, 1:87.

4 The Baulche stream flows from the southwest and joins the Yonne shortly north of Auxerre.

5 Vaux, 5 km south of Auxerre.

6 There used to be places called Poizy and Nantelle in the commune of Vaux.

7 St-Georges, 3 km west of Auxerre.

in Graciaco uilla iuxta Sanctum Priscum,[8] et in Valente uilla,[9] et in circuitu monasterii uineas et terras aquarum cursus cum mancipiis utrusque sexus ibidem commorantibus; Clamiciacum quoque uillam in eodem comitatu sitam;[10] in pago quoque Aquitanico uillam que uocatur Sisina,[11] et in comitatu Senonico uilla Mitiganna,[12] in comitatu Wastinensi Ipduaco uillam.[13] Cuius suggestionem ac rationabilem petitionem annuere placuit et quicquid ut predictum est postulauit ad effectum perducere curauimus.

Proinde hos nostre auctoritatis apices erga predictas monasterii basilicas uirginesque inibi Domino seruientes diuino inspirante amore fieri iussimus, per quos decernimus atque sancimus ut loca supra nominata cum omnibus ad se iuste et legaliter pertinentibus, sicut a sepe dictis imperatoribus et regibus collata sunt, ita per hanc nostram auctoritatem in earum iure ac potestate absque alicuius diminoratione aut retractione permaneant, et ut nullus successor abbas uidelicet aut rector memorati monasterii ab earum donatione ea quoquo modo auferre aut in aliam partem transferre presumat, quatenus sublata omni indigencia uictus et uestimentorum pro nobis coniuge proleque nostra et pace ac stabilitate tocius regni a Deo nobis commissi alacrius eas indesinenter Dei misericordiam exorare delectet. Et hec nostre confirmationis auctoritas pleniorem in Dei nomine obtineat firmitatem, de anulo nostro subter iussimus sigillari.

Hugh 'the Abbot' was lay abbot of St-Julien; see the preceding document. Although the document cannot be dated more exactly than by the reign of Charles the Bald as king (before he bcame emperor), it was most likely relatively early in his reign.

4

Auxerre, 18 February 1043

Count Geoffrey reaches an agreement with Emma, abbess of St-Julien, over claims that his father, also named Geoffrey, had made against the nunnery. The

8 There used to be a hamlet called Grisy in the commune of St-Bris, which is 10 km southeast of Auxerre.

9 Vallan, 7 km south-southwest of Auxerre.

10 Clamecy, 37 km south of Auxerre. It, as well as Vaux and Migennes, was among the original property given the nuns in the seventh century.

11 I have not identified this villa, located in Aquitaine; it was among the original property given the nuns.

12 Migennes, in the Senonais, 21 km north-northwest of Auxerre.

13 I have not identified this villa, located in the Gâtinais.

count acts with his mother, Adelaide, and his brothers, Archbishop Gilduin of Sens and Rainard.

MANUSCRIPTS: St-Julien cartulary, fol. 2r. Arch. Yonne H 1668, fols. 1v–2r.
EDITIONS: GC 12, instr. cols. 101–2, no. 3, dated 1044. Q 1:178–80, no. 93; dated 1043, from GC and the cartulary.

In nomine sancte et indiuidue trinitatis. Ego Gaufridus comes notum uolo fieri quod uenit ad nostram presentiam Emma uenerabilis abbatissa monasterii Sancte Marie Sanctique Iuliani martyris quod est situm extra muros Autissiodorensis ciuitatis, deprecans ut in ipso monasterio Deo seruientibus certam fieri iuberem de quibusdam malis consuetudinibus, quas domnus Gaufredus pater meus in uita sua uuirpiuit Deo et Sancte Marie uirgini, et Sancto precissimo Christi martyri Iuliano, per deprecationem matris mee Aahelaidis, consensu et consilio meo et fratrum meorum, Gilduini uidelicet archiepiscopi Senonensis,[1] et Rainardi, et fidelium ministrorumque nostrorum.

Ego igitur Gaufredus filius eius post obitum patris confirmo ea que ipse fecit pro remedio anime sue, ut qui particeps fui in peccato quod habuit, fiam particeps in penitencia qua penituit, et in elemosina si qua sit. In comitatu Senonico et in uilla que uocatur Mitiganna[2] uuirpio totas malas consuetudines et usurpationes quas per malos ministros inueni, pro anima mea et ancessorum meorum, Deo et sanctis eius, acceptis de bonis ipsius loci exceptis banno raptu et incendio. Vt nullus umquam aliqua accipere presumat in ipsa uilla nec minister nec seruiens in perpetuum, nisi ancille Dei iam dicti monasterii almi Iuliani, ut possint Deo seruire quiete per tempora succedencia. Si quis uero quod absit hoc infringere uoluerit, uel cupiditate cecatus aliquid acceperit, cum dyabolo et angelis eius dampnatus in inferno cum malis et perditis hominibus ardeat, et perpetue maledictioni et excommunicationi subiaceat, et hec carta firma in eternum permaneat.

Vt autem firma sit et firma hec nostra uuirpio uigeat, firmaui manu propria et manibus fratrum meorum, id est archiepiscopi et Fulconis, cuius consilio facta est, manibusque fidelium meorum tradidi firmandam. Actum publice Autissiodoro in monasterio Sancti Iuliani gloriosi martyris, sub die xii kalendas Martii, regnante Henrico Francorum rege,[3] anno xii. Que quidem carta signata est signo predicti comitis, signo ministeris et fratrum ipsius et aliorum plurimorum, et sigillata sigillo Gilduini archiepiscopi Senonensi et eiusdem comitis fratris.

1 Gilduin, archbishop of Sens (1030–49).
2 Migennes, 21 km north-northwest of Auxerre.
3 Henry I, king of France (1031–60).

Although Count Geoffrey is not explicitly identified, it seems certain that he was the count of Joigny.

5

Sens, 1164

Archbishop Hugh of Sens and two cardinals settle a quarrel between Abbess Agnes of St-Julien and Count Rainard of Joigny, over four men that both claimed. When the abbess had complained to the archbishop, the count had appealed to the pope. The count now frees the men and their families from his jurisdiction, influenced in part by his sister, a nun at St-Julien.

MANUSCRIPTS: St-Julien cartulary, fol. 2r–v. Arch. Yonne H 1668, fol. 2r. Arch. Yonne H 1711; a seventeenth-century copy, from the cartulary.
EDITIONS: GC 12, instr. cols. 128–9, no. 42. Q 2:165–7.

Nos Hugo Dei gratia Senonensis archiepiscopus[1] et Humbaudus Hostiensis episcopus et Odo diaconus cardinalis Sancti Nicholai in carcere Tulliano. Notum fieri uolumus presentibus et futuris quod inter Agnetem abbatissam S. Iuliani Autissiodorensis et Rainardum comitem Ioigniaci[2] controuersia agitabatur super quatuor hominibus, Gosberto, Anulfo, Rainardo, Horrico, quos predicta abbatissa in potestate Migrannie[3] seruientes suos constituerat. Que controuersia per querelam predicte abbatisse ad audientiam unius nostrum Hugonis Senonensis archiepiscopi deducta fuisset, predictus comes ad audientiam domini pape Alexandri,[4] qui tunc Senonis erat, appellauit. Cum autem utraque pars pro eadem appellatione ad presenciam domini pape conuenisset, dominus papa eandem causam nobis Humbaudi Hostiensi episcopo et Odoni cardinali audiendam terminandamque commisit.

Post diutinam autem et prolixam eiusdem cause uentilationem, causa illa per concordiam et transactionem hoc modo finita et determinata est, quod comes predictos quatuor homines et uxores eorum et liberos in perpetuum liberos et absolutos dimisit abbatisse et monasterio Sancti Iuliani, ita ut in eis nullam habeat iustitiam exacturam seu requisituram, seu in uxoribus siue liberis eorum, quandiu seruientes fuerint, et ministeriales predicti monasterii extiterint. Cum autem seruientes seu ministeriales esse desierint, habeat in eis sicut in propriis

1 Hugh of Toucy, archbishop of Sens (1143–68).
2 Count Rainard IV of Joigny (1137–72). Joigny, 25 km north-northwest of Auxerre.
3 Migraine was the name of the area just northwest of Auxerre.
4 Pope Alexander III (1159–81).

hominibus Sancti Iuliani. Confessus est etiam et protestatus predictus comes in presencia nostra se nichil in nemore Sancti Iuliani quod est in Otha,[5] excepta gruaria. Quod autem predictus comes a controuersia illa, tam super predictis hominibus quam super nemore omnino discessit, hoc fecit intuitu sororis sue que in eodem erat monasterio,[6] et respectu gratie et amoris abbatisse eiusdem et nostrarum etiam precum interuentu.

Huius autem transactionis seriem presentis scripti pagina iussimus annotari, et sigillorum nostrorum impressione et mandato utriusque partis iussimus insigniri. Huius rei testes sunt Stephanus abbas Sancti Remigii Senonensis, Guillermus Senonensis ecclesie prepositus, Guido Sancti Stephani Autissiodorensis prepositus, Stephanus Autissiodorensis archipresbiter, magister Henricus Autissiodorensis canonicus, Obertus de Madriaco,[7] Petrus Rusellus capellanus abbatisse, Odo maior abbatisse, Rainaudus Cheneuox. Ex parte uero comitis, Garinus filius uicecomitis Senonensis, Odo Liboz, Stephanus Coeniz, Hugo prepositus Ioigniaci, Guillermus Burgaudus. Actum est hoc publice Senonis, anno ab incarnatione Domini MCLXIIII, Alexandro papa presidente, regnante Ludouico rege Francorum,[8] Hugone archiepiscopo Senonensi.

Although this quarrel was supposedly settled at this time, it dragged on for another eighteen years; see the following document.

6

Lateran, 21 January 1182

Pope Lucius III recalls the quarrel between Abbess Agnes of St-Julien and Count Rainard of Joigny over four men that both had claimed. The pope confirms the earlier settlement at the request of Abbess Heluise.

MANUSCRIPTS: St-Julien cartulary, fol. 2v. Arch. Yonne H 1668, fol. 2r–v.

EDITIONS: GC 12, instr. cols. 137–8, no. 54. PL 201:1098, no. 27, from GC; mistakenly dated 27 January.

SUMMARIES: Q 2:167, no. 150; dated 1181–5. Philip Jaffe, *Regesta pontificum Romanorum*, new ed. by Wilhelm Wattenbach, vol. 2, p. 436, no. 14572 (9446).

---

5 The forest of Othe, northeast of Auxerre and Joigny.

6 His sister Heluise later became abbess; GC 12, instr. cols. 139–40, no. 57.

7 Merry, 28 km south of Auxerre.

8 King Louis VII of France (1137–80).

Lucius episcopus seruus seruorum Dei,[1] dilectis in Christo filiabus Hel[uise] abbatisse[2] et sororibus Sancti Iuliani Autissiodorensis, salutem et apostolicam benedictionem. Ex tenore scripti autentici nobis innotuit, quod cum inter Agnetem abbatissam eiusdem monasterii uestri, et R[ainardum] comitem Ioigniaci,[3] super quatuor hominibus, Gosberto uidelicet, Anulpho, Rainardo et Hurrico, quos abbatissa in potestate Migannie suos constituerat seruientes, controuersia mota per appellationem ad sancte recordationis Alexandris pape predecessoris nostri,[4] qui tunc erat Senonis, audientiam peruenisset eam nobis et bone memorie Odoni Sancti Nicholai in carcere Tulliano diacono cardinali terminandam commisit. Post diutinam autem et prolixam uentilationem ipsius cause, de uoluntate partium mediantibus nobis finem per huius transactionem accepit. Quod comes predictos quatuor homines, uxores eorum et liberos imperpetuum absolutos ipsi abbatisse et monasterio uestro dimisit, ita ut in eis nullam iustitia habeat exactionem uel requisitionem, quandiu seruientes et ministeriales monasterii predicti extiterint. Cum uero seruientes siue ministeriales esse desierint, habeant in eis sicut in propriis hominibus monasterii uestri. Confessus est etiam et protestatus ipse comes se nichil habere in nemore Sancti Iuliani quod est in Otha,[5] excepta gruaria. Sed quod a controuersia hominum et nemoris omnino discessit pro reuerencia nostrarum precum et intuitu sororis sue que in monasterio uestro erat, et propter abbatissam hoc egit. Quia igitur compositionem prescriptam ut maiorem habeat firmitatem scripto nostro queritis confirmari. Nos uestris postulationibus annuentes, eam sicut a partibus sponte recepta est et seruata auctoritate apostolica confirmamus, et presentis scripti patrocinio communimus, statuentes ut nulli omnino hominum liceat hanc paginam nostre confirmationis infringere, uel ei ausu temerario contraire. Si quis autem hoc attemptare presumpserit, indignationem omnipotentis Dei et beatorum Petri et Pauli apostolorum eius se nouerit incursurum. Datum Laterani, xii kalendas Februarii.

For this quarrel, see the preceding document. The charter can be dated to 1182 because that was the only year that the pope was at the Lateran in January. The cartulary scribe was clearly very selective, because she did not copy other charters from roughly the same period, covering similar quarrels, which still exist.

---

1 Pope Lucius III (1181–5).

2 Heluise of Joigny, abbess of St-Julien. She was sister of the count; GC 12, instr. cols. 139–40, no. 57.

3 Count Rainard IV of Joigny (1137–72).

4 Alexander III (1159–81). This is a reference to the preceding document.

5 The forest of Othe.

7

March 1209

Philip, official of the curia of Sens, settles a quarrel between the count of Joigny and the abbess of St-Julien. The nuns had complained that the count and his men had stayed in one of their houses without permission and fished in their pond, especially undesirable because men should not be in a nuns' house. The quarrel is settled in favour of the abbess.

MANUSCRIPTS: St-Julien cartulary, fol. 2v. Arch. Yonne H 1668, fol. 2r.

Magister Philippus curialis Senonensis officialis, omnibus presentes litteras inspecturis, in Domino salutem. Nouerint uniuersi quod cum in curia Senonensis diutius litigassent nobilis comes Ioigniaci ex una parte et uenerabilis abbatissa et conuentus Sancti Iuliani Autissiodorensis ex altera. Pars abbatisse et conuentus componebant contra dictum comitem quod contra iusticiam, et tam regule quam iuris ordinem in domo sua de Sancto Angelo hospitabatur eis inuitis et in proprio stanno eiusdem domus piscabatur, quod ei non lidcebit. Tamque satis inhonestum est quod tantus uir et qui tales homines secum ducit in domo religiosa et maxime ubi moniales habitant hospitentur. Tamque iure alterius nemo de iure sine uoluntate Domini debet presumere. Opponebat etiam eidem comiti quod quoddam nemus quod Chasnetum[1] uocatur posuerat in foresta que ei non licebat et quod in nemore Sancti Iuliani quatuor posuerat forestarios, ubi non nisi unicum ponere debebat. E contrario procurator comitis datus ad totam causam et de speciali mandato in animam ipsius comitis iuratus respondebat quod re uera comes iacuerat in domo Sancti Angeli, et quod in stanno eiusdem comus piscatus fuerat, sicut pater eius qui multociens ibi expensis propriis iacuerat et piscatur fuerat in stanno.

Requisitus etiam utrum credetur quod de iure ibi debetur iacere uel piscari nichil aliud rendit nisi quod ita fecerant multociens pater eius et antecessores sui. Licebat etiam ei ut asserebat in nemore predicto ponere quotquot uellet seruientes ad suas feras ratione gruarie quam in illo nemore habebat conseruandas, nec eos habebat pro forestariis, sed unicum posuerat et poneret, nec nemus de Thasneto nisi quantum ad homines suos posuerat in foresta. Saluo tamen iure tam ecclesie Sancti Iuliani, quam hominum suorum in omnibus et per omnia.

Tandem auditis super hiis omnibus allegoribus rationibus et confessoribus utriusque partis, cum ex parte comitis melius fuisset ostensium per quod ius usus, uel seruitus in predictis et competeret, et petitorio coram nobis ageretur iudicio, de prudentum in usque iure consilio per senteniam diffinitiuam

1 Chastenay, 22 km southwest of Auxerre.

iudicauimus quod dictus comes secundum ea que allegata fuerunt et proposita, nec in domo Sancti Angeli hospitari, nec in stanno piscari, nec etiam nemus quod Chasnetum uocatur in foresta ponere poterat sine licenciam abbatisse. Iudicamus etiam quod in predicto nemore Sancti Iuliani non potest ponere nisi unicum forestarium. Sed ratione guarie que secundum confessionem utriusque partis ad ipsum comitem pertinet, licebit ei quattuor uel quinque uel etiam sex seruientes ponere qui custodiant feras suas. Ita quod ex illa custodia uel seruientum apponere ecclesie Sancti Iuliani nullum generetur preiudicum uel grauamen. Actum anno gratie MCC octauo, mense Marcio.

This document has not been previously printed. Although the count is not named, he was William I (1177-1221). The date is 1209 in 'new style.'

8

June 1214

William I, count of Joigny, settles his quarrel with St-Julien over the woods of Othe. They will both have rights there, including that of pasturing pigs. William's wife, Countess Beatrix, confirms.

MANUSCRIPTS: St-Julien cartulary, fol. 3r–v. Arch. Yonne H 1668, fols. 2v–3v.
EDITION: Q 3:67–8, no. 148; from the cartulary.

Ego Willelmus comes Ioigniaci[1] notum facio uniuersis tam presentibus quam futuris quod cum controuersia uersaretur inter me ex una parte et uenerabilem abbatissam Sancti Iuliani Autissiodorensis et conuentus eiusdem ecclesie ex altera parte super nemore de Otha[2] quod dicitur nemus Sancti Iuliani, tandem de consilio bonorum uirorum et discretorum talis inter nos compositio facta est, quod de consensu partium, scilicet mei comitis et abbatisse et conuentus Sancti Iuliani, tercia pars illius nemoris quam comes Ioigniaci uoluerit ponetur in foresta usque ad triginta annos, ita quod de illa tercia parte alter sine altero nec dare nec uendere aliquid poterit, nec accipere usque ad finem illius termini. Sed ex tunc abbatissa Sancti Iuliani illam terciam partem uendere poterit per loca et monstratas si uoluerit, ita quod comes Ioigniaci qui in fundo tocius nemoris illius octauam habet partem pro bono pacis. De cetero per compositionem de consilio bonorum uirorum inter nos factam, quartam partem habebit precii

1 Count William I of Joigny (1177–1221).
2 The forest of Othe, which stretches northeast of Joigny.

omnium uenditionum nemoris et panagii, salua parte Yterii[3] militis de Brione[4] qui in fundo illius nemoris sextadecimam habet partem. Abbatissa uero ponere poterit quinquaginta porcos tantum, comes similiter Ioigniaci quinquaginta et non plures moraturos in illa foresta, a festo Sancti Remigii usque ad Natale Domini annuatim, ita quod neuter alia animalia ponere poterit nisi de mutuo consensu. Post terminum autem triginta annorum elapsum, si abbatissa illam terciam partem que in foresta posita erat uendere uoluerit, ei licebit per monstratas et loca, comite non requisito, ita quod de aliis duabus partibus medietas quam comes Ioigniaci uoluerit in foresta ponetur ab illo termino in triginta annos, sicut superius dictum est de prima tercia parte, ita quod supradicta forma pacis semper duret de nemore uendendo. De aliis autem duabus partibus dictum fuit et hinc inde concessum quod abbatissa per loca et monstratas pro uoluntate sua uendere poterit, ita quod si aliquam monstratam uendiderit, aliam monstratam uendere non poterit donec monstrata illa sublata sit et ab emptore relicta. Sed per loca uendere poterit interim et in uendita monstrata nec comes Ioigniaci nec abbatissa currere poterunt quousque sit ab emptore relicta. Successiue autem uendite monstrate in foresta ponentur usque ad quindecim annos nec infra uendi poterunt nisi de consensu mutuo. Quindecim autem annis elapsis, abbatissa uendere poterit, sicut prius. Verumtamen comes Ioigniaci quartam partem precii nemoris illius habebit, siue per monstrata uendita sit uel per loca. Si autem per monstratam abbatissa uendere uoluerit, significabitur hoc comiti, uel senescallo, uel preposito Ioigniaci, uel illi qui loco prepositi erit infra octo dies postquam palmata uenditionis facta fuerit. Et si ab illa die qua comiti uel alicui predictorum significatum fuerit aliquis emptor apparuerit infra mensem qui uenditionem ab abbatissa factam de sexta parte uel plus annuitare uoluerit, eam habebit per manum abbatisse, et hoc modo crescere poterit uenditio usque ad prefatum terminum, consideratis omnibus circumstanciis, tam circa terminos de pagis faciendis quam circa alia commoda. Si autem per loca uendiderit abbatissa, significabit hoc forestario comitis, et si ab illa die qua significatum fuerit aliquis emptor apparuerit infra octo dies qui uenditionem ab abbatissa factam uel a mandato eius de sexta parte aut de plus annuitare uoluerit, eam habebit omnibus circumstanciis consideratis sicut superius dictum est. Et si aliquis pro palmata annuitate uenditionis aliquid habuerit, de communi soluetur. Si uero infra terminos memoratos nullus emptor apparuerit qui modo predicto annuitaret, prima teneret uenditio. Si autem illi qui usuarium habent in nemore in monstratis uenditis uellent currere, sicut prius, comes Ioigniaci et abbatissa tenentur bona fide garentire uenditionem factam quantum ius permitteret.

3 The cartulary reads 'Yteri.'

4 Brion, 6 km northeast of Joigny.

Domus Sancti Angeli cum pourprisia et palicio a porta usque ad posticum iuxta ulmum et inde usque ad furnum, et a furno usque ad eandem portam, libera est ab omni iusticia comitis Ioigniaci, excepto quod si aliquis aliquid forefactum perpetraret ibi propter quod debeat mori uel mutilari, ibidem iudicatus ab abbatissa nudus comiti traderetur Ioigniaci, uel eius mandato. Extra pourprisiam predictam comes Ioigniaci totalem habet iusticiam, excepto forefacto de nemore facto. De proprio uino suo propriam tabernam facere poterunt moniales, alii autem in pourprisia sepedicta tabernam facere non poterunt, nec in propria pourprisia monialium in taberna potatores sedebunt ad potandum uel ludendum. De cuniculis dictum fuit quod si forte infra dictam pourprisiam fortuito casu uenerit, si eos moniales uel aliquis de earum familia ceperit, sine iniuria comitis Ioigniaci et offensa erit. Alia autem animalia nec infra nec extra capere poterunt. Et notandum quod abbatissa supradicto modo uendere poterit, non obstante griaria uel iusticia comitis Ioigniaci quas habet comes in totali nemore. Abbatissa uero tres habebit forestarios et comes duos ad custodiendum nemus. Forefactum uero de nemore factum quod forestarius comitis Ioigniaci inueniret per se comitis erit. Et si forestarius abbatisse inueniret per se, abbatisse erit. Si autem ad forefactum uenirent simul forestarius comitis et forestarius abbatisse, equaliter inter eos emenda forefacti diuidetur. Comes autem Ioigniaci quotquot uoluerit seruientes in nemore ponere poterit ad custodiendum uenationem suam qui non erunt forestarii. Et si uiolencia dictis forestariis uel alicui eorum inferretur, dicti seruientes eos iuuare poterunt. Preterea de prima tercia parte que primo posita est in foresta usque ad triginta annos dictum fuit et hinc inde concessum quod quando per monstratas uendetur, si aliquis emptor infra mensem apparuerit, uel per loca infra ebdomadam, ita erit sicut de aliis uenditoribus et annuntiatoribus dictum est.

Has igitur conuentiones superius annotatas et istius formam compositionis, ego Willelmus comes Ioigniaci bona fide me obseruaturum iuraui, et si quod absit me uel meos super premissis in aliquo articulo contingeret intercipere, a facta commonitione postquam inde essemus requisiti infra quindenam teneremur emendare. Quod ut ratum sit et firmum et imperpetuum robur obtineat, in harum conuentionum et istius compositionis et tocius facti memoriam necnon et testimonium presentem cartam sigilli mei munimine feci fidelicter roborari.

Ego uero Beatrix comitissa Ioigniaci[5] has conuentiones et istius formam compositionis totumque factum a domino meo nobili uiro Willelmo comite Ioigniaci ordinatum, sicut in presenti cartula continetur, laudo, concedo, et ratum habeo. In cuius facti memoriam presentem cartam sigilli mei impressione signaui.

---

5 Beatrix, countess of Joigny. She later acted as regent for their son, William II. Theodore Evergates, *The Aristocracy in the County of Champagne*, p. 159.

Actum anno dominice incarnationis duecentesimo quatrodecimo, mense Iunio.

This agreement was repeated, in essentially the same terms, throughout the rest of the thirteenth century; see the following documents.

9

May 1236

Count William II of Joigny settles his quarrels with the abbess of St-Julien. He recognizes that the woods of Boulay belongs to the nuns. He also reconfirms the agreement with St-Julien reached by his father, William I.

MANUSCRIPTS: St-Julien cartulary, fols. 3v–4r. 1236. Arch. Yonne H 1668, fols. 3v–4r.
SUMMARY: Q 3:68, no. 148.

Ego Guillelmus comes Ioigniaci[1] notum facio omnibus tam presentibus quam futuris quod de querelis que erant inter me ex una parte et abbatissam Sancti Iuliani Autissiodorensis ex altera pacificatum est in hunc modum, quod de boscho de Boeleto[2] qui est in terram Sancti Iuliani recognosco et concedo quod abbatissa et conuentus Sancti Iuliani in eo possunt capere alto basso omnia necessaria ad usum suum et domorum suarum, et debeo dictum boschum bona fide custodire. Recognosco etiam quod dicta abbatissa habet medietatem in omnibus hayis de Buissiaco[3] ubique sint et teneor dictas hayas tenere in foresta, custodire et garentire, bona fide secundum ius, nec possum de dictis hayis aliquid capere, dare, uendere uel partiri sine assensu abbatisse, nec abbatissa sine me, et si contigerit dictas hayas exartari, terra abbatisse remanebit ad uoluntatem suam faciendam. De nemore usuagii in quo homines de Migenna, de Buissiaco, et de Brione[4] habent usuagium, recognosco et concedo quod abbatissa et conuentus in eo possunt capere alto basso omnia necessaria ad usum suum et domorum suarum, et de eodem nemore potest uendere abbatissa per loca et monstratas sicut uoluerit, item tamen quod habeam quartam partem precii uenditionis que fiet ab abbatissa, et abbatissa tres partes dicti precii, salua

1 Count William II of Joigny (1225–44).

2 Boulay, 30 km east-northeast of Joigny.

3 Bussy, 9 km northeast of Joigny.

4 Migennes, 7 km east of Joigny; Bussy; and Brion, 6 km northeast of Joigny.

sextadecima parte heredum defuncti Iterii de Brione militis,[5] de qua sextadecima parte teneor soluere quartam dictis heredibus partem, et abbatissam erga eos liberare. Ego uero de dicto nemore nichil possum uendere, nec circularios, nec carbonarios in eo mittere, nec ad proprium usum sine uenditione aliqua facienda. Et cum dicta abbatissa de dicto nemore per loca uel monstratas uenditerit, significabit hoc forestario meo, et si ab illa die qua significatum fuerit aliquis emptor apparuerit infra octo dies qui uenditionem ab abbatissa factam, uel a mandato eius, de sexta parte aut de plus augmentare uoluerit, omnibus circumstanciis consideratis, tam circa terminos de pagis faciendis, quam circa alia commoda, eam habebit. Et si aliquis pro palmata augmentare uenditionis aliquid habuerit de communi soluetur. Recognosco etiam et concedo quod in toto nemore, foreste, hayarum, usuagii, et boeleti predictorum non possum domum stanguum uel aliud edificium facere uel habere, nec partiri dicta nemora, siue partionem requirere, nec abbatissa partiri similiter.

Recognosco etiam et concesso quod illam partem nemoris quod dicitur Sancti Iuliani que posita est in foresta, a bone memorie Willelmo patre meo,[6] et dictis abbatissa et conuentu, tenere teneor in foresta custodire et garentire,[7] erga omnes bona fide secundum ius, nec possum de eo aliquid dare, capere, uel uendere, nec partiri siue partitionem requirere, nec similiter dictis abbatisse et conuentui licet de dicto nemore aliquid capere, dare, uel partiri, sine meo assensu. Sed de eodem nemore uendere poterit abbatissa comite non requisito per loca et monstratas. Successiue uendite monstrate in foresta ponentur usque ad quindecim annos, nec infra uendi poterunt, nisi de mutuo consensu. Quindecim autem annis elapsis abbatissa uendere poterit, uerumptamen comes Ioigniaci quartam partem precii nemoris uenditi habebit, siue per monstratas uendiderit siue per loca. Si autem abbatissa per monstratas siue per loca uendiderit, significabit hoc comiti uel senescallo uel preposito Ioigniaci uel illi qui loco prepositi erit infra octo dies postquam palmata uenditionis facta fuerit. Et si ab illa die qua comiti uel alicui predictorum significatum fuerit aliquis emptor apparuerit infra mensem qui uenditionem ab abbatissa factam de sexta parte uel plus augmentare uoluerit, eam habebit per manum abbatisse, et hoc modo crescere poterit uenditio usque ad prefixum terminum, consideratis omnibus circumstanciis, tam circa terminos de pagis faciendis quam circa alia commoda. De quarta parte sextedecime partis precii uenditionis teneor liberare abbatissam erga heredes defuncti Yterii de Brione militis, qui in totali nemore foreste et usuagii sextamdecimam habent partem. Teneor insuper garentire et

5 He is also mentioned in the preceding document.

6 Count William I of Joigny (1177–1221).

7 This is a reference to document 8.

deffendere bona fide secundum ius omnes uenditiones que a dicta abbatissa de dicto nemore fient inperpetuum. Recognoso etiam et concedo quod abbatissa et conuentus uendiderunt de dicto nemore circiter mille et trecenta arpenta, etiam dicte abbatissa et conuentus associauerunt me ad medietatem precii uenditionis que fiet a dicta abbatissa de residuo predicte foreste, hac sola et unica uice, ita quod postquam hac sola et unica uice uendita fuerit, nequam postea potero petere in uenditionibus predicte foreste quantumque fient, nisi quartam partem. Et teneor garentire istam uentam ad quam dicte abbatissa et conuentus associauerunt me ad medietatem, hoc modo quod si aliquis super illo nemore dampnum mercatoribus intulerit uel uenditionem nemoris arrestauerit, ego dampna teneor reddere sine abbatissa et conuentu, et dictum nemus mercatoribus garentire, et mercatores solutionem partis pecunie que me continget de dicta uenditione quoniam fiet diffendere poterunt, quousque dampna sua dictis mercatoribus fuerint restituta, et uenditio nemoris liberata. Et quantum arrestatio durauerit, tantum liberatoris dicti nemoris prorogabitur tempore, nec propter hoc retardabitur uel impedietur solutio pecunie abbatisse, nec de aliquo impedimento aut arrestatione dicti nemoris, mercatores aliquam actionem uel recursum ad abbatissam habere poterunt. Teneor insuper in me suscipere omnem garenciam et omnem defensionem dicte uenditionis quoniam fiet contra omnes qui in nemore uendito ratione usuagii, uel aliqua alia ratione uoluerint aliquid reclamare, et de omnibus hiis teneor me obligare erga mercatores dicte uente, etiam pro hiis conuentionibus a me comite adimplendis associauerunt me dicte abbatissa et conuentus ad medietatem precii dicte uenditionis, et sub eisdem conuentionibus faciet dicta abbatissa uenditionem. Teneor insuper soluere heredibus dicti defuncti Yterii medietatem dicte sextedecime partis istius uente, ad quam abbatissa et conuentus me associauerunt ad medietatem, et eas teneor erga dictos heredes de dicta medietate sextedecime partis liberare. Recognosco etiam et concedo me habere octauam partem tamen in totali fundo nemorum foreste et usuagii, et in uenditionibus quartam partem. Dominium uero omnium uenditionum predictorum nemorum foreste et usuagii inperpetuum futurarum pertinet ad abbatissam. Recognosco etiam et concedo quod abbatissa potest habere tres forestarios in dicto nemore foreste et usuagii, et ego duos ad custodiendum nemus. Forefactum uero de nemore factum si forestarius meus per se inueniret meum erit. Et si forestarius abbatisse per se inueniret abbatisse erit. Si autem ad forefactum uenirent insimul, forestarius meus et forestarius abbatisse, equaliter inter nos emenda forefacti diuidetur. Recognosco etiam et concedo quod omnes excasure hominum et feminarum de candela tam mobilium quam immobilium quantumque sint de candela inter me et dictam abbatissam per medium diuidentur cum decesserint sine herede ad usum manus mortue. Et terre que a dicta abbatissa tenentur ad terciam ad ipsam deuenient et deuenire debent ab omnibus illis qui eas tenent, siue sint de candela siue non, cum decesserint sine herede ad usum manus mortue. Recognosco etiam et concedo quod abbatissa habet manum mortuam in omnibus hominibus suis apud Ioigniacum, Buissiacum, Colengias Vinosas, Vallem Marcy, et Escoliuas[8] morantibus sanguinem et de homine ecclesie interficto plenariam emendationem. Concedo etiam et promitto quod de propriis rebus dicte ecclesie que tam in uilla de Migenna quam in aliis uillis ad eandem potestamen pertinentibus nichil deinceps accipiam nec ego nec mei.

Hec omnia prenotata ego comes concessi et iuramento corporaliter prestito promisi me in futurum et imperpetuum bona fide obseruaturum, et heredes meos ad hec omnia fideliter obseruanda imperpetuum obligaui, ita quod quicumque de heredibus meis dictam partem dictorum nemorum retinerit, infra quadraginta dies postquam a dicta abbatissa uel eius mandato dicte abbatisse patentes litteras super hoc deferente fuit requisitus, hoc iuramentum facere teneatur abbatisse et conuentui apud Autissiodoro in ecclesia sua de omnibus predictis fideliter obseruandis. Rogaui etiam reuerendum patrem Galterum archiepiscopum Senonis[9] ut super hiis omnibus litteras suas patentes dictis abbatisse et conuentui faciat, in quibus contineatur quod si me uel heredes meos contra predicta in aliquo uenire contigerit, ipse personam meam et dictos heredes excommunis sententie supponeret, et tamdiu suppositas teneret donec essent abbatisse et conuentui omnia plenius emendata. Confirmo etiam et concedo ecclesie Sancti Iuliani omnia que eidem ecclesie concessa sunt a bone memorie Willelmo quodam patre meo comite Ioigniaci et aliis antecessoribus meis sicut in eorum litteris plenius continetur.

Actum anno domini MCC trecesimo sexto, mense Mayo.

The nuns had property located in two principal areas over 30 km apart, one south of Auxerre and the other northeast of Joigny – itself located 24 km northwest of Auxerre. Count William II quarrelled with Pontigny as well as with St-Julien, although most members of his dynasty were generous to that house.[10] There is a blank space, enough for about fifteen lines, at the top of fol. 4v, suggesting the scribe wanted to leave enough space for the preceding document but had already begun copying the next one.

8 The places are Joigny; Bussy, 9 km northeast of Joigny; Coulanges-la-Vineuse, 11 km south of Auxerre; Val-de-Mercy, 14 km south of Auxerre; and Escolives, 9 km south-southeast of Auxerre.

9 Walter III, archbishop of Sens (1223–41).

10 *Le premier cartulaire de l'abbaye cistercienne de Pontigny (XIIe–XIIIe siecles)*, ed. Martine Garrigues, pp. 237–8, no. 190.

10

May 1236

Archbishop Walter of Sens attests to the end of the quarrel between Count William II of Joigny and the abbess and convent of St-Julien. He repeats the concessions that the count had made.

MANUSCRIPTS: St-Julien cartulary, fols. 4v–5v. Arch. Yonne H 1668, fols. 5r–6r.

Omnibus presentes litteras inspecturis, Galterus Dei gratia Senonensis archiepiscopus,[1] salutem in Domino. Nouerit uniuersitas uestra quod in nostra presencia constitutus nobilis uir Willelmus comes Ioigniacensis[2] recognouit quod de querelis que erant inter ipsum ex una parte et abbatissa et conuentus Sancti Iuliani Autissiodorensis ex altera pacificatum erat in hunc modum, quod dicte abbitissa et conuentus Sancti Iuliani in nemore de Booleto[3] possent capere alto et basso omnia necessaria sua ad usum suum et domorum suarum, recognoscens se teneri dictum nemus custodire bona fide. Recognouit etiam quod dicte abbatissa et conuentus habent medietatem in omnibus ayis de Buisiaco[4] ubique sint et quod dictis hayis tenetur tenere in foresta, custodire et garentire bona fide secundum ius, et quod non potest de dictis ayis aliquid capere, dare, uendere uel partiri sine abbatisse assensu, nec abbatissa sine ipsius assensu, et quod si contigerit dictis ayis exartari, terra abbatisse remanebit ad suam uoluntatem faciendam. De nemore usuagii in quo homines de Migenna, de Bussiaco, et de Brione[5] habent usuagium ut dicebant, idem comes recognouit et concessit quod abbatissa et conuentus in eo possunt capere alto et basso omnia necessaria sua ad usum suum et domorum suarum, et quod de eodem nemore potest uendere abbatissa per loca et monstratas, ita tamen quod comes habeat quartam partem precii uenditionis que fiet ab abbatissa, et abbatissa tres partes dicti precii, salua sextadecima parte heredum defuncti Iterii de Brione militis, de qua sextadecima parte dictus comes recognouit se teneri soluere quartam partem dictis heredibus, et abbatissam erga eos liberare. Recognouit etiam prefatus comes quod de dicto nemore nichil potest uendere, nec circularios, nec carbonarios in eo mittere, nisi ad proprium usum sine uenditione aliqua facienda, et quod cum dicta abbatissa de dicto nemore per loca et monstratas uendiderit significabit hoc forestario comitis, et si ab illa die qua significatum fuerit aliquis

1 Walter III, archbishop of Sens (1223–41).

2 Count William II of Joigny (1225–44).

3 Boulay, 30 km east-northeast of Joigny.

4 Bussy, 9 km northeast of Joigny.

5 Migennes, 7 km east of Joigny; Bussy; and Brion, 6 km northeast of Joigny.

emptor apparuerit infra octo dies qui uenditionem ab abbatissa factam uel a mandato eius de sexta parte aut de plus augmentare uoluerit, omnibus circumstanciis consideratis tam circa terminos de pagis faciendis quam circa alia commoda eam habebit per manum abbatisse, et si aliquis pro palmata augmentare uenditionis aliquid habuerit de communi soluetur. Recognouit etiam et concessit dictus comes quod in toto nemore foreste ayarum usuagii et boolety non potest domum stanguum uel aliud edificium facere uel habere, nec partiri dicta nemora siue partitionem requirere, nec abbatissa partiri similiter. Recognouit etiam prefatus comes quod illam partem nemoris quod dicitur Sancti Iuliani que posita est in foresta ut dicebat comes a bone memorie Willelmo patre dicti comitis[6] et dictis abbatissa et conuentu tenere tenetur dictus comes in foresta custodire, garentire, et deffendere erga omnes bona fide secundum ius, nec potest de ea aliquid dare, capere, uel partiri, nec uendere, nec inde partitionem requirere, nec similiter dictis abbatisse et conuentui licet de dicto nemore aliquid capere, dare, uel partiri sine assensu comitis. Sed de eodem nemore uendere poterit dicta abbatissa comite non requisito per loca et monstratas, ita quod successiue monstrate in foresta ponetur, usque ad quindecim annos, nec infra uendi potuerit nisi de mutuo assensu. Quindecim autem annis elapsis, abbatissa uendere poterit. Verumtamen comes Ioigniaci quartam partem precii uenditi habebit siue per loco[7] siue per monstratas uendiderit abbatissa. Si autem abbatissa per monstratas siue per loca uendiderit, significabit hoc comiti, uel senescallo, uel preposito Ioigniaci, uel illi qui loco prepositi erit infra octo dies postquam palmata uenditionis facta fuerit. Et si ab illa die qua comiti uel alicui predictorum significatum fuerit, aliquis emptor apparuerit infra mensem qui uenditionem ab abbatissa factam de sexta parte uel de plus augmentare uoluerit, eam habebit per manum abbatisse, et hoc modo crescere poterit uenditio usque ad prefixum terminum, consideratis omnibus circumstanciis, tam circa terminos de pagis faciendis quam circa alia commoda. Recognouit insuper prefatus comes quod de quarta parte sextedecime partis precii uenditionis tenetur liberare abbatissam erga heredes defuncti Iterii de Brione militis qui in totali nemore foreste et usuagii sextamdecimam habeant partem. Tenetur insuper garentire dictus comes sicut recognouit coram nobis et deffendere bona fide secundum ius omnes uenditiones que a dicta abbatissa fient de dicto nemore imperpetuum. Recognouit etiam et concessit quod abbatissa et conuentus uendiderunt de dicto nemore circiter mille et trecenta arpenta, et quod dicte abbatissa et conuentus associauerunt comitem ad medietatem precii uenditionis que fiet a dicta abbatissa de residuo predicte foreste, ita quod postquam hac sola et

6 Count William I of Joigny (1177–1221).

7 The correct form would be ‘loca.’

unica uice uendita fuerit, nunquam postea poterunt comes et eius heredes petere in uenditionibus predicte foreste quacumque fient nisi quartam partem, et tenentur dicti comes et eius heredes garentire istam uentam ad quam dicte abbatissa et conuentus associauerunt comitem ad medietatem, hoc modo quod si aliquis super illo nemore dampnum mercatoribus intulerit uel uenditionem nemoris arrestauerit comes tenetur dampna reddere sine abbatissa et conuentu, et dictum nemus mercatoribus garentire et mercatores solutionem partis pecunie que comitem continget de dicta uenditione quoniam fiet diffendere poterunt, quosque dampna sua fuerint dictis mercatoribus restituta, et uenditio nemoris liberata, et quantum arrestatio duruerit tantum liberatoris dicti nemoris prorogabitur nec propter hec retardabitur uel impedietur solutio pecunie abbatisse, nec de aliquo impedimento aut arrestatione dicti nemoris mercatores aliquam actionem uel recursum ad abbatissam habere poterunt. Recognouit etiam prenotatus comes se teneri in se suscipere omnem garentiam et omnem deffensionem dicte uenditionis quoniam fiet, contra omnes qui in nemore uendito ratione usuagii uel aliqua alia ratione uoluerint aliquid reclamare, et de omnibus hiis tenetur dictus comes se obligare erga mercatores dicte uente et pro hiis conuentionibus a predicto comite adimplendis associauerunt dicte abbatissa et conuentus dictum comitem ad medietatem precii dicte uenditionis, et sub eisdem conuentionibus faciet abbatissa dictam uenditionem. Recognouit insuper prenominatus comes se teneri soluere heredibus dicti defuncti Iterii medietatem dicte sextedecime partis istius uente, ad quam abbatissa et conuentus associauerunt dictum comitem ad medietatem et eas terras teneatur prefatus comes erga dictos heredes de dicta medietate sextedecime partis liberare.

Recognouit etiam et concessit prefatus comes se habere octauam partem tamen in totali fundo nemorum foreste et usuagii, et in uenditionibus quartam partem, recognoscens quod dominium omnium uenditionum predictorum nemorum foreste et usuagii imperpetuum futuraram pertinet ad abbatissam. Recognouit etiam et concessit prenotatus comes quod abbatissa poterit habere tres forestarios in dicto nemore foreste et usuagii, et comes duos ad custodiendum nemus. Forefactum uero de nemore factum quod forestarius comitis inueniret per se comitis erit. Et si forestarius abbatisse per se inueniret forefactum abbatisse erit. Si autem ad forefactum uenirent insimul forestarius comitis et abbatisse forestarius, equaliter inter comitem et abbatissam emenda forefacti diuidetur. Recognouit etiam et concessit dictus comes quod omnes excasure hominum et feminarum de candela tam mobilium quam immobilium quantumque sint de candela inter dictum comitem et abbatissam per medium diuidentur cum decesserint sine herede ad usum manus mortue, et terre que a dicta abbatissa tenentur ad terciam ad ipsam deuenient et deuenire debent ab omnibus illis qui eas tenent, siue sint de candela siue non, cum decesserint sine herede ad usum manus mortue, sicut recognouit comes. Recognouit etiam et concessit dictus comes quod abbatissa habet manum mortuam in omnibus hominibus suis apud Ioigniacum, Bussiacum, Colongias Vinosas, Vallem Marcy, et Escoliuas[8] morantibus sanguinem et de homine ecclesie interfecto plenariam emendationem. Concessit etiam et promisit dictus comes quod de propriis rebus dicte ecclesie que tam in uilla de Migenna quam aliis uillis ad eandem potestatem pertinentibus nichil deinceps accipient nec ipse nec sui. Hec omnia prenotata dictus comes concessit et iuramento corporaliter prestito promisit se in futurum, et imperpetuum bona fide obseruaturum. Et heredes suos ad hec omnia prenotata fideliter obseruandi imperpetuum obligauit. Ita tamen quod quicumque de heredibus comitis dictam partem dictorum nemorum tenuerit, et infra quadraginta dies postquam a dicta abbatissa uel eius mandato dicte abbatisse patentes litteras super hoc defferente fuerit requisitus, hoc iuramentum facere teneatur abbatisse et conuentui apud Autissiodoro in ecclesia sua et de omnibus predictis fideliter obseruandis. Voluit etiam et concessit dictus comes quod si ipsum uel heredes suos contra predictum in aliquo uenire contigerit, nos personas dicti comitis et heredum ipsius excommunis sententie supponeremus et tamdiu suppositas teneremus donec essent abbatisse et conuentui omnia plenius emendata. Confirmauit etiam et concessit dictus comes ecclesie Sancti Iuliani Autissiodorensis omnia que eidem ecclesie concessa sunt a bone memorie Willelmo patre dicti comitis et aliis antecessoribus dicti comitis sicut in eorum litteris plenius continetur. Quod ut ratum et firmum permaneat et ad petitionem partium presentes litteras sigillo nostro duximus roborandas.

Actum anno Domini MCC trecesimo sexto, mense Mayo.

This document is the archbishop's confirmation of the preceding one. It has not been previously printed.

11

1238

Odo, official of the curia of Sens, attests to the end of a quarrel that Count William II of Joigny and his wife, Elizabeth, had with the abbess and convent of St-Julien. He repeats the details of the count's concessions to the nuns.

MANUSCRIPTS: St-Julien cartulary, fols. 5v–6v. Arch. Yonne H 1668, fols. 6r–7r.

8 Bussy, 9 km northeast of Joigny; Coulanges-la-Vineuse, 11 km south of Auxerre; Val-de-Mercy, 14 km south of Auxerre; and Escolives, 9 km south-southeast of Auxerre.

Omnibus presentes litteras inspecturis, magister Odo Senonensis curie officialis, in Domino salutem. Nouerit uniuersitas uestra quod in nostra presencia constituti nobilis uir Guillelmus comes Ioigniaci et Helisabeth eius uxor[1] recognouerunt quod de querelis que erant inter dictum comitem ex una parte et abbatissam et conuentum Sancti Iuliani Autissiodorensis ex altera pacificatum erat in hunc modum, quod dicte abbatissa et conuentus Sancti Iuliani in nemore de Boeleto[2] possent capere alto et basso omnia necessaria sua ad usum suum et domorum suarum, recognoscentes se teneri dictum nemus custodire bona fide. Recognouerunt etiam quod dicte abbatissa et conuentus habent medietatem in omnibus hayis de Buissiaco ubique sint, et quod dictas hayas tenentur tenere in foresta, custodire et garentire bona fide secundum ius, et quod non possunt de dictis hayis aliquid capere, dare, uendere, uel partiri sine abbatisse assensu, nec abbatissa sine ipsorum assensu. Et quod si contigerit dictas hayas exartari, terra abbatisse remanebit ad suam uoluntatem faciendam. De nemore usuagii in quo homines de Migenna, de Buissiaco et de Brione[3] habent usuagium ut dicebant, idem comes et eius uxor recognouerunt et concesserunt quod abbatissa et conuentus in eo possunt capere alto et basso omnia necessaria sua ad usum suum et domorum suarum. Et quod de eodem nemore potest uendere abbatissa per loca et monstratas. Ita tamen quod comes habeat quartam partem precii uenditionis que fiet ab abbatissa, et abbatissa tres partes dicti precii, salua sextadecima parte heredum defuncti Yterii de Brione militis, de qua sextadecima parte dicti comes et comitissa recognouerunt se teneri soluere quartam partem dictis heredibus, et abbatissam erga eos liberare.

Recognouerunt etiam prefati comes et comitissa eius uxor quod de dicto nemore nichil possunt uendere, nec circularios, nec carbonarios in eo mittere, nisi ad proprium usum siue uenditione aliqua facienda. Et quod cum dicta abbatissa de dicto nemore per loca uel monstratas uendiderit significabit hoc forestario comitis et si ab illa die que significatum fuerit aliquis emptor apparuerit infra octo dies qui uenditionem ab abbatissa factam uel a mandato eius de sexta parte aut de plus augmentare uoluerit, omnibus circumstanciis consideratis tam circa terminos de pagis faciendis quam circa alia commoda eam habebit per manum abbatisse. Et si aliquis pro palmata augmentare uenditionis aliquid habuerit de communi soluetur. Recognouerunt etiam et concesserunt dicti comes et eius uxor quod in toto nemore foreste hayarum usuagii et boeleti non possunt domum stanguum uel aliud edificium facere uel habere, nec partiri dicta nemora siue partionem requirere, nec abbatissa partiri similiter. Recognouerunt

1 Count William II of Joigny (1225–44) and his wife, Elizabeth.

2 Boulay, 30 km east-northeast of Joigny.

3 Migennes, 7 km east of Joigny; Bussy, 9 km northeast of Joigny; and Brion, 6 km northeast of Joigny.

etiam prescripti comes et eius uxor quod illam partem nemoris quod dicitur Sancti Iuliani que posita est in foresta ut dicebant comes et comitissa a bone memorie Willelmo patre dicti comitis et dictis abbatissa et conuentu tenere tenentur dicti comes et comitissa in foresta custodire et garentire erga omnes bona fide secundum ius, nec possunt de eo aliquid dare, capere, uel partiri, nec uendere, nec partitionem requirere, nec similiter dictis abbatisse et conuentui licet de dicto nemore aliquid capere, dare, uel partiri sine assensu comitis. Sed de eodem nemore uendere poterit abbatissa comite non requisito per loca et monstratas. Ita quod successiue monstrate in foresta ponantur, usque ad quindecim annos, nec infra uendi poterunt nisi de mutuo consensu. Quindecim autem annis elapsis, abbatissa uendere poterit. Verumptamen[4] comes Ioigniaci quartam partem precii uenditi habebit siue per loca siue per monstratas uendiderit abbatissa. Si autem abbatissa per monstratas siue per loca uendiderit, significabit hoc comiti uel senescallo uel preposito Ioigniaci, uel illi qui loco prepositi erit infra octo dies, postquam palmata uenditionis facta fuerit, et si ab illa die qua comiti uel alicui predictorum significatum fuerit, aliquis emptor apparuerit infra mensem qui uenditionem ab abbatissa factam de sexta parte uel de plus augmentare uoluerit, eam habebit per manum abbatisse, et hoc modo crescere poterit uenditio usque ad prefixum terminum, consideratis omnibus circumstanciis, tam circa terminos de pagis faciendis, quam circa alia commoda. Recognouerunt insuper prefati comes et comitissa quod de quarta parte sextedecime partis precii uenditionis tenetur liberare abbatissam erga heredes defuncti Yterii de Brione militis qui in totali nemore foreste et usuagii sextamdecimam habent partem. Tenentur insuper garentire dicti comes et comitissa sicut recognouerunt coram nobis et defendere bona fide secundum ius omnes uenditiones que a dicta abbatissa fient de dicta nemore imperpetuum. Recognouerunt etiam et concesserunt quod abbatissa et conuentus uendiderunt de dicto nemore circiter mille et trecenta arpenta, et quod dicte abbatissa et conuentus associauerunt comitem ad medietatem precii uenditionis que fiet a dicta abbatissa de residuo predicte foreste, ita quod postquam hac sola et unica uice uendita fuerit, nequaquam postea potuerint comes et eius heredes petere in uenditionibus predicte foreste quantumcumque fient nisi quartam partem, et tenentur dicti comes et comitissa et eorum heredes garentire istam uentam ad quam dicte abbatissa et conuentus associauerunt comitem ad medietatem, hoc modo quod si aliquis super illo nemore dampnum mercatoribus intulerit, uel uenditionem nemoris arrestauerit, comes tenetur dampna reddere sine abbatissa et conuentu, et dictum nemus mercatoribus garentire, et mercatores solutionem partis pecunie que comitem continget de dicta uenditione quoniam

4 The correct form would be 'Verumtamen.'

fiet diffendere poterunt, quousque dampna sua dictis mercatoribus fuerint restituta et uenditio nemoris liberata, et quantum arrestatio durauerunt tamen liberatoris dicti nemoris prorogabitur ipse nec propter hec retardabitur uel impedietur solutio pecunie abbatisse, nec de aliquo impedimento aut arrestatione dicti nemoris mercatores aliquam actionem uel recursum ad abbatissam habere poterunt. Recognouerunt etiam prenotatus comes et comitissa se teneri in se suscipere omnem garentiam et omnem deffensionem dicte uenditionis quoniam fiet, contra omnes qui in nemore uendito ratione usuagii uel aliqua alia ratione uoluerint aliquid reclamare, et de omnibus hiis tenentur dicti comes et eius uxor se obligare erga mercatores dicte uente et pro hiis conuentionibus a predictis comite et comitissa adimplendis associauerunt dicte abbatissa et conuentus dictum comitem ad medietatem precii dicte uenditionis, et sub eisdem conuentionibus faciet abbatissa dictam uenditionem. Recognouerunt insuper prenominati comes et comitissa se teneri soluere heredibus dicti defuncti Yterii medietatem dicte sextedecime partis istius uente, ad quam abbatissa et conuentus associauerunt dictum comitem ad medietatem et eas tenentur prefati comes et eius uxor erga dictos heredes de dicta medietate sextedecime partis liberare. Recognouerunt etiam et concesserunt prefati comes et comitissa se habere octauam partem tamen in totali fundo nemorum foreste et usuagii, et in uenditionibus quartam partem, recognoscentes quod dominium omnium uenditionum predictorum nemorum foreste et usuagii imperpetuum futuraram pertinet ad abbatissam. Recognouerunt etiam et concesserunt prenotati comes et comitissa quod abbatissa potest habere tres forestarios in dicto nemore foreste et usuagii, et comes duos ad custodiendum nemus. Forefactum uero de nemore factum quod forestarius comitis inueniret per se comitis erit. Et si forestarius abbatisse per se inueniret forefactum abbatisse erit. Si autem ad forefactum uenirent insimul forestarius comitis et abbatisse forestarius, equaliter inter comitem et abbatissam emenda forefacti diuidetur. Recognouerunt etiam et concesserunt dicti comes et comitissa quod omnes excasure hominum et feminarum de candela tam mobilium quam immobilium quantumque sint de candela inter dictum comitem et abbatissam per medium diuidentur cum decesserint sine herede ad usum manus mortue, et terre que a dicta abbatissa tenentur ad terciam ad ipsam deuenient et deuenire debent ab omnibus illis qui eas tenent, siue sint de candela siue non, cum decesserint sine herede ad usum manus mortue, sicut recognuerunt comes et comitissa. Recognouerunt etiam et concesserunt dicti comes et comitissa quod abbatissa habet manum mortuam in omnibus hominibus suis apud Ioigniacum, Buissyacum, Colongias Vinosas, Vallem Marcy, et Escoliuas[5]

5 Bussy, 9 km northeast of Joigny; Coulanges-la-Vineuse, 11 km south of Auxerre; Val-de-Mercy, 14 km south of Auxerre; and Escolives, 9 km south-southeast of Auxerre.

morantibus sanguinem et de homine ecclesie interfecto plenariam emendationem. Concesserunt etiam et promiserubt dicti comes et comitissa quod de propriis rebus dicte ecclesie que tam in uilla de Migenna quam in aliis uillis ad eandem potestatem pertinentibus nichil deinceps accipient nec ipse nec sui. Hec omnia prenotata dicti comes et comitissa concesserunt et iuramento corporaliter prestito promiserunt se in futurum, et imperpetuum bona fide obseruaturos. Et heredes suos ad hec omnia prenotata fideliter obseruanda imperpetuum obligauerunt. Ita tamen quod quicumque de heredibus comitis et comitisse dictam partem dictorum nemorum tenuerit, infra quadraginta dies postquam a dicta abbatissa uel eius mandato dicte abbatisse patentes litteras super hoc deferente fuerit requisitus, hoc iuramentum facere teneatur abbatisse et conuentui apud Autissiodoro in ecclesia sua de omnibus predictis fideliter obseruandis. Voluerunt etiam et concesserunt dicti comes et comitissa quod si ipsos uel heredes suos contra predictum in aliquo uenire contigerit, nos personas dictorum comitis et comitisse et heredum ipsorum excommunis sententie supponeremus et tamdiu suppositas teneremus donec essent abbatisse et conuentui omnia plenius emendata. Confirmauerunt etiam et concesserunt dicti comes et comitissa ecclesie Sancti Iuliani Autissiodorensis omnia que eidem ecclesie concessa sunt a bone memorie Willelmo patre dicti comitis et aliis antecessoribus dicti comitis sicut in eorum litteris plenius continetur. Quod ut ratum et firmum permaneat ad petitionem partium presentes litteras sigillo curie Senonensis duximus sigillandas.

Actum anno Domini MCC trecesimo octauo, mense Ianuario.

This document has not been previously printed. It is nearly word for word the same as the archbishop's charter from two years earlier (document 10), except for the addition of the countess to the agreement.

12

August 1244

Robert, official of the curia of Sens, attests that William III, count of Joigny, has agreed to the quarrel settlement reached by his father, William II, with the abbess and convent of St-Julien. He repeats the terms of that settlement.

MANUSCRIPTS: St-Julien cartulary, fols. 6v–7v.[1] Arch. Yonne H 1668, fols. 7r–8v.

1 A modern hand mistakenly dates this document 1254 in the margin.

Omnibus presentes litteras inspecturis, magister Robertus officialis curie Senonensis, in Domino salutem. Notum facimus quod in nostra presencia constitutus nobilis uir Guillelmus comes Ioigniaci[2] recognouit quod de querelis que quondam fuerant inter bone memorie Guillelmum quondam comitem Ioignaci patrem suum[3] ex una parte et abbitissam et conuentum Sancti Iuliani Autissiodorensis ex altera pacificatum fuit inter eos in hunc modum.

Videlicet quod dicte abbitissa et conuentus in bosco de Boleto[4] qui est in terra Sancti Iuliani poterant capere alto et basso omnia necessaria sua ad usum suum et domorum suarum. Recognouit etiam idem comes quod predictus Guillelmus quondam pater suus et defuncta Elisabeth quondam mater sua recognouerant quod de abbatissa et conuentus habebant medietatem in omnibus hayis de Buissiaco[5] ubique essent et quod dictas hayas tenebantur tenere in foresta, et garentire dictis abbatisse et conuentui bona fide secundum ius, et quod non poterant de dictis hayis aliquid capere, dare, uendere uel partiri sine abbatisse assensu, nec abbatissa sine eorum assensu, et quod si contingerit dictas hayas exartari, terra abbatisse ad uoluntatem eidem abbatisse faciendam remaneret, et quod etiam de nemore usuagii in quo homines de Migenna, de Bussiaco, et de Brione[6] habent usuagium recognouerant et concesserantt idem defuncti comes et comitissa quod abbatissa et conuentus in eo poterant capere alto et basso omnia necessaria sua ad usum suum et domorum suarum, et quod de eodem nemore poterat uendere eadem abbatissa per loca et monstratas, ita tamen quod comes habeat quartam partem precii uenditionis que fieret ab abbatissa, et abbatissa tres partes dicti precii, salua sextadecima parte heredum defuncti Iterii de Brione militis, de qua sextadecima parte precii dicte uenditionis recognouit idem comes Ioigniaci quod predicti defuncti comes et comitissa tenebantur erga dictos heredes liberare de dicta quarta parte. Recognouit item et concessit idem comes quod prefati defuncti comes et comitissa recognouerant quod de dicto nemore nichil uendere poterant, nec circularios, nec carbonarios in eo mittere, nisi ad proprium usum sine aliqua uenditione facienda, et quod cum dicta abbatissa de dicto nemore per loca uel per monstratas uendidisset, hoc significaret forestario comitis, et quod si ab illa die qua significatum esset aliquis emptor apparuerit infra octo dies qui uenditionem ab abbatissa factam uel a mandato eius de sexta parte aut de plus augmentare uellet, omnibus circumstanciis consideratis tam circa terminos de pagis faciendis quam circa alia commoda eam haberet per manum abbatisse, et quod etiam si aliquis

2 William III, count of Joigny.

3 William II, count of Joigny (1225–44).

4 Boulay, 30 km east-northeast of Joigny.

5 Bussy, 9 km northeast of Joigny.

6 Migennes, 7 km east of Joigny; Bussy; and Brion, 6 km northeast of Joigny.

pro palmata augmentate uenditionis aliquid haberet de communi soluetur. Recognouit item dictus comes et concessit quod prenominati defuncti comes et comitissa recognouerant et concesserant quod in toto nemore foreste hayarum usuagii et boeleti non poterant domum stanguum uel aliud edificium facere uel habere, nec partiri dicta nemora siue partitionem requirere, nec abbatissa partiri similiter, et quod iidem defuncti comes et comitissa partem illam nemoris quod dicitur nemus Sancti Iuliani que posita erat in foresta ut dicebat comes a bone memorie Guillelmo patre dicti defuncti comitis[7] et dictis abbatissa et conuentu tenere tenebantur prefati defuncti comes et comitissa in foresta custodire et garentire abbatisse et conuentui erga omnis bona fide secundum ius, nec poteranat de eo aliquid capere, dare, uendere, uel partiri, nec partitionem requirere, nec similiter dicte abbatissa et conuentus sine assensu comitis. Sed de eodem nemore uendere poterat abbatissa comite non requisito per loca et per monstratas, ita quod successiue monstrate uendite in foresta ponerentur, usque ad quindecim annos, nec infra uendi possent nisi de mutuo consensu, et elapsis quindecim annis, abbatissa uendere poterat. Verumtamen comes Ioigniaci quartam partem precii uenditionis haberet, siue per loca siue per monstratas uendideret abbatissa. Recognouit etiam idem comes Ioigniaci quod si abbatissa per loca uel per monstratas uendidisset, hoc significare tenebatur comiti, uel senescallo, uel preposito Ioigniaci, uel illi qui loco prepositi esset infra octo dies postquam palmata uenditionis facta fuisset, et quod si ab illa die qua comiti uel alicui predictorum significatum fuisset, aliquis emptor apparuerit infra mensem qui uenditionem ab abbatissa factam de sexta parte uel de plus augmentare uellet, eam habret per manum abbatisse, et hoc modo crescere posset uenditio usque ad prefixum terminum, consideratis omnibus circumstanciis, tam circa terminos de pagis faciendis quam circa alia commoda. Recognouit item idem comes quod prefati defuncti comes et comitissa recognouerant quod de quarta parte sextedecime partis precii uenditionis tenebantur liberare abbatissam erga heredes predicti defuncti Iterii qui in totali nemore foreste et usuagii sextamdecimam parte habere dignoscitur. Recognouit etiam quod prescripti defuncti comes et comitissa tenebantur deffendere dictis abbatisse et conuentui bona fide secundum ius omnes uenditiones que a dicta abbatissa fierent imperpetuum. Et quod iidem defuncti comes et comitissa recognouerant quod abbatissa et conuentus uendiderant de dicto nemore circiter mille et trecenta arpenta, et quod dicta abbatissa et conuentus associauerant dictum comitem ad medietatem precii uenditionis que fieret a dicta abbatissa de residuo dicte foreste, ita quod postquam hac sola et unica uice uendito factum fuisset, nequaquam postea possent comes et eius heredes aliquid petere in uenditionibus dicte foresta

7 Count William I of Joigny (1177–1221).

quoniam fierent nisi quartam partem, et quod tenebantur prenotati comes et comitissa et eorum heredes garentire abbatissa et conuentui uenditionem illam ad quam abbatissa et conuentus associauerant comitem ad medietatem, hoc modo quod si aliquis super illo nemore dampna mercatoribus inferet uel uenditionem nemoris arrestaret comes tenebatur dampna reddere sine abbatissa et conuentu, et dictum nemus mercatoribus garentire, et quod mercatores solutionem partis pecunie que comitem contingeret de dicta uenditione quoniam fieret diffendere possent, quosque dictis mercatoribus dampna sua essent restituta, et uenditio nemoris liberata, et quod quantum arrestatio duraret tam liberatoris dicti nemoris prorogaretur tempore, nec propter hec impediretur uel retardaretur solutio pecunie abbatisse, nec de aliquo impedimento aut arrestatione dicti nemoris aliquam actionem uel recursum ad abbatissam habere possent. Recognouit etiam idem comes quod predicti defuncti comes et comitissa tenebantur in se suscipere omnem garentiam dicte uenditionis quoniam fieret, contra omnes qui in nemore uendito ratione usuagii uel alia ratione uellent aliquid reclamare, et quod de hiis omnibus tenebantur dicti defuncti comes et comitissa se obligare erga mercatores dicte uenditionis et quod etiam pro istis conuentionibus a dictis comite et comitissa obseruandis associauerant dicte abbatissa et conuentus dictum comitem ad medietatem precii dicte uenditionis, et quod sub hiis conuentionibus faciet dictam abbatissa uenditionem. Recognouit insuper dictus comes quod prefati defuncti comes et comitissa tenebantur soluere heredibus dicti defuncti Iterii medietatem sextedecime partis illius uenditionis, ad quam abbatissa et conuentus associauerant comitem ad medietatem et eas tenebantur erga dictos heredes de illa uenditione sextedecime partis liberare. Recognouit item dictus comes Ioigniaci quod memorati defuncati comes et comitissa recognuerant et concesserant se habere octauam partem tamen in totali fundo nemorum foreste et usuagii, et in uenditionibus quartam partem, et quod etiam recognouerant quod dominium omnium uenditionum predictorum nemorum foreste et usuagii imperpetuum futuraram pertinebat ad abbatissam. Recognouit item quod predicti defundcti comes et comitissa recognouerant et concesserant quod abbatissa poterat habere tres forestarios in dicto nemore foreste et usuagii, et comes duos ad custodiendum nemus, et quod forefactum de nemore factum quod forestarius comitis inueniret comitis esset. Et si forestarius abbatisse per se inueniret forefactum abbatisse esset forefactum, et si insimul uenirent ad forefactum forestarius comitis et forestarius abbatisse, equaliter inter comitem et abbatissam emenda forefacti diuideretur. Recognouit item prefatus comes quod prenotati defuncti comes et comitissa recognouerant et concesserant quod omnes excasure hominum et feminarum de candela tam mobilium quam immobilium quantumque essent de candela inter dictum comitem et abbatissam per medium diuidentur cum decedent sine herede ad usum manus mortue. Et terre que ab abbatissa tenebantur ad terciam ad ipsam deuenirent et deuenire debebant ab omnibus illis qui eas tenebant, siue essent de candela siue non, cum decedent sine herede ad usum manus mortue. Recognouit etiam dictus comes quod prefati defuncti comes et comitissa recognuerant et concesserant quod abbatissa habebat manum mortuam in omnibus hominibus suis apud Ioigniacum, Buissiacum, Colongias Vinosas, Vallem Mercy, et Escoliuas[8] morantibus sanguinem et de homine ecclesie interfecto plenariam emendationem. Et quod etiam ipsi comes et comitissa quondam Ioigniaci de propriis rebus dicte ecclesie que tam in uilla de Migenna quam aliis uillis ad eandem potestatem pertinentibus nichil acciperent nec ipse nec sui. Et quod et hec omnia predicti defuncti comes et comitissa concesserant et iuramento prestito promiserant se imperpetuum seruatoros, et quod heredes suos imperpetuum obligauerant ad hec omnia obseruandi et tenenda. Ita tamen quod quicumque de heredibus comitis et comitisse quondam Ioigniaci dictam partem dictorum nemorum teneret, infra quadraginta dies postquam a dicta abbatissa uel eius mandato dicte abbatisse patentes litteras super hoc deferente esset requisitus, hoc iuramentum facere tenetur apud Autissiodoro in ecclesia sua et de omnibus predictis fideliter obseruandis. Recognouit item comes prefatus quod dicti defuncti comes et comitissa uoluerunt et concesserunt quod officialis curie Senonis ipsos uel eorum heredes si contra predictam uenirent in aliquo uenire excommunicaret, et pro excommunicatis haberet donec essent abbatisse et conuentui omnia plenius emendata, prout in litteris curie Senonis inde confectis plenius dicitur contineri. Recognouit item idem comes quod prefati defuncti comes et comitissa confirmauerunt et concesserunt ecclesie Sancti Iuliani Autissiodorensis omnia ea que eidem ecclesie concessa sunt a bone memorie Guillelmo patre dicti Guillelmi comitis et aliis antecessoribus dicti comitis prout in eorum litteris plenius continetur. Recognouit item prenominatus comes Ioigniaci predicta omnia prout superius sunt expressa et confirmans ea et concedens ecclesie supradicte. Et quantum ad hoc heredes suos sub predictis conuentionibus obligans promisit per fidem suam se predicta omnia fideliter obseruare, et non contra uenire. Preterea uoluit et concessit et bona fide promisit predictus Guillelmus comes Ioigniaci quod infra annum in quo uxor eius in terra sua erit mansionaria iuramentum faciet ipsa spontanea non coacta apud Autissiodoro in predicta ecclesia Sancti Iuliani de predictis omnibus similiter et inuiolabiliter obseruandis et tenendis.

Datum anno Domini MCC quadragesimo quarto, mense Augusto.

---

8 Bussy, 9 km northeast of Joigny; Coulanges-la-Vineuse, 11 km south of Auxerre; Val-de-Mercy, 14 km south of Auxerre; and Escolives, 9 km south-southeast of Auxerre.

This document has not been previously printed. It is a confirmation of document 11, presumably done when William III had just inherited from his father.

13

St-Julien, 1283

The official of the curia of Auxerre attests that Count John of Joigny recognizes the quarrel settlement his predecessors reached with the abbess and convent of St-Julien. He spells out the terms of that settlement.

MANUSCRIPTS: St-Julien cartulary, fols. 7v–8r. Arch. Yonne H 1668, fols. 8v–9v.

Omnibus presentes litteras inspecturis, officialis Autissiodorensis salutem in Domino. Noueritis quod in nostra presencia constitutus nobilis domicellus Iohannes comes Ioigniaci[1] recognouit quod per compositionem olim habitam inter predecessorem suum scilicet bone memorie Guillelmum quondam comitem Ioigniaci ex una parte et abbatissam Sancti Iuliani Autissiodorensis que tunc temporem erat ex altera, abbatissa et conuentus Sancti Iuliani Autissiodorensis de boscho de Boeleto[2] qui est in terram Sancti Iuliani in eo possunt capere alto et basso omnia necessaria ad usum suum et domorum suarum, et quod ipse comes debet dictum boscum bona fide custodire. Recognouit etiam item comes quod dicta abbatissa habet medietatem in omnibus ayis de Buissiaco[3] ubique sint et tenetur idem comes dictas hayas tenere in foresta, custodire et garentire, bona fide secundum ius, nec potest idem comes de dictis hayis aliquid capere, dare, uendere uel partiri sine assensu abbatisse, nec abbatissa sine ipso, et si contingeret dictas hayas exartari, terra abbatisse remanebit ad uoluntatem suam faciendam. De nemore usuagii in quo homines de Migenna, de Buissiaco, et de Brione[4] habent usuagium, recognouit et concessit idem comes quod abbatissa et conuentus in eo possunt capere alto et basso omnia necessaria ad usum suum et domorum suarum, et de eodem nemore potest uendere abbatissa per loca et monstratas sicut uoluit, ita quod comes habeat quartam partem precii uenditionis que fiet ab abbatissa, et abbatissa tres partes dicti precii, salua sextadecima parte heredum defuncti Iterii de Brione militis, de qua sextadecima parte tenetur comes soluere quartam partem heredibus

1 John, count of Joigny.

2 Boulay, 30 km east-northeast of Joigny.

3 Bussy, 9 km northeast of Joigny.

4 Migennes, 7 km east of Joigny; Bussy; and Brion, 6 km northeast of Joigny.

antedictis, et abbatissam erga eos liberare. Dictus uero comes de dicto nemore nichil potest uendere, nec circularios, nec carbonarios in eo mittere, nec ad proprium usum sine uenditione aliqua facienda. Et cum dicta abbatissa de dicto nemore per loca uel monstratas uenditit, significabit hoc forestario comitis, et si ab illa die qua significatum fuerit aliquis emptor apparuerit infra octo dies qui uenditionem ab abbatissa factam, uel a mandato eius, de sexta parte aut de plus augmentare uoluit, omnibus circumstanciis consideratis, tam circa terminos de pagis faciendis, quam circa alia commoda, eam habebit. Et si aliquis pro palmata augmentare uenditionis aliquid habuerit de communi soluetur. Recognouit etiam et concessit dictus comes quod in toto nemore, foreste, hayarum, usuagii, et boeleti predictorum non potest ipse comes domum stanguum uel aliud edificium facere uel habere, nec partiri dicta nemora, siue partitionem requirere, nec abbatissa partiri similiter.

Recognouit etiam et concessit quod illam partem nemoris quod dicitur Sancti Iuliani que posita fuit in foresta, a pater prefati Guillelmi comitis,[5] et dictis abbatissa et conuentu, tenere tenetur ipse Iohannes comes in foresta custodire et garentire, erga omnes bona fide secundum ius, nec potest de eo aliquid capere, dare, uel uendere, nec partiri siue partitionem requirere, nec similiter dictis abbatisse et conuentui licet de dicto nemore aliquid capere, dare, uel partiri, sine assensu comitis. Sed de eodem nemore uendere poterit abbatissa comite non requisito per loca et monstratas. Successiue uendite monstrate in foresta ponentur usque ad quindecim annos, nec infra uendi poterunt, nisi de mutuo consensu. Quindecim autem annis elapsis abbatissa uendere poterit, uerumptamen comes Ioigniaci quartam partem precii nemoris uenditi habebit, siue per monstratas uendiderit siue per loca. Si autem abbatissa per monstratas siue per loca uendiderit, significabit hoc comiti uel senescallo uel preposito Ioigniaci uel illi qui loco prepositi erit infra octo dies postquam palmata uenditionis facta fuerit. Et si ab illa die qua comiti uel alicui predictorum significatum fuerit aliquis emptor apparuerit infra mensem qui uenditionem ab abbatissa factam de sexta parte uel plus augmentare uoluerit, eam habebit per manum abbatisse, et hoc modo crescere poterit uenditio usque ad prefixum terminum, consideratis omnibus circumstanciis, tam circa terminos de pagis faciendis quam circa alia commoda. De quarta parte sextedecime partis precii uenditionis tenetur idem comes liberare abbatissam erga heredes defuncti Yterii de Brione militis, qui in totali nemore foreste et usuagii sextamdecimam partem habere dicuntur. Tenetur insuper idem Iohannes comes garentire et deffendere bona fide secundum ius omnes uenditiones que a dicta abbatissa de dicto nemore fient inperpetuum. Recognouit etiam et concessit dictus Iohannes comes se

5 Count William I of Joigny (1177–1221).

habere octauam partem tamen in totali fundo nemorum foreste et usuagii, etiam in uenditionibus quartam partem.

Dominium uero omnium uenditionum predictorum nemorum foreste et usuagii inperpetuum futurarum pertinet ad abbatissam prout confessus et idem comes coram nobis. Recognouit etiam et concessit idem comes quod abbatissa potest habere tres forestarios in dicto nemore foreste et usuagii, et dictus comes duos ad custodiendum nemus. Forefactum uero de nemore factum si forestarius comitis per se inueniret suum erit. Et si forestarius abbatisse per se inueniret abbatisse erit. Si autem ad forefactum uenirent insimul, forestarius comitis et forestarius abbatisse, equaliter inter comitem et abbatissam emenda forefacti diuidetur. Recognouit etiam et concessit Iohannes comes quod omnes excasure hominum et feminarum de candela tam mobilium quam immobilium quantumque sint de candela inter comitem et abbatissam per medium diuidentur cum decesserint sine herede ad usum manues mortue. Recognouit etiam et concessit idem comes quod abbatissa habet manum mortuam in omnibus hominibus suis de Appoigniacum, Buissiacum, Colengias Vinosas, Vallem Marci, et Escoliuas[6] morantibus sanguinem et de homine interficto scilicet homine ecclesie plenariam emendationem. Recognouit etiam quod terre que a dicta abbatissa tenentur ad terciam, ad ipsam abbatissam deuenient et deuenire debent ab omnibus illis qui eas tenere siue sint de candela siue non cum decesserint sine herede ad usum manus mortue. Concessit etiam et promisit quod de propriis rebus dicte ecclesie que tam in uilla de Migenna quam in aliis uillis ad eandem potestamen pertinentibus nichil deinceps accipiet nec ipse nec sui.

Hec autem omnia prenotata dictus Iohannes comes concessit et iuramento ab ipso corporaliter prestito coram nobis in ipsa ecclesia Sancti Iuliani presentibus abbatissa et conuentu ipsius ecclesie et multis bonis uiris ad hoc specialiter uocatis tactis sacrosanctis euangeliis promisit idem Iohannes comes se in futurum et imperpetuum bona fide obseruaturum, et successores suos ad hec omnia fideliter obseruanda imperpetuum obligauit, ita quod quicumque erit comes Ioigniaci et dictam partem dictorum nemorum tenuerit, infra quadraginta dies postquam a dicta abbatissa uel eius mandato dicte abbatisse patentes litteras dicte abbatisse super hoc deferente fuit requisitus, hoc iuramentum facere teneatur abbatisse et conuentui apud Autissiodoro in ecclesia sua de omnibus predictis fideliter obseruandis, et se quantum ad hec et successores suos supposuit iuridictioni curie Autissiodorensis, ita quod si ipsum comitem uel successores suos qua predicta in aliquo uenire contingerit, nos et successores nostri

6 The places are Appoigny, 10 km north-northwest of Auxerre; Bussy, 9 km northeast of Joigny; Coulanges-la-Vineuse, 11 km south of Auxerre; Val-de-Mercy, 14 km south of Auxerre; and Escolives, 9 km south-southeast of Auxerre.

personam suam et dictos succcessores excommunicationis sentenie supponamus, et tamdiu suppositos teneamus donec fuerint abbatisse et conuentui omnia plenius amendata. Nos uero officialis Autissiodorensis in testimonium premissorum omnium et munimine presentibus litteris sigillum curia Autissiodorensis datum apponendum

Datum et actum apud Sanctum Iulianum, anno Domini MCC octogesimo secundo, die dominica ante ramos palmarium.

Because this charter was given before Easter, it should be dated 1283 in 'new style.' It has not been previously printed. It follows the text of document 9 very closely.

14

Auxerre, 1 October 1291

Count John of Joigny agrees to the settlement agreement earlier reached between St-Julien and Count William II, after it is read out to him in the vernacular.

MANUSCRIPTS: St-Julien cartulary, fols. 8v–9r. Arch. Yonne H 1668, fols. 9v–10v.

In nomine Domini amen. Anno natiuitate eius MCC nonagesimo primo, indictione quinta, quarta kalendas Octobris, pontificatus Domini Nicholai pape quarti[1] anno quarto, per presens publicum instrumentum cunctis pateat euidenter, quod in presencia nostrorum officialium curie Autissiodorensis et curie decani Autissiodorensis et in presentia mei Petri de ecclesia clerici auctoritate sacrosancti Romane ecclesie publici notarii et testium subscriptorum accedente nobili uiro Iohanne comite Iogniaci[2] Senonensis dyocesis personaliter in ecclesia religiosarum monialum abbatissa et conuentus Sancti Iuliani Autissiodorensis, dictis religiosis presentibus ex parte dictorum religiosorum dicto comite presente lecte fuerant quedam littere sigillo recolende memorie Guillelmi quondam comitis Ioigniaci ut prima facie apparebat sigillate, in principio dictorum litterarum que sic incipiunt.

Ego Guillelmus comes Ioigniaci notum facio omnibus tam presentibus quam futuris iisque ad illam clausulam in dictis litteris contentam. Recognosco et concedo quod abbatissa et conuentus uendiderunt de dicto nemore circiter mille et trecenta arpenta usque ad illam clausulam. Recognosco etiam et concedo me

1 Pope Nicholas IV (1288–92).

2 John, count of Joigny.

habere octauam partem tamen in totali fundo nemoris, foreste et usuagii, et a dicta clausula usque ad finem dictarum litterarum et exposita fuerunt dicto Iohanni comiti ea que in dictis litteris continebantur lingua materna. Omnium litterarum tenor sequens in hoc uerba.

Ego Guillelmus comes Ioigniaci[3] notum facio omnibus tam presentibus quam futuris quod de querelis que erant inter me ex una parte et abbatissam Sancti Iuliani Autissiodorensis ex altera pacificatum est in hunc modum, quod de bosco de Boeleto[4] qui est in terram Sancti Iuliani recognosco et concedo quod abbatissa et conuentus Sancti Iuliani in eo possunt capere alto et basso omnia necessaria ad usum suum et domorum suarum, et debeo dictum boscum bona fide custodire. Recognosco etiam quod dicta abbatissa habet medietatem in omnibus hayis de Buissiaco[5] ubique sint et teneor dictas hayas tenere in foresta, custodire et garentire, bona fide secundum ius, nec possum de dictis hayis aliquid capere, dare, uendere uel partiri sine assensu abbatisse, nec abbatissa sine me, et si contingerit dictas hayas exartari, terra abbatisse remanebit ad uoluntatem suam faciendam. De nemore usuagii in quo homines de Migenna, de Buissiaco, et de Brione[6] habent usuagium, recognosco et concedo quod abbatissa et conuentus in eo possunt capere alto et basso omnia necessaria ad usum suum et domorum suarum, et de eodem nemore potest uendere abbatissa per loca et monstratas sicut uoluerit, item tamen quod habeam quartam partem precii uenditionis que fiet ab abbatissa, et abbatissa tres partes dicti precii, salua sextadecima parte heredum defuncti Yterii de Brione militis,[7] de qua sextadecima parte teneor soluere quartam dictis heredibus partem, et abbatissam erga eos liberare. Ego uero de dicto nemore nichil possum uendere, nec circularios, nec carbonarios in eo mittere, nec ad proprium usum sine uenditione aliqua facienda. Et cum dicta abbatissa de dicto nemore per loca uel monstratas uenditerit, significabit hoc forestario meo, et si ab illa die qua significatum fuerit aliquis emptor apparuerit infra octo dies qui uenditionem ab abbatissa factam, uel a mandato eius, de sexta parte aut de plus augmentare uoluerit, omnibus circumstanciis consideratis, tam circa terminos de pagis faciendis, quam circa alia commoda, eam habebit. Et si aliquis pro palmata augmentare uenditionis aliquid habuerit de communi soluetur. Recognosco etiam et concedo quod in toto nemore, foreste, hayarum, usuagii, et boeleti predictorum non possum domum stanguum uel aliud edificium facere uel habere, nec partiri dicta nemora, siue partionem requirere, nec abbatissa partiri similiter.

3 Count William II of Joigny (1225–44).
4 Boulay, 30 km east-northeast of Joigny.
5 Bussy, 9 km northeast of Joigny.
6 Migennes, 7 km east of Joigny; Bussy; and Brion, 6 km northeast of Joigny.
7 He is also mentioned in the preceding document.

Recognosco etiam et concedo quod illam partem nemoris quod dicitur Sancti Iuliani que posita est in foresta, a bone memorie Willelmo patre meo,[8] et dictis abbatissa et conuentu, tenere teneor in foresta custodire et garentire,[9] erga omnes bona fide secundum ius, nec possum de eo aliquid capere, dare, uel uendere, nec partiri siue partitionem requirere, nec similiter dictis abbatisse et conuentui licet de dicto nemore aliquid capere, dare, uel partiri, sine meo assensu. Sed de eodem nemore uendere poterit abbatissa comite non requisito per loca et monstratas. Successiue uendite monstrate in foresta ponentur usque ad quindecim annos, nec infra uendi poterunt, nisi de mutuo consensu. Quindecim autem annis elapsis abbatissa uendere poterit, uerumptamen comes Ioigniaci quartam partem precii nemoris uenditi habebit, siue per monstratas uendiderit siue per loca. Si autem abbatissa per monstratas siue per loca uendiderit, significabit hoc comiti uel senescallo uel preposito Ioigniaci uel illi qui loco prepositi erit infra octo dies postquam palmata uenditionis facta fuerit. Et si ab illa die qua comiti uel alicui predictorum significatum fuerit aliquis emptor apparuerit infra mensem qui uenditionem ab abbatissa factam de sexta parte uel de plus augmentare uoluerit, eam habebit per manum abbatisse, et hoc modo crescere poterit uenditio usque ad prefixum terminum, consideratis omnibus circumstanciis, tam circa terminos de pagis faciendis quam circa alia commoda. De quarta parte sextedecime partis precii uenditionis teneor liberare abbatissam erga heredes defuncti Yterii de Brione militis, qui in totali nemore foreste et usuagii sextamdecimam habent partem. Teneor insuper garentire et defendere bona fide secundum ius omnes uenditiones que a dicta abbatissa de dicto nemore fiant inperpetuum. Recognoso etiam et concedo quod abbatissa et conuentus uendiderunt de dicto nemore circiter mille et trecenta arpenta, et dicte abbatissa et conuentus associauerunt me ad medietatem precii uenditionis que fiet a dicta abbatissa de residuo predicte foreste, hac sola et unica uice, ita quod postquam hac sola et unica uice uendita fuerit, nequam postea potero petere in uenditionibus predicte foreste quantumque fiant, nisi quartam partem. Et teneor garentire istam uentam ad quam dicte abbatissa et conuentus associauerunt me ad medietatem, hoc modo quod si aliquis super illo nemore dampnum mercatoribus intulerit uel uenditionem nemoris arrestauerit, ego dampna teneor reddere sine abbatissa et conuentu, et dictum nemus mercatoribus garentire, et mercatores solutionem partis pecunie que me continget de dicta uenditione quoniam fiet diffendere poterunt, quousque dampna sua dictis mercatoribus fuerint restituta, et uenditio nemoris liberata. Et quantum arrestatio durauerit, tantum liberatoris dicti nemoris prorogabitur tempore, nec propter hoc retardabitur uel

8 Count William I of Joigny (1177–1221).

9 This is a reference to document 8.

impedietur solutio pecunie abbatisse, nec de aliquo impedimento aut arrestatione dicti nemoris, mercatores aliquam actionem uel recursum ad abbatissam habere poterunt. Teneor insuper in me suscipere omnem garenciam et omnem deffensionem dicte uenditionis quoniam fiet contra omnes qui in nemore uendito ratione usuagii, uel aliqua alia ratione uoluerint aliquid reclamare, et de omnibus hiis teneor me obligare erga mercatores dicte uente, et pro hiis conuentionibus a me comite adimplendis associauerunt me dicte abbatissa et conuentus ad medietatem precii dicte uenditionis, et sub eisdem conuentionibus faciet abbatissa dictum uenditionem. Teneor insuper soluere heredibus dicti defuncti Yterii medietatem dicte sextedecime partis istius uente, ad quam abbatissa et conuentus me associauerunt ad medietatem, et eas teneor erga dictos heredes de dicta medietate sextedecime partis liberare. Recognosco etiam et concedo me habere octauam partem tamen in totali fondo nemoris foreste et usuagii, et in uenditionibus quartam partem. Dominium uero omnium uenditionum predictorum nemorum foreste et usuagii inperpetuum futurarum pertinet ad abbatissam. Recognosco etiam et concedo quod abbatissa potest habere tres forestarios in dicto nemore foreste et usuagii, et ego duos ad custodiendum nemus. Forefactum uero de nemore factum si forestarius meus per se inueniret meum erit. Et si forestarius abbatisse per se inueniret abbatisse erit. Si autem ad forefactum uenirent insimul, forestarius meus et forestarius abbatisse, equaliter inter nos emenda forefacti diuidetur. Recognosco etiam et concedo quod omnes excasure hominum et feminarum de candela tam mobilium quam immobilium quantumque sint de candela inter me et dictam abbatissam per medium diuidantur cum decesserint sine herede ad usum manus mortue. Et terre que a dicta abbatissa tenentur ad terciam ad ipsam deuenient et deuenire debent ab omnibus illis qui eas tenent, siue sint de candela siue non, cum decesserint sine herede ad usum manus mortue. Recognosco etiam et concedo quod abbatissa habet manum mortuam in omnibus hominibus suis apud Ioigniacum, Buissiacum, Colengias Vinosas, Vallem Marcy, et Escoliuas[10] morantibus sanguinem et de homine ecclesie interficto plenariam emendationem. Concedo etiam et promitto quod de propriis rebus dicte ecclesie que tam in uilla de Migenna quam in aliis uillis ad eandem potestamen pertinentibus nichil deinceps accipiem nec ego nec mei.

Hec omnia prenotata ego comes concessi et iuramento corporaliter prestito promisi me in futurum et imperpetuum bona fide obseruaturus, et heredes meos ad hec omnia fideliter obseruanda imperpetuum obligaui, ita quod quicumque de heredibus meis dictam partem dictorum nemorum retinerit, infra quadraginta dies postquam a dicta abbatissa uel eius mandato dicte abbatisse patentes

10 The places are Joigny; Bussy, 9 km northeast of Joigny; Coulanges-la-Vineuse, 11 km south of Auxerre; Val-de-Mercy, 14 km south of Auxerre; and Escolives, 9 km south-southeast of Auxerre.

litteras super hoc deferente fuit requisitus, hoc iuramentum facere teneatur abbatisse et conuentui apud Autissiodoro in ecclesia sua de omnibus predictis fideliter obseruandis. Rogaui etiam reuerendum patrem Galterum archiepiscopum Senonis[11] ut super hiis omnibus litteras suas patentes dictis abbatisse et conuentui faciat, in quibus contineatur quod si me uel heredes meos contra predicta in aliquo uenire contigerit, ipse personam meam et dictos heredes excommunis sententie supponeret, et tamdiu suppositas teneret donec essent abbatisse et conuentui omnia plenius emendata. Confirmo etiam et concedo ecclesie Sancti Iuliani omnia que eidem ecclesie concessa sunt a bone memorie Willelmo quodam patre meo comite Ioigniaci et aliis antecessoribus meis sicut in eorum litteris plenius continetur.

Actum anno domini MCC trecesimo sexto, mense Mayo.

Omnibus litteris sic lectis et predicto comiti expositis lingua materna. Religiosa domina Eustachia abbatissa Sancti Iuliani Autissiodorensis nomine suo et conuentus sui dicto conuentu presente in eorum monasterio in choro dicti monasterii sui predicti requisiuit dictum Iohannem comitem Ioigniaci ut ipse tam de omnibus et singulis supradictis in dictis litteris contentis quam in aliis litteris et instrumentis a predecessoribus ipsius Iohannis comitis dictis religiosis et eorum monasterio concessis prestaret iuramentum. Etiam comes in presencia nostrorum officialium et mei notarii et testium subscriptorum tactis sacrosanctis euangeliis iurauit et promissit se tenere et complere inuiolabiliter obseruare ea que in dictis litteris continentur et in aliis litteris et instrumentis a predecessoribus ipsius Iohannis comitis dictis religiosis et eorum monasterio concessis et contra non uenire, prout predecessores sui uoluerunt et concesserunt.

Presentibus uenerabilis uiris et clericis Gaufrido decano ecclesie Autissiodorensis, magistro Hugone de Hermento archidiacono Autissiodorensis, Hugone de Plasseyo[12] archidiacono in ecclesia Autissiodorensis, Iohanne de Sancto Prisco[13] canonico torfrio in ecclesia Autissiodorensis, Petro de Poilliaco[14] sigillatore curia Autissiodorensis, Guillelmo de Cheuannis[15] sigillatore curie decani Autissiodorensis, Hugone de Sancto Iangulpho et Petro de Charriaco presbiteris, et pluribus aliis tam clericis quam laicis uocatis testibus et rogatis.

Actum in monasterio predicto Sancti Iulianii Autissiodorensis, anno indictione quarto, kalendas Octobris et pontificatu predictis.

Most of this charter is a verbatim transcription of document 9. Folio 9v is blank, so this was always the end of the cartulary.

11 Walter III, archbishop of Sens (1223–41).
12 Plécy, 29 km southeast of Auxerre.
13 St-Bris, 10 km southeast of Auxerre.
14 Poilly, 16 km northwest of Auxerre.
15 Chevannes, 8 km southwest of Auxerre.

THE BISHOPS OF AUXERRE, TWELFTH AND THIRTEENTH CENTURIES

The following men held the office of bishop during the period covered by the episcopal cartulary.

Hugh of Mâcon, 1136–51
Had been first Cistercian abbot of Pontigny (*Gesta*, 2:97).

Alain, 1152–67
Had been Cistercian abbot of Larrivour, in the diocese of Troyes (*Gesta*, 2:107).

William of Toucy, 1167–81
Brother of the archbishop of Sens (*Gesta*, 2:113).

Hugh of Noyers, 1183–1206
Acted as lord of Noyers in his own right (*Gesta*, 2:143, 155).

William of Seignelay, 1207–20
A cousin of his predecessor and brother of Bishop Manasses of Orléans. In 1220 was promoted to the diocese of Paris (*Gesta*, 2:207, 225, 265).

Henry of Villeneuve, 1220–35
Of a middle-class background in the diocese of Paris. Had been cantor (*Gesta*, 2:281).

Bernard of Sully, 1235–45
Had been dean of the cathedral according to Alberic de Trois-Fontaines, archdeacon according to his episcopal biography, which added that he had refused election to the see of Nazareth.[1]

1 Alberic de Trois-Fontaines, *Chronica* 1233, MGH SS 23:933; *Gesta*, 2:285.

Raynald of Seignelay, 1245–7[2]
Had been dean of the cathedral (*Gesta*, 2:291).
Gui of Mello, 1247–70
Son of William of Mello, lord of St-Bris (*Gesta*, 2:293).
Erard of Lézinnes, 1270–8[3]
His predecessor Gui was his *avunculus*. His mother was Bishop Gui's sister (*Gesta*, 2:335).
William III of Grez, 1279–93

2 In the modern scholarly literature, Raynald is usually called 'of Saligny.' It seems more likely, however, that this short-lived bishop was from Seignelay, in the diocese of Auxerre (a lordship that had already produced an earlier bishop), than from Saligny, in the Bourges region. The *Gesta* of the bishops refers to his family as *de Siligniaco*, the Latin for Seignelay; *Gesta*, 2:291.

3 GC 12, instr. col. 175, no. 111.

APPENDIX
INVENTORY OF DOCUMENTS IN THE EPISCOPAL ARCHIVES

Here I present the inventory of documents in the episcopal archives that was attached to the cartulary in the fourteenth century. It may initially appear like a table of contents to the cartulary, but in fact this inventory and the cartulary were derived separately from the archives (see the introduction). Although the way that a particular document is characterized is often identical in the two sources, this is doubtless because both were copying the brief summary typically written on the back of a charter. There is of course a great deal of overlap between this inventory and the cartulary, and thus I give in brackets the document numbers of those documents mentioned in this inventory that were copied into the cartulary. The documents mentioned here that are not in the cartulary may have been issued after the cartulary was compiled, or may have been among those the cartulary scribe skipped over.

Bishops' cartulary, fols. 8r–11v.

Hic incipit inuentarium cartarum et priuilegiorum que faciunt ad ius et iurisdictionem episcopi Autissiodorensis et inuenientur in scriniis suis signatis per ordinem alphabeti et ita scripta sunt et signata in hoc libro.

In scrinio signato per A inuenientur littere siue carte que faciunt ad ius et iurisdictionem episcopi in ciuitate Autissiodorensis et pertinenciis.

Item littere Sancti Bernardi [1].

Item confirmacio littere papalis Sancti Bernardi [3].

Item littere episcopi Lingonensis super declaracione iuris et consuetudinis inter episcopum et comitem iuxta formam littere Sancti Bernardi [2].

Item littera Guidonis comitis Niuernensis de approbacione cartarum predictarum facta coram rege [4].

Item ultime confirmaciones papales, uidelicet una uetus et una noua, ab episcopo Guidone impetrate.

Item littere de concessione hominum Varziaci facta episcopo pro quibus episcopus fundauit altare Sancte Crucis in ecclesia Sancti Stephani Autissiodorensis in redditibus suis de Giiaco.

Item littere de iurisdictione et iusticia concessis canonicis Autissiodorensis in domibus eorundem [6].

In scrinio signato per B inuenientur littere comitum et baronum qui dominum episcopum portare tenentur.

In scrinio signato per C inuenientur littere de homagiis comitum et baronum.

Item littera super composicione inter episcopum et decanum [21].

Item littera quod iurisdicio uacante decanatu spectat ad episcopum [22].

Item compromissio inter dominum episcopum et decanum super ultima contencione et articuli.

In scrinio signato per D inuenientur littere et processus super discordia porte pendentis, porte claustri, et super apertura murorum in clauso episcopi.

Item arbitrium siue siuna prolata super dicto facto [23].

Item multi processus excommunicacionum et agrauacionum contra prepositum et bailiuum occasione dictorum excessuum.

In scrinio signato per E inuenientur littere regis super quittacione regalium duplicate et confirmacio papalis.

Item littera regis super quittacione procuracionum pro feodo de Giemo [26].

Item littera regis super communia non facienda apud Autissiodorem sine uoluntate episcopi [25].

In scrinio signato per F inuenientur littere de moneta Autissiodorensis et totus processus.

Item littere regis super excercitibus que sunt in quadrige pridie.

In scrinio signato per G inuenientur littere de institutione prioris Sancti Amatoris debita fieri ab episcopo et confirmacio papalis.

Item littera de permutacione uini quod canonici Sancti Amatoris habebant in domo episcopi [29].

Item littera de yudaido super pontem Autissiodorensis [30].

Item littera super institutione lectorie [31].

Item littera de scolastica [32].

Item quatuor littere de castello de Ortis [34, 35].

Item due littere de domibus de tanneria Autissiodorensis [36, 37].

Item due littere de obediencia abbatis Sancti Mariani et de cura ei tradita ab episcopo Autissiodorensis [38].

Item littere de electione Sancti Iuliani de licencia eligendi requisita.

Item tres littere de subiectione prioris de Marciaco.

In scrinio signato per H inuenientur littere de franchisia Appoignii [39].

Item littera Iohannis et Milonis de Autissiodorensis militum de uendicione censuum quos habebant apud Appoigniacum.

Item littera Milonis de Autissiodorensis militis de permutacione quitquid habebat apud Appoigniacum ad molendinum de Boufant.

Item littera confirmacionis ad permutacionem predictam ab Agnete uxore dicti Milonis.

Item littera de uendicione molendini dicti de Bofant.

Item littera quod omnia que habet Milo de Autissiodorensis miles apud Appoigniacum obligata sunt episcopo pro vi libris Turonenses.

Item plures littere de sentenciis latis contra Gaillardum et plures alios de Appoigniacum.

Item littera de homagio et recognicione Guidonis Bailledart.

Item alia littera Guidonis Bailledart de recognicione iuris episcopi apud Bailliacum et Appoigniacum in bicheto banno poto et mensuris.

Item due littere de Petranis de Gurgiaco.

Item littera comitis Sacri Cesaris quod dedit episcopo Autissiodorensis quitquid habebat in decimis uini et bladi apud Appoigniacum.

Item tres littere de conquestibus factis ab episcopo apud Charbuiacum.

Item due littere de usagio concesso hominibus de Appoigniaco a Theobaldo de Barro in nemoribus de Chaulon et de Arcia ab omnia necessaria.

Item littera de empcione census de Lindriaco.

In scrinio signato per I inuenientur littere super constitucione seu diuisione archidiaconatuum.

Item littere quod canonici Auttisiodorensis non possunt comedere unus apud alium in x festiuitatibus [40].

Item due littere super decimis acquirendis et quod dominus possit habere partem decimarum.

Item littera contra usuarios quod dominus possit eos compellere ad desistendum.

Item littera episcopalis[1] quod dominus episcopus non teneatur ad prouisionem.
Item due littere de salagio ad archiepiscopum utiles.
Item quedam littera siunalis legati contra Templarios.

In scrinio signato per K inuenientur littere quod Guido comes Niuernensis dedit episcopo Autissiodorensis quicquid habebat apud capellam Sancti Andree [42].
Item quatuor littere de domino Castellionis pro feodo de Cepense et de Varziaco [43].
Item omnes littere de empcione et inuadiacione terre Saciaci [45, 46, 47, 48, 49].
Item due littere de feodo de Vilers lou Sec [50, 51].
Item littera de feodo Vlmi [44].
Item littera quod dominus Droco de Melloto tenet Villers lo Sec in feodo de episcopo Autissiodorensis [58].
Item quatuor littere de uendicione burgi de Couches et una littera de permutacione cum capitulo [52, 53].
Item due littere de burgense de Varziaco facto milite qui emendauit [54].
Item antiqua littera de uendicione molarum apud Varziacum.
Item littera de quittacione nemoris de Liermois et de Codicto.
Item littera de quittacione decimarum Varziaci [56].
Item littera papalis quod episcopus probare possit per testes non per duellum homines suos de corpore [57].
Item littera de recognicione feodi de Villari Sicco [55].
Item littera Yolendis de recognicione feodi de Colongiis et Betriaci et Malliaci [59].
Item littera H. de Vlmo super homagio de Vlmo [60].

In scrinio signato per L inuenientur littere Heruei comitis de feodo et tradicione castellorum uidelicet Sancti Saluatoris, Conade, Castri Noui [61].
Item littera Petri comitis de recognicione feodi Mailliaci et Betriaci et de tradicione dictorum castellorum [62, 63].
Item alia littera Petri comitis de recognicione feodi Mailliaci.
Item alia littera eiusdem Petri de recognicione homagii de Colongiis super Yonem [65].
Item littera regis super eadem recognicione.
Item littera Petri comitis Autissiodorensis et Tornodorensis quod Mailliacum et Betriacum sunt de feodo episcopi et debent ei tindi quocienscumque uoluerit episcopus [66].

---

1 The cartulary, summarizing this document, refers to 'littera papalis,' which seems more likely.

Item littera Manasse episcopi Aurelianensis, Droconis de Melloto, et Guillelmi eiusdem Droconis filii militum testimonialis super feodo Malliaci et Betriaci [64].
Item littera Manasse episcopi Aurelianensis et Henrici comitis de feodo Murati.
Item due littere Heruei comitis Niuernensis et Matildis comitisse de feodo Murati et de tradicione dicti castri.

In scrinio signato per M inuenientur littere de feodo de Petra·Ficta, de Monputois et de Lineriis [68].
Item sex parta litterarum de feodo de Belcha, et quod si plures heredes fuerint omnes facient homagium episcopo et si aliquid acquisierint iuxta domum illam quod non sit de alterius feodo de feodo episcopi erit [76, 77, 78, 79, 80, 81, 82].
Item littera de feodo Odanti [69].
Item littera de feodo de Gurgi [70].
Item littera capelle de Intrannis et de uicaria de Giemo [71, 73].
Item littera de Breteschia de Corbolano attestata [75].
Item littera de collacione de Intramno [72].
Item littera de collacione uicarii de Giemo [74].

In scrinio signato per N inuenientur littere de fundacione parrochiarum de Karitate [83].
Item littere super discordiis et arbitriis et processibus de Karitate [86, 87, 88].

In scrinio signato per O inuenientur multe littere de subiecione Sancti Germani et multe similie et recogniciones [90, 91, 92, 93, 94, 95, 96].
Item quedam littera de hospitacione fratrum minorum Autissiodorensis in loco ubi sunt et ad quid tenentur [97].
Item de abbatia Pontigniaci super capellam quam habunt apud Sanctum Priscum [98].

In scrinio signato per P inuenientur carte Conade et plures littere de Conada [99, 100, 101].
Item due littere de nemore de Codreto et de Liermois.
Item littera quod ecclesia de Nuisiaco non debet procuracionem archidiacono.

In scrinio signato per Q inuenientur littera de capella de Betleem apud Clameciacum et littere bullate de confirmacione dicte simile [103].
Item littera Regnaudi comitis Ioigniacum quod tenet in feodo ab episcopo Autissiodorensis castellatum de Mons, duas uillas scilicet Rollen et Marsengi.

In scrinio signato per R inuenientur littere quod H. Sillons de Autissiodoro miles uendidit episcopo Auttissiodorensis clausum de Vaunoise.

Item littera quod Iohannes de Prenso armiger uendidit quitquid habebat apud Floriacum episcopo Autissiodorensis.

Item littera de emptione decime de Giiaco.

Item littera de emptione pratorum terrarum apud Appoigniacum.

Item littera de emptione decimarum de Boya.

Item littera de emptione decem et septem decimarum censualium in territorio quod est in ualle de Tayno.

Item alia littera[2] de emptione decimarum de Boyaco.

Item littera de portacione quam comitissa Sacri Cesaus habebat in bosco de Aillentois.

Item littera Odonis dicti Cutbet de emptione terra apud Floriacum.

Item alia littera de emptione de Boyaco ab Hugone de Anges.

Item littera Regnaudi de Preaus de emptione eorum que habebit in parrochia de Lindriaco.

Item littera de rendicione census apud Lindriacum facta a Guillemo episcopo Autissiodorensis.

In scrinio signato[3] per S inuenientur omnes littera de emptione domus Parisis per multas particulas.

In scrinio signato per T inuenientur littere de ordinibus factis a domino episcopo et de nominibus ordinatorum.

2 The manuscript reads 'alia littera alia littera.'

3 The manuscript reads 'signato signato.'

BIBLIOGRAPHY OF SOURCES CITED

Arbois de Jubainville, H. d'. *Histoire des ducs et des comtes de Champagne*. 6 vols. Paris: 1859–66.

Böhmer, J.F. *Regesta imperii*. New edition by Engelbert Mühlbacher. Vol. 1. Innsbruck, 1908; rpt. 1966.

Bouchard, Constance B. 'Episcopal *Gesta* and the Creation of a Useful Past in Ninth-Century Auxerre.' *Speculum* 84 (2009): 1–35.

– *Spirituality and Administration: The Role of the Bishop in Twelfth-Century Auxerre*. Speculum Anniversary Monographs 5. Cambridge, MA, 1979.

– *Sword, Miter, and Cloister: Nobility and the Church in Burgundy, 980–1198*. Ithaca, NY, 1987.

– *'Those of My Blood': Constructing Noble Families in Medieval Francia*. Philadelphia, 2001.

Brequigny, M. de. *Table chronologique des diplômes, chartes, titres et actes imprimés concernant l'histoire de France*. 8 vols. Paris, 1769–1876.

Bullarium sacri ordinis Cluniacensis. Lyon, 1589.

The Cartulary of Countess Blanche of Champagne. Edited by Theodore Evergates. Medieval Academy Books 112. Toronto, 2010.

The Cartulary of Byland Abbey. Edited by Janet Burton. Publications of the Surtees Society 208. Woodbridge, Suffolk, 2004.

Catalogue général des manuscrits des bibliothèques publiques de France. Départements. Vol. 6. Paris, 1887.

Delisle, Léopold. *Catalogue des actes de Philippe-Auguste*. Paris, 1856; rpt. Brussels, 1968.

Depreux, Philippe. *Prosopographie de l'entourage de Louis le Pieux (781–840)*. Sigmaringen, 1997.

Duru, L.-M., ed. *Bibliothèque historique de l'Yonne*. Vol. 1. Paris, 1850.

Evergates, Theodore. *The Aristocracy in the County of Champagne, 1100–1300*. Philadelphia, 2007.

– *Feudal Society in the Bailliage of Troyes under the Counts of Champagne, 1152–1284*. Baltimore, 1975.

Gesta pontificum Autissiodorensium. 3 vols. Edited by Guy Lobrichon et al. Paris, 2002–9.

Les gestes des abbés de Saint-Germain d'Auxerre. Edited by Noëlle Deflou-Leca and Yves Sassier. Paris, 2011.

Jaffe, Philip. *Regesta pontificum Romanorum ad annum post Christum natum MCXCVIII*. New edition by Wilhelm Wattenbach. 2 vols. Leipzig, 1885–8.

Keyser, Richard. 'The Transformation of Traditional Woodland Management: Commercial Sylviculture in Medieval Champagne.' *French Historical Studies* 32 (2009): 353–84.

Lebeuf, Abbé. *Mémoires concernant l'histoire civile et ecclésiastique d'Auxerre*. Vol. 2. Paris, 1743.

– *Mémoires concernant l'histoire civile et ecclésiastique d'Auxerre et de son ancien diocèse*. New edition by A[mbrose] Challe and M[aximilien] Quantin. Vol. 4. *Recueil de monuments, chartes, titres et autres pièces inédites*. Auxerre, 1855.

Lespinasse, René de. *Le Nivernais et les comtes de Nevers*. 3 vols. Paris, 1909–14.

Luchaire, Achille. *Etudes sur les actes de Louis VII*. Paris: Alphonse Picard, 1885.

Mabillon, Jean. *De re diplomatica*. Paris, 1681.

Monumenta Vizeliacensia: Textes relatifs à l'histoire de l'abbaye de Vézelay. Ed. R.B.C. Huygens. Corpus christianorum continuatio mediaevalis 42. Turnhout, 1976.

Murauer, Rainer, and Andrea Sommerlechner, eds. *Die Register Innocenz' III*. Vol. 10. Vienna, 2007.

Pardessus, J.M. *Diplomata chartae epistolae leges ad res Gallo-Francicas spectantia*. New edition. Vol. 2. Paris, 1849.

Perard, Estienne, ed. *Recueil de plusieures pièces curieuses servant à l'histoire de Bourgogne*. Paris, 1664.

Petit, Ernest. *Histoire des ducs de Bourgogne de la race capétienne*. Vols. 4, 5. Paris, 1891, 1894.

Plancher, Urbain, ed. *Histoire générale et particulière de Bourgogne*. 4 vols. Dijon, 1739–81; rpt. 1968.

Potthast, August. *Regesta pontificum Romanorum inde ab a. post Christum natum MCXCVIII ad a. MCCCIV*. 2 vols. Berlin, 1874–5.

Le premier cartulaire de l'abbaye cistercienne de Pontigny (XIIe–XIIIe siècles). Edited by Martine Garrigues. Paris, 1981.

Le premier registre de Philippe-Auguste: Reproduction heliotypique du manuscrit du Vatican. Edited by Léopold Delisle. Paris, 1883.

Quantin, Maximilien. *Dictionnaire topographique du département de l'Yonne.* Paris, 1862.

Quantin, Maximilien, ed. *Cartulaire général de l'Yonne.* 2 vols. Auxerre, 1854–60.

– *Recueil de pièces pour faire suite au Cartulaire général de l'Yonne.* Auxerre, 1873.

Recueil des actes de Charles II le Chauve, roi de France. Edited by Arthur Giry, Maurice Prou, and Georges Tessier. Vol. 2. Paris 1952.

Recueil des actes de Philippe Auguste, roi de France. Edited by H.-Fr. Delaborde et al. 4 vols. Paris, 1916–79.

Rosenwein, Barbara H. *Negotiating Space: Power, Restraint, and Privileges of Immunity in Early Medieval Europe.* Ithaca, NY, 1999.

Sassier, Yves. *Louis VII.* Paris, 1991.

– *Recherches sur le pouvoir comtal en Auxerrois du Xe au début du XIIIe siècle.* Auxerre, 1980.

Stein, Henri. *Bibliographie générale des cartulaires français.* Paris, 1907.

Tabbagh, Vincent. *Diocèse de Sens.* Fasti ecclesiae Gallicanae 11. Turnhout, 2009.

INDEX OF PEOPLE

This index references, by document number, the people mentioned in the cartularies. It does not cover the introduction. When a name appears in several different forms (even for the same person in the same document), I have normalized it here to the most common form. Cross-references are provided for different versions of names, except where the reference is an immediately adjacent entry. In arranging entries, I have put the ecclesiastics before the laymen, more important dignitaries before simple ecclesiastics or laymen, and those of whom nothing is known but the name itself at the end of the entry.

INDEX OF PLACES

Place names are here given in their modern form. Cross-references are provided for the Latin form, although I have not given a cross-reference for what would be an immediately adjacent entry. This index does not include Auxerre, mentioned in nearly every document. For places in the region of the Auxerrois, I give their location, generally in terms of direction and distance from that city.

INDEX OF TOPICS

This index lists topics by English words, rather than by the Latin. Thus for example references to any kind of toll may be located by looking under the entry 'tolls,' without necessarily having to know the different medieval Latin terms.

www.ingramcontent.com/pod-product-compliance
Lightning Source LLC
LaVergne TN
LVHW090155080826
844660LV00013B/819/J

* 9 7 8 1 4 4 2 6 4 5 2 8 8 *